Oct. 2012

For [illegible] —

Great [illegible]

Women Gone Wild

The adventures of two city slickers who leave their urban footprints behind and learn to love rattlers, bears, pot growers, two dachshunds and each other

& Cherry Creek

by Jane Futcher

Irregulars,

Love,

Jan

JANE FUTCHER

❧

With special thanks to the Helene Wurlitzer
Foundation of New Mexico.
Portions of this book were published in the San
Francisco Chronicle Magazine.

❧

Book cover design & e-publication technical
services by
Emerald Chasm Entertainment

❧

For more information about the author and her other
publications go to www.janefutcher.com

❧

DEDICATION

To my beloveds . . . Erin, Woody and Luna

"Twenty years from now you will be more disappointed by the things you didn't do than by the ones you did do." *Mark Twain.*

CONTENTS

CHAPTER 1

LOOKING FOR LAND IN ALL THE WRONG PLACES!

We stood before a shingled shack that had been described in that day's classifieds as a "see-to-believe creekside getaway near the Russian River, with guest cottage and private redwood grove."

The creek, now barely a trickle, apparently ran *through* this house in the winter, which might explain why the entire structure listed to one side. The redwood grove was a single looming tree growing so close to the foundation that its roots had hoisted the garage six inches off the ground. We could almost hear the buzz of happy termites munching on the floor joists.

"Keep an open mind," Erin whispered as we walked into the knotty pine hallway carpeted with an orange shag rug. We'd been together 10 years and a place in the country was the lift we thought our relationship needed. But this place was a downer. To the left was the kitchen, where dozens of teddy bears dressed in pink bikinis dangled from the ceiling. Dead ahead was a bathroom barely large enough for a family of small frogs.

"Fabulous, isn't it?" A suntanned woman in a white kaftan appeared from nowhere, her eyes unnaturally blue and teeth so white they threatened to blind us. She waved her manicured fingernails vaguely in the direction of the creek, her gold charm bracelet jingling. "This was originally a summer cottage. Could use some TLC, but there's so much you can do with it."

"Except live in it," I mumbled, sneaking a second look at those weird dolls. "What's with the teddy bears?"

"Wonderful, aren't they?" swooned the agent. "The owner is an artist. Very creative."

"It's much smaller than we. . ." Erin opened a closet door before slamming it shut fast to keep a ski boot and a cast iron skillet from falling on her head.

It was happening again: real estate hell. Home prices were soaring, thanks, in part, to President Bill Clinton, who had just been summoned by the independent counsel to testify before a grand jury on his relationship with Monica Lewinsky. We were bummed. All the country houses in our price range were a mess: They had dry rot in the casements or mold lurking in the closets or were too close to the road to be safe for our dachshunds, Woody and Luna. This one fit right in. In a corner of the bedroom, the plaster was crumbling onto the head of a six-foot Hello Kitty doll. The paint peeling off the room's only window reminded me of the blistering sunburns I used to get as a kid.

"Looks like that meth lab house we saw in Healdsburg," Erin whispered, pulling me toward the front door

"Look," I yelled. Out the back door, three dark, hairy pigs were snorting through a pile of empty Pampers cartons by a corrugated metal shed.

"The guest cottage?" I said to the agent.

"Adorable, isn't it? Oozing potential." She winked at me. "I've got other listings. Are you the writer or the midwife?"

"My pager just went off." Erin charged past her and out the front door. "I've got a client who's seven centimeters."

"You're the midwife," the agent called. "So marvelous. To bring new life into the world. Let me give you my card. If I see something. . ."

We roared out of the driveway before she could finish her sentence. Erin's pager had, happily, not gone off, and moments later we were sipping organic two-percent decaf lattes at the natural grocery store in the nearby town of Sebastopol, in Sonoma County.

"Don't be discouraged." Erin licked milk foam from her lips. "We're just exploring our options.

3

These outings are little adventures that give us special time together and a chance to see what's out there. This is a lot more fun than watching the 49ers lose, don't you think? Or fretting over one of your editorials."

My stomach coiled. At that moment, someone, probably the county hospital's CEO--a volatile, tenacious woman who taught "Body Sculpting by Margaret" at a local gym--was complaining to the publisher about my editorial in this morning's paper. We had run a mildly worded piece suggesting that the hospital might want to look into the reasons why someone on the ER staff had waved away an ambulance carrying the victim of a fatal car crash.

I slugged down my latte, while wishing the clerk had spiked it with some caffeine and pondering whether Erin and I would ever find rural paradise. How far north would we have to go to find something we could afford? A midwife and a newspaper editorial writer couldn't telecommute from Alaska, and neither of us was ready to quit our job.

"Can you drive home?" Erin rubbed her shoulder and gulped down some Advil. She'd been rear-ended twice in the past few months, and her neck and shoulder pains were aggravated by the pretzel positions required to coax babies through the birth canal. Her practice was booming, but the long nights, pain from the car accidents, and the traffic in the Bay Area were taking a toll.

"Erin?" We looked up to see a young woman with gold studs riveting her body from her eyebrows to her bellybutton. She wore a skimpy tank top, tie-dyed pajama bottoms and combat boots, and was now charging toward us, a small child running after her. "Is that you?"

"Hey," Erin smiled, turning to me. "Uh oh. What's her name? She has a band, and her cat scratched my arm just as the baby crowned."

"It *is* you, Erin." The woman practically sat in Erin's lap, suddenly remembering her barefoot toddler trailing behind her pushing a miniature shopping cart as raspberry yogurt dripped down his tiny coveralls. "Paprika, Sweetie. This is Erin, the woman who brought you into the world. Do you remember her, Pappy? Can you say hello? She was your midwife."

Paprika glanced mutely at Erin, lurching past her to grab a rack of VW camper buses made of toasted marzipan. "Mine!" he yelled, toppling the case and ecstatically loading the marzipan Volkswagens into his cart. "Mine!"

"Silly Pappy," smiled the woman, righting the case and turning back to Erin.

"How have you been, Tarragon?" Erin said, finally remembering the woman's name.

"Got a new band," she said, wiping yogurt off of Pappy's mouth and pulling a chair over to our table. "I think this one is going somewhere." As she effervesced about the Icelandic belly dancer that she and Paprika's father, a flute player, had met and fallen in love with while hamster dancing on the Web, I wandered off to check the store's sleep remedies. If I got more sleep, I told myself, these little encounters with unsuitable real estate listings and Erin's former clients wouldn't be so challenging.

At the checkout counter I noticed a copy of *Country Life* magazine, featuring color photos of graying Baby Boomers in jeans and fleeces, tool belts slung around their waists, hammering, plastering, and painting their rural dream houses from Nova Scotia to Las Cruces. I chewed my lip. Our country fantasy was nothing but a cliché. Everyone our age was hoping to get out of the rat race and live off the grid. Baby Boomers had made Frances Mayes a millionaire by mainlining *Under the Tuscan Sun*. Our whole generation had been doing this country-living thing since the Sixties, devouring tomes like *The Whole Earth Catalog* and *Stalking the Wild Asparagus*. If I hadn't moved to New York in the Seventies to live in Greenwich Village, work at a publishing house and become a lesbian, I'd probably have joined a commune in Vermont, raised a few goats, and shivered through a winter before admitting that surviving in rural America isn't all that easy.

I heard Erin laughing and looked up at her short hennaed hair, green blouse and open, freckled face. She and Tarragon were deep into the topic of love triangles, to the delight of several eavesdroppers. No wonder pregnant mothers loved Erin; her easy laugh, calm competence, and amused blue eyes were deeply reassuring. Plus, she had chutzpah; nursing degree in hand, she'd practiced home birth for nearly 20 years, safely catching nearly 1,000 babies while working in the trenches to rewrite state law so that lay midwives could practice home birth legally.

"Hey," I said, pointing to my watch, "I thought you had a woman in labor."

Erin rose. "Tarragon, it's been great."

Erin and I walked to the parking lot with Tarragon right behind us--Pappy asleep in her arms--ecstatically extolling the energizing properties of the flotation tank she and Pappy's dad had been using to increase their Kama Sutra. Wistfully, I watched a storm of 10-speed cyclists whoosh through the intersection in their shiny black skintight suits, sucking their water bottles en route to the Zen Bookstore and the Middle Earth Bakery down the road. Erin and I had mountain bikes, but they'd been hanging from rafters in our garage collecting dust since Erin's accidents. What was happening to us? Was 50 too old for strenuous physical activity? Were we too tired from our jobs and too stuck in our routines to zoom around anything?

I glanced at Tarragon, all young and exuberant and strong, holding that heavy kid in her arms. Did we really think we could chop wood or put in a vegetable garden if we couldn't ride our bikes for an hour without tossing down Advil? Would we miss daily newspapers and movies and Castro Street and antiwar demonstrations and Costco if we moved away?

I wasn't a laid-back California girl like Erin. I was the anxious type. I'd gone to an East Coast girls' school, been a reluctant debutante, majored in English, moved to New York to work in publishing and stayed away from smoking pot at rock concerts or anywhere else because I got stuck in Edvard Munch's "Scream" when I got stoned. The most offbeat thing I'd done in my life was become a lesbian, primarily because the alternative was jumping off a bridge.

Erin was born confident and happy near the corner of Haight and Ashbury streets. She'd danced her teens away to the Grateful Dead and

Janis Joplin at the Fillmore and the Avalon, dropped acid with her boyfriend in Golden Gate Park, and at 20 married a wandering Jew from the Bronx 10 years her senior at a wedding in the high desert of Northern New Mexico, presided over by their yoga teacher from the Punjab and attended by a band of chanting, cherubic hippies. She became a Sikh, thanks to her teacher, studied home birth midwifery, had two daughters at home in the ashram, and put herself through nursing school. She divorced her husband when she realized he was never going to get a job, and she embraced change gracefully. She watched more TV on the couch than I thought was good for her, and when I told her so, she glared at me, explaining that being up for days in a row bringing babies into the world was stressful and that I was judgmental and condescending. Sometimes I was.

Back in the parking lot, Erin had finally extracted herself from Tarragon with the help of Luna and Woody, our miniature long-haired dachshunds, who barked so viciously at the sight of Paprika's yogurt-covered hand reaching in to the car to pet them that he was now screaming more loudly than Tarragon could talk.

"Good dogs," I said, patting their happy, licking faces as we headed south on Highway 101 to our house in Marin County. "She was a jolly sort," I offered tentatively.

Erin laughed. "We should go hear her band sometime. Klezmer jazz, she says. She plays electric mandolin, he plays the flute and clarinet and the belly dancer plays trumpet and trombone."

"Could be interesting," I said, as our Magic Genie garage door opened, allowing us to cruise into our clean, termite-free, one-level Western-style tract house in the Northern Marin suburb of Novato. Maybe this was as much of a ranch as I needed. With Trader Joe's enchiladas bubbling in the microwave, *Sixty Minutes* on the tube and Masterpiece Theatre's opera-loving sleuth, Inspector Morse, waiting for us, I stretched out on the couch and picked up the remote. Life in the 'burbs, from where I sat--10 feet away from our 52-inch TV screen--seemed pretty darned good. Sure, traffic was horrible on Highway 101. And, yes, we had neighbors so close their little girls could count the bubbles swirling in our hot tub. So what if Erin's job was mangling her shoulders and mine hurt my brain. We had a good life. We had two lovable, impossible, hardheaded dachshunds; close friends who lived nearby; jobs that engaged us, and miles of hiking trails right behind our house. I, for one, was willing to let my rural fantasies slip to that familiar mental junkyard where unrealized dreams quietly fade.

And then something happened.

CHAPTER 2

EAT, DRINK AND BE MERRY. . .

Erin and I died.

Metaphorically speaking.

With eight other women from our Buddhist meditation center, we pretended we had one year to live.

We wanted to be ready when death came a knocking. It had knocked hard recently, and it hurt a lot.

My cousin Ruffin in San Francisco had died of AIDS at age 54. My closest friend and former partner, Catherine, has been diagnosed with advanced ovarian cancer, dying two year later, at 52. My favorite Japanese student at the English language school where I'd recently taught had been killed at age 20 in a horrific automobile crash.

Were Erin and I ready for the Big Knock? We didn't think so. I, for one, had a lot of questions. Where had Ruffin and Catherine and Mie, my student, gone when they died? Were they now high-nitrogen soil in the cosmic compost? Were they living in white togas up in the clouds? Was there a way to prepare ourselves for death? Did we have the emotional resources to help Erin's elderly mother in Sonoma County when her time came? Would I be able to assist my nearly 90-year-old father, who lived in Baltimore, if he became ill? How easily would *we* let go if we received a fatal diagnosis? Since it would happen to all of us, why did the Big D always seem a stranger?

Something else nagged at us. The year 2000 was imminent. In the newsroom where I worked, every reporter was gearing up for the new millennium, interviewing future forecasters, politicians and security experts on what 2000 might bring. The newswires hummed with frightening predictions of global technological catastrophe, even Armageddon, if the date change from 1999 to 2000 caused worldwide computer systems to fail. If the subsequent oil spills, air collisions or nuclear accidents didn't wipe us out, terrorists, always lurking in the wings since the World Trade Center bombing in 1993, might exploit the chaos to stage their own attack.

Guided by Stephen Levine's book *A Year to Live*, our group of 10 met one Saturday a month at each other's homes to ponder how to meet our maker. We were awkward at first, since we didn't know each other well and hadn't ever formally pretended that we were about to die. After an opening meditation each week, we'd "check in" about our lives, losses, screw ups and accomplishments, then consider the spiritual, emotional, legal, or financial issues that Stephen Levine recommended we discuss that month.

Each of us kept a record of our dreams and life goals and the obstacles that kept us from achieving them. We noted hang-ups and beliefs about death that scared us. We talked of loved ones we had lost and what we wished we'd said to them before they'd died. We wrote our own obituaries and read them aloud in graveyards. We practiced letting go of material belongings by putting our names in a hat and giving the person whose name we'd drawn one of our most precious possessions. Yes, I cheated a little, presenting a silver goddess rattle I liked but didn't adore to a group member who had joined an evangelical church halfway through our dying process. The gift exercise was instructive--letting go of material things on our deathbeds would be easier if we got some practice ahead of time.

Many of us wrote or rewrote our wills, signed durable powers of attorney for healthcare and advance directives requesting that no extraordinary measures be taken to keep us alive if we were near death and recovery was impossible.

All of us made changes. One of our members, who'd longed to be a nightclub singer, joined a "peak performance" group and, with all of us in the audience, belted out show tunes at a San Francisco pub. Another reconciled with a child she had given up for adoption as a teenager, having been raped and impregnated by a close friend's father. One member learned to ride horses blindfolded, training them without whips or spurs. A psychotherapist in the group began writing a book on healing that she'd been afraid to start. The woman who'd initially launched our circle quit her job as a respiratory therapist to lead Year to Live groups professionally.

Erin, struggling with agonizing shoulder pain from whiplash, made the difficult decision to wind down her midwifery practice.

I resolved to finish the novel I'd been writing on weekends, begging my boss to let me work part time. He nixed my proposal, but I'd planted the seed and won hugs from the group for speaking up.

At the end of our year together, we rented a house by the ocean and died, molding small clay sculptures of ourselves and constructing death masks by wrapping gooey bandages of orthopedic gauze and Elmer's glue on each other's faces. On Sunday morning, we said farewells at the beach, cried and chanted and hugged, burying each other in the sand. Then we tossed our clay selves into the sea. Back at the house, we held a wake and spoke of ourselves in the past tense.

Dying had been a blast, and we learned something. Now was the time to make changes if we wanted our dreams to come true. Tomorrow might be too late.

Drum roll. Trumpet fanfare.

Both Erin and I had written the same goal at the top of our list of dreams: Find a place in the country--soon.

CHAPTER 3

NORTH TO MENDOCINO

Just before our death, Gina and Lin, two friends from my fiction writing group in Berkeley, mentioned that they were buying 320 acres somewhere in northern Mendocino County. The land was ruggedly beautiful, they said, with Douglas fir forests and oak-studded pastures interrupted by dramatic rock escarpments. Year-round creeks ran through the valleys, feeding tributaries of the Eel River.

"Where is it exactly?" Erin put *Seinfeld* on pause as Woody, our blind, two-year-old doxie, licked my face and snuggled down into my arms.

"Mendocino County."

She sat up. "Where in Mendocino County?"

"I don't know," I said. "Someone in the group told me none of the characters in my novel are likable. My mind went blank after that."

"Don't listen to them." Erin placed the phone receiver in my hands. "You're a wonderful writer. Now call Gina and Lin and find out more about that land."

"You call," I looked at my watch. "It's late. And maybe they don't want us horning in on their territory."

"Don't be silly. They're you're friends. You want to live in the country, don't you?"

"Yes, but. . . "

"You keep saying in the Year to Live group that you want to be more forceful in pursuing your dreams?"

"It's 10 p.m."

"Call."

I dialed, praying they wouldn't pick up, but Gina answered. She said there were several more parcels for sale near theirs in Mendocino County and gave me the number of a woman named Stephanie, who was the owner's caretaker and would show us around.

"By the way," Gina said sweetly. "I think your characters are fine."

"Really?" I said, relieved. "They're not dreary and negative?"

"They're quirky. Like you. Keep writing. You can

16

always make changes in a later draft." We both laughed.

I told Erin the news. "Gina doesn't think the book's that bad."

"But the land?" Erin stared at me.

"There are more parcels for sale, and they're very beautiful, and we have the number of a woman who can show them to us," I said. "Are you happy?"

She was very happy indeed.

The next weekend, as wind and rain rattled the palm fronds in our front yard, we loaded the car with enough peanut-butter pretzels, carrots, energy bars, dog treats, water bottles and sodas to survive for a week if we were swallowed up by the El Nino floods. We were headed north to Mendocino County.

Woody was curled comfortably behind us on the back seat on his flannel-lined redwood-chip bed. His sister and littermate, Luna, trembled in my lap, convinced that she faced grave danger because we'd departed from our daily morning routine--a drive to the nearby open space to hike in the hills.

The rain had turned the wetlands next to San Francisco Bay into a vast, tidal lake, the water rising dangerously close to Highway 101. At least we had the road to ourselves. Normal people were in bed reading the newspaper or loading their animals into their arks.

We churned through Santa Rosa, usually jammed with traffic, surfing past the plucked, naked vineyards of Sonoma County.

"Why are we doing this today?" I said. Rain pelted the windshield. "We could drown if it keeps up like this."

Erin turned on the radio. "Just be quiet and find us some music."

I popped open a vanilla cream soda and pressed the button for KPFA, the community radio station in Berkeley that played Bach on Sunday morning. But the host was doing his segment called "All the news that's fit to spit," reading headlines from the *Sunday New York Times*, and rattling off more bad news about President Clinton's pending impeachment trial in the Senate.

"What about all the people we're killing in Kosovo?" I fumed. "What about 'Don't ask, don't tell'? Why don't they spend their energy on something other than what he did with an intern?"

"No rants, please." Erin popped a Grateful Dead tape into the cassette player. Her ex-husband had managed the Dead for a while in the Sixties, and the band had taken Erin and him with them to Woodstock in a helicopter. I hadn't known one Dead tune from another until Jerry Garcia died in a Marin County rehab hospital, and I had to write a farewell eulogy to him for the editorial page. Erin had given me a crash course on his catchiest tunes.

"Drivin' that train, high on cocaine," Jerry sang now. *"Casey Jones you better watch your speed."*

I had to admit, I was a tiny bit excited about seeing this land up north even if there was no chance in hell we were going to buy it. We had friends, family and jobs in Marin, so Sonoma was as far north as either one of us wanted to move. Did they even have newspapers in northern Mendocino County?

At the turnoff for the Russian River resorts, Erin

ripped open the pretzel bag with her teeth. "I loved living in the country in the Seventies."

I knew what was coming next. She would tell me about how she and her wuzband--her word for her ex-husband--lived in a house near the town of Sonoma during their itinerant hippie period, before they had children. They'd grown vegetables and baked pies from the apples in their orchard. A farmer down the road sold them goat cheese; they bought milk from a neighbor and honey from the bee man.

"Our chickens laid eggs, and we had ducks, too. And we used the cistern as a swimming pool."

I shivered at the thought of swimming today, with the sky looking as dark and nasty as the characters in my novel apparently were. "You'd probably still be living there if that CIA agent who owned the place hadn't moved to Mexico."

"That was the place we lived in Mendocino County, not Sonoma," she corrected. "The owner freaked out because of the Viet Nam War and got pissed at the U.S. government and offered to sell the place to us, but we didn't have any money. Wuz was philosophically opposed to paid work, and he didn't want me to work either. The point is, I loved growing our own food, and living outside and seeing the seasons change. You'd really like that, too."

"While you were raising bean sprouts, I was roaming the asphalt jungles of New York having drunken dinners at Mother Courage in the Village and trying to meet women at the Duchess."

Erin laughed. "Poor little Janie had to wait another 20 years to find her perfect partner."

"Worth the wait," I said, sinking into the seat as

Erin began recounting her time in the tiny village of Elk, on the Mendocino coast, when she and Wuz had organized a yoga retreat for their spiritual teacher and lived in a tent in a redwood forest with their first child. Her big problem was that her daughter had weaned herself of breast milk and needed cow's milk, which was impossible to keep cool because they had no refrigeration.

"I'm not sure I could live without a fridge," I said. It was about time I started to draw some lines in the mud or I might end up growing celery in the Pacific Northwest.

"Don't get all squirrelly on me. We're just looking today. We're not buying anything."

"I know, I know. We're having an adventure. But what about Paris?"

Erin glanced at me. "What about it?"

"Spending time in Paris was one of my top three Year to Live goals."

Erin tapped the steering wheel. "We could live in Paris if you really wanted to. I wish my French were better."

"Trouble ahead, trouble behind," came Jerry's raspy voice. *"And you know that notion just crossed my mind."*

When we crossed the Mendocino County line, I craned my neck to get a better look at the Russian River, foamy and turbulent as it hurled itself against the huge rocky precipice above its west bank. Sometimes, a lot of times, I wished I were more like Erin. She welcomed change--and most new things--with calm good humor. At the home births she'd taken me to, she was like a big warm rock that her laboring mothers could cling to as they screamed and swore and moaned their way through childbirth. New things that rattled me didn't faze her at all. Like when we met. I was so panicked about getting off on the wrong, dysfunctional footing that I'd insisted she listen to a dozen of my self-help tapes on avoiding co-dependent relationships. One of my favorite tapes had warned that you should not even consider kissing someone until your sixth date, so when I accidentally touched Erin's elbow with my pinky finger on Date Three, as we stood in line waiting for a movie, I jumped three feet and apologized profusely.

When we finally did hook up, we had our work cut out. Erin loved doing everything together and was hurt when I'd go back to my own house, exhausted, to have some time and space alone. I was so jumpy about commitment that when Erin suggested we have a joint session with her psychotherapist, who practiced in a little cabin with a crackling wood stove in a eucalyptus grove near Muir Beach, I agreed. The shrink asked us to lie on the floor under a down quilt as she played a deafeningly loud classical music tape. At the end of the session, she deduced from the imagery we'd reported while under the covers that our inner children were upsetting each other. Erin's "little girl" was afraid I was abandoning her when I spent the night at my house, and my little girl felt lost and claustrophobic if I stayed too long at Erin's. Under the shrink's supervision, our inner children negotiated some compromises, and it had worked. Ten years later, I now felt so safe with Erin that I worried I'd turned nearly all my life decisions over to her. If I didn't stand up for my vision of our place in the country, she'd have us moving to a cozy dacha in Siberia.

"So who's the woman selling this land?" Erin asked as we entered a green valley between two mountain ridges. "How does Gina know her?

"Her name is Liz and she's an heiress from Los Angeles who spends a lot of time in Northern California. In the Seventies, she ran a women's retreat on the Russian River called Birches or Oaks or something."

"Willow!" Erin cried. "I know that place. We had a midwives' meeting there. It was great. They had a communal kitchen and cabins and a huge swimming pool and a hot tub, and they didn't allow men."

I pressed a stick of sugarless peppermint gum into my mouth. "I have some bad associations with Willow. My ex fell in lust with some hot young babe she met there."

"Catherine?"

"Yep."

"Why shouldn't she have? You left her because you fell for some babe of your own."

"My babe wasn't so young," I said quickly, not wishing to be reminded of my double standard. "And my babe was crazy. Anyway, the resort is closed now. According to Gina and Lin, Liz bought a lot of land at this former cattle ranch to have as a wildlife refuge. They said be sure to ask Stephanie to show us parcels 39 and 40. They have fantastic views."

Erin squinted into the rain as we began to climb higher into the green, wooded Coastal Range Mountains. "Why's this woman selling?"

I snapped my gum. "I've told you everything I know."

"Maybe she's trying to reduce her carbon footprint. Speaking of which. . ." Erin turned off the freeway toward the town of Ukiah. "I need a bio break."

"What?"

"Got to pee," she said. "So do the dogs."

I looked around at the bungalow-style houses near the freeway. "I feel like I've been here before."

"You have." Erin parked in front of a McDonald's, zipped up her rain jacket and leashed the dogs. "Remember that reading you did for the short story collection? This is the place. Ukiah. County seat of Mendocino."

"That was here?" I lurched away as Woody yanked on the leash, sniffing, pawing, gingerly scratching and reluctantly peeing on a brown spot in the wet grass. Our dogs hated wet grass and rain.

"Remember all those country women we ate dinner with before the show?"

I perked up as I thought of that night. I'd read my story--set in the Fifties--about an eight-year-old girl who seduces her blond, zaftig second-grade teacher after driving her to lunch at the country club in her Pontiac convertible. One member of the audience had complained that my story was sexually exploitative because the teacher had taken advantage of the child.

"But the kid seduced the teacher," I'd said. "It wasn't the teacher's fault. Anyway, it's a fantasy."

The editor had smiled. "We loved the story. That's why it's in the anthology."

The women at dinner before the reading had talked in a different language--who was living off the grid and who was on, who had composting toilets and had indoor plumbing, who lived in yurts and who was building a straw bale or a cob house, and who used generators and who had solar electricity. One woman had lowered her voice, confessing to me that she craved hot water, central heating and paved roads and was thinking of moving to town.

Erin scooped a Luna poop into a plastic bag and popped it into the trash barrel as we entered McDonald's. A group of men had taken over half the tables and seemed to be reading the Bible together.

"Christians," I whispered.

"It's AA," Erin sighed. "That's the Big Book. Those are your people." She was referring to the fact that I'd had a little problem with alcohol when I was younger and went to AA meetings every day when she and I first met. I wasn't an AA Nazi, but I liked the companionship meetings offered and the 12-step suggestions for how to live a good life.

"The Big Book is blue," I said. "That book is black."

Erin studied the menu, ordered, then thumbed through a real estate guide she'd picked up by the door, pointing to a grainy black and white photo of a ranch house in the town of Willits, just north of here. A collapsed jungle gym, three junker cars and a deflated plastic swimming pool littered the back yard. "Only $127, 000. You can't buy a dog house in Marin for that."

She could see I wasn't impressed.

"Check this one out. A 300-acre dude ranch in Covelo. We could buy it with friends and create a community. Maybe co-housing."

Uh-oh. I was flashing back to a dinner we'd had

with our good friends Douglas and Stephen a couple of months earlier. Stephen had mentioned that he and Douglas wanted to buy a weekend place in West Marin, somewhere near the ocean. Erin had proposed that we buy property together.

Stephen had stopped chewing the perfectly marinated lamb their personal chef had prepared and stared at her. "With you and Jane?"

"We could pool our resources, get more for our money, and create community."

"Community?" Stephen scowled. "The four of us?"

"We could have more people if you want," she continued bravely. "If we join forces, we'll get more for our money and have the satisfaction of, you know, living. . .together."

Stephen poured himself another glass of wine, leaning away from the table. "Darling, I adore you," he said, running his hands through his wavy silver hair, "but you and I would kill each other. We're both too controlling."

"I'm not controlling." Erin reddened. I stepped on her foot, but she marched on. "You're the one who always insists on having your own way."

Stephen's nostrils flared. "Don't blame me for being bossy when you're exactly the same way."

"That hurts my feelings." Erin was about to cry. I reached for her hand.

Douglas turned to me. "Well, my dear," he said, raising his eyebrows. "Our Utopian community is off to an interesting start."

I sighed. Douglas and Steve ended up buying and remodeling an amazing house overlooking Stinson Beach, in Marin County, while we were driving to the outer limits of civilization searching for a place we could afford.

Back at McDonald's, I sipped my decaf McCoffee, sneaking looks at the Bible study group. "I thought we gave up the idea of having land partners or group living after that dinner with Steve and Doug," I said.

"They're just two people," Erin said. "We have other friends."

I glanced at another of the Christians. "That man just put 11 sugars in his coffee."

Erin cornered a home fry with a plastic fork. "What you may not know is that there are very cool people in Mendocino County. There's a whole Buddhist city just across the freeway here, in the old state mental hospital. And there are all sorts of progressive folks who've been here since the Sixties. There's Judy Bari, who fought the logging companies. . ."

"And got blown up by the FBI," I reminded her.

"Julia Butterfly's living in that redwood tree. . ."

"That's Humboldt County."

Erin kept going. "Almost every town has a farmers' market and. . ."

"Pot growers. . ."

The men at the table looked up from their Bibles.

Erin nodded. "Maybe we'll grow pot, and I won't have to get a nursing job."

"Sure," I said. "We could open a head shop and sell bongs and roach clips and hemp pajamas."

"Okay, okay." Erin tossed her Egg McMuffin wrapper into the waste bin and jingled the car keys. Outside, the rain had gotten heavier. She straightened my rain hat and kissed my cheek right in front of the Christian men. "I love you. I'm having fun. Are you having a little fun?"

"I think so," I said. "I think they put some caffeine in the decaf. I'm feeling more positive."

"Yes!" Erin said, opening the car door. "We're going to have fun, and we're going to look at this land, and we're going to keep an open mind."

"Yes, we are," I said, as the dachshunds lunged for the Egg McMuffin I'd saved for them.

We surfed back to Highway 101, twisting higher through the hills, past pastures dotted with cattle and oaks and occasional vineyards. For long stretches we saw no cars at all, just unrelenting gray hills.

"There are things you can replace," sang the Dead. *"And others you cannot. The time has come to weigh those things. This space is getting hot."*

"Kind of remote," I shivered, turning up the heater.

Erin dialed the heat back down as water cascaded off the rocks above the freeway and down to the road.

"You've got to admit, this is desolate." I said again.

"Look at these beautiful hills and big old oaks. I feel like I can breathe."

As we descended into Willits, the freeway narrowed to two lanes. Some scruffy, one-story shops in Quonset-hut buildings flanked Highway 101--a gun shop with a huge plastic elk on wheels in front, a farm equipment supply place, a tire shop, two auto parts stores, a beauty salon, a Jack in the Box, a McDonald's and a Burger King.

"Bright lights, big city," I said.

"Time for an attitude adjustment," Erin said evenly. "The Safeway should be just ahead."

We had to find the Safeway to call Stephanie, the woman who was going to show us the land. She had said it would take her the same amount of time to drive from her house to the main gate of the ranch as it would take us to drive to the same gate from Safeway in Willits.

I reached her on the second ring, making plans to meet her at the Cherry Creek gate in 20 minutes. Mission accomplished, we passed acres of flooded farmland on the north side of town, then twisted back up into the hills, the redwood forest closing ominously around us. My stomach felt sort of queasy and tight. Was it the coffee, or was I scared of what was coming?

Hidden among the redwoods were clusters of dilapidated houses and mobile homes, smoke curling from the chimneys, driveways littered with dead cars, old appliances and piles of trash.

"Do you think it's better to be poor in the country or poor in the city?" I said, unwrapping a stick of peppermint gum and peering into the woods. It was noon, but now so dark I could see a string of blinking Christmas lights strung around a soggy settlement of trailers.

Erin squinted at the roadway. "At least in the country there's nature and trees and fresh air and beauty."

I wondered. "I read somewhere that rural poverty can be worse than urban poverty because country people don't have the same access to libraries and hospitals and public transportation and other services that we have in cities."

"Could be. The lumber and fishing industries tanked here in the Seventies and Eighties. I've heard pot cultivation keeps the county alive."

"You call this alive?" I said. Mistake.

"Be positive, hon," Erin warned, pointing to a road sign that said the rest area was just ahead.

And there she was at the gate, a pretty woman in her thirties, with long blond hair, pink cheeks and a friendly smile. She was wearing a bright yellow slicker, blue jeans and black rain boots.

CHAPTER 4

WELCOME TO CHERRY CREEK

Stephanie waved us in and introduced herself, which launched a full frontal barking blast from Woody and Luna. They scrambled into Erin's lap to get a better view.

"Hello, little ones." The earthy blond woman reached through the window; Luna wriggled over the door and melted into her arms.

"That's a first," Erin laughed. "She's not known for her kindness to strangers." Woody peered at

Stephanie, his tail wagging frenetically as he tried to get closer.

"Welcome to Cherry Creek." Stephanie glanced at our low-to-the-ground city slicker car. "You'd better ride with me. I've got four-wheel drive that works most of the time."

We followed her down the road a few hundred yards, leaving our car at a turnout where the asphalt became dirt and the road took a sharp right up a steep, wooded hill.

"She seems nice," I whispered to Erin as we gave the dogs a last chance to pee and put them back in the car.

"I used to have hair that long," Erin said wistfully, running her hand through her short, hennaed spikes. "I could sit on it."

Long hair had been required by Erin's erstwhile spiritual teacher, who had expected his yoga students and most devout followers to become Sikhs, as he was, taking Sikh names and following Sikh practices, like not cutting their body hair, donning white turbans and wearing traditional Indian clothing. Erin, still in her early twenties and eager for more structure in her peripatetic life with Wuz, had complied. She and Wuz became leaders in the ashram; she managed food buying and preparation and began assisting with home births for women in the community. Her parents' help with childcare, and the availability of ashram members for babysitting allowed her to enroll in home birth midwifery school and eventually nursing school.

As she matured, Erin bridled under her teacher's patriarchal caveats and her husband's casual indifference to making money. Despite the dark predictions of her teacher that she'd end up in the gutter if she left the Sikh community, she divorced Wuz, cut her hair, renamed herself Erin and took a job in the family practice of a doctor who attended home births. Eventually, she launched a successful midwifery business with offices in Marin, Berkeley, and San Francisco.

Wuz and Erin's older daughter, Jiwan, were still Sikhs. Their teacher's condemnation of homosexuality added to the challenges Erin and I had faced when I moved in with Erin. Her younger daughter, Nam Kirn, 16 at the time, had just moved back to live with her mother after five years of Sikh boarding school in India.

"Puppy Schnoodles only bites if you make a sudden, unexpected move," Stephanie was saying to me, as Erin took the front seat of the SUV, and I climbed into the back--with a blue heeler and a very wet Australian shepherd, who both growled when I opened the door.

"No worries," Stephanie said, seeing my expression in the rear view mirror. "They're rescue dogs; Schnoodles is very docile and deaf as a post. And Chips is a pussycat once you get to know her."

Slowly, to avoid alarming Puppy Schnoodles or Chips, I hugged the door as we ascended a steep and winding road through Douglas fir and madrone trees for move than a mile. Stephanie talked the whole way. Cherry Creek Ranches, she said, had been a 7,000-acre, family owned timber and cattle operation before it was bought by a developer in the 1980s and subdivided into about 50 parcels-- half 40 acres in size, the rest 160 acres. The old ranch headquarters, she said, had burnt down many years before, but some of the barns and outbuildings were still there, owned by a gay man from San Francisco who'd built a small, pre-cut "kit" cabin there. The land we were going to see was much higher up--nearly 2,500 feet--and five miles southeast of the gate. Many of the owners, she explained, were Bay Area folks who camped on their parcels a few times a year. Some never came at all. Every parcel had a potential home site and a water source, or what she called a developed spring--a water tank placed below ground in a wet area with an open bottom to capture spring water. Above ground about three feet was a capped PVC pipe extending from the tank to the surface.

At the crest of a long hill, we came to a clearing, where a road called Black Bear jogged off to the right. We spotted a covered bulletin board with a few community announcements; next to it was a hand-painted sign that showed what was unmistakably a green marijuana leaf in a red circle with a red slash cutting through it.

"Guess somebody doesn't like pot," Erin laughed, turning to glance at me. "I've never seen a sign like that before."

Stephanie nodded. "There was a pot bust here before Ken and I arrived and the developer wanted to put the kibosh on growers. Good thing, too. In some areas around Laytonville, which is just up the road, you take your life into your hands if you drive around the back roads during the pot harvest season."

"What happens?" I craned forward to hear more.

"A lot of the growers have guns, and they'll

shoot if they think you're trespassing."

"They'll kill you?"

"It happens."

I was amazed.

"Marijuana is Mendocino County's economic engine," Stephanie, running a hand through her long blond tresses. "But you don't have to worry about getting shot here. Nobody's growing, as far as I know, although with 160 acres, you can plant just about anything you want and no one would know. Not the neighbors, anyway. If the DEA flew over or you hired too many trimmers, then there'd be a problem."

"Trimmers?" I scratched my head. This was fascinating.

"They prep the pot for market," she said matter of factly. "You've got to do everything by hand, and that takes labor. The guy who got busted here had a lot of trimmers driving in and out during harvest season, going way too fast. That's not acceptable."

"Wow," I said, ready to ask more questions. But Erin turned to give me a dirty look, so I focused on the surroundings. We were driving through an open valley next to a bubbling creek, its muddy, turgid water rising close to the road. In the hills on either side stood a few arthritic, twisted oaks covered with lichen, pale green moss, and occasional clumps of mistletoe. Black stumps of giant trees that had been felled decades ago poked intermittently through the fields, giving the valley the desolate look of a World War I battlefield.

"How many people did you say live here?" Erin craned to see a big canvas teepee up on a hill to our left.

Stephanie counted on her fingers. "Ten, I think. Including Ken and me." She pointed to a driveway on our right that disappeared into the woods. "An inventor and his wife, Woody and Linda, live in a big house they built by themselves up in those trees. They have a barn, and they've added a stone bridge and a castle turret for reenactments of medieval battles."

"For what?" Erin stared through the trees trying to catch a glimpse of the house.

"They pretend it's the Middle Ages and stage battles around the property. The Society for Creative Anachronism, it's called. Ken and I have been to a few of their events. The members camp on their land and dress up in Medieval costumes-- tights and chain mail and tunics--and they speak Old English and have battles with swords and lances and battering rams.

"Kind of like the Renaissance Faire," I said. "And they have the same names as our dogs?"

"Woody and *Linda*," Erin corrected. "Not Woody and Luna."

"Okay," I said, straining to see someone in chain mail cavorting in the woods with a swinging mace. "Do they talk in Elizabethan when you see Woody and Luna on the road?"

"Woody and *Linda*!" Erin repeated.

"Only when the society is meeting. They're very nice, smart people."

In the open valley along Cherry Creek, we passed a little manzanita forest on the left, and through the round, shiny green leaves we could make out the roof of a shed.

"That's where Mike and Robin, the Los Angeles cop and his wife, have a cabin," Stephanie said.

"You'll love them. They camp here for a month every summer. He's a National Guard disaster expert, and she's a riot, sometimes hikes around in her Girl Scouts jacket with her all badges. He wears camouflage fatigues and a Vietnam belt buckle. They plan to quit their jobs and move here permanently next summer."

I looked behind us. "That road we passed back there--Black Bear? Is it called that because there are. . ."

"Oh, yes," Stephanie laughed. "We have bears, mountain lions, wild pigs, bobcats, elk, deer, coyotes, rattlesnakes, bald eagles, quail and grouse, to name a few. There's no hunting allowed, so the ranch is a paradise for animals."

"It's. . .beautiful." Erin stared out at the gushing creek and the wet, green ridges on either side of the valley.

Was it beautiful? I wasn't sure. It was remote and wet and kind of forbidding. "When did you and Ken come here?"

"Two years ago."

Torrents of water rushed down the hillside into the creek.

"From where?"

"Hollywood."

"Hollywood!" Puppy Schnoodles glared at me, sending me even closer to the door. "Wasn't this place kind of a shock to your system? Didn't you feel isolated?"

"Not for minute," said Stephanie, explaining that Liz's wildlife preserve kept them very busy. Plus, they had Liz's horses to feed and care for and goats and a garden and their birds. "There's always too much to do when you live in the country," she said. "You'll find out soon enough."

Was Stephanie suggesting that we would move to this soggy outpost? Probably just her way of being hospitable.

"How on earth did you find this place?" I stared up at three turkey vultures circling over the ridge to our right. "It's so far from Los Angeles."

"Exactly right," Stephanie smiled.

I noticed that Stephanie's hair seemed to release a pleasant aroma of oranges or cloves or wintergreen--something delicious--whenever she brushed it away from her eyes. "Did you have to leave your jobs? Did you work in the film industry? Can you still do that here? How many birds do you have?"

"Well. . ." Stephanie coughed.

"Don't feel you have to answer her." Erin waved me quiet with her hand. "She makes her living asking questions, Stephanie. She doesn't know when to stop."

"That's quite alright," Stephanie said a little stiffly, making me wonder if maybe Erin was right and she really didn't like all my questions. "The short version to how we got here is that a friend of mine from Los Angeles was collecting her two parrots that had been staying here after Liz's caretaker had died suddenly. My friend asked me to come up here with her, and I said I would on the condition that I could interview for the job of caretaker."

"Just like that? And you'd never been here?" This was too much. How could anyone make a decision to move to the middle of nowhere so quickly?

She shrugged. "I knew from my friend's

description of the place that it was exactly what I was looking for. When we got here, I called Ken and told him I was moving."

A city girl leaving everything behind to live in this. . .what was it? "Was Ken okay with that?"

"He had to be," she said, her blue eyes finding mine in the rear-view mirror. "When I make up my mind, that's it. I don't go back."

The road came to a T, where we turned left and climbed higher through a manzanita forest. "This is the road your parcel is on," Stephanie said. She was doing it again--assuming we were buying the place.

"What did the previous caretaker die of?" Erin probed quietly. "I'm a nurse, so these things interest me."

Stephanie took a breath. "It was a drug overdose. One of the owners found her body near Liz's gate. Liz needed someone else right away for the animals. Since then she's decided to let go of a few of her parcels and has agreed to sell us the Emerald Chasm."

"The Emerald what?" Erin said, without removing her eyes from the spectacular view of the valley we'd just passed through.

"That's our name for the parcel along Cherry Creek that Ken and I are buying. Each one of Liz's parcels is beautiful. You'll see that. But we love our parcel because the creek runs through it and has created a stunning chasm. It's dramatic. Very much like a film set."

For some reason, the mention of a film set reassured me. Stephanie hadn't completely left L.A. behind.

Erin rolled down her window. The sky had

lightened and the rain tapered as we twisted up a red clay road. "Why does Liz want to sell her land?"

Stephanie sucked in a breath. "She started a small animal rescue in Sonoma and doesn't get up here as much as she used to. Quite frankly, since the horses were murdered, she doesn't feel the same about the place."

"What?" Erin gasped.

Stephanie pushed a strand of aromatic gold hair from her eyes and tightened her hands on the steering wheel. "Liz adopted some wild horses from a large animal shelter and released them here several years ago. Three were murdered last year."

"They were murdered?" I shivered.

Stephanie clenched her jaw. "We know who did it. And Liz will make them pay."

"Really?" I said, wondering how this payment was going to be exacted, but this time I kept my mouth shut.

"It's a long story that I'd rather not go into," Stephanie said. "But suffice it to say that Liz is suing them."

Erin zipped up her rain jacket and rolled down her window. "Will we see these horses? The live ones?"

"I wouldn't be surprised," Stephanie said, as we reached the top of the ridge. "They have the run of the ranch." Before we could ask more about the horses and their murderers, we found ourselves on a ridge gazing out at the edge of the world, overlooking a series of mountain ranges culminating in some snow-capped peaks in the far distance. Directly below us was a long rolling hillside descending into canyons thick with green firs. Stephanie stopped the car so we could walk around. As I opened the door for a better look, Chips and Puppy Schnoodles flew over me, taking off down the hill.

"Sorry," I said. "Should I try to catch them?"

"No worries. They'll come back."

We stood in the wind gazing out at miles of mountain wilderness in every direction. It was cold here. Much colder than Marin County.

"What do you think?" Stephanie kicked some mud off her rubber boots.

"Dramatic," I said, wishing I'd brought my down coat. "Really beautiful." Why did I feel so reluctant to admit it?

"Incredible." Erin's freckles had turned pink; her blue eyes were bright.

"I knew you'd like it." Stephanie smiled. "So this is Parcel 40, which your friends mentioned to you."

"This view is for sale?" I said.

"Yes, it is," she nodded. "Those snowcapped peaks you're looking at are part of the Mendocino National Forest--miles and miles of undeveloped land. Sanhedrin Mountain is the one that towers over the others."

We stood in silence, breathing the fresh, cold air. I pressed my hands into my rain jacket to slow the cartwheels in my stomach.

"How far down the hill does this parcel go?" Erin stared into the forested canyon.

"To the bottom of the first meadow."

"What's below that?"

"Parcel 39. And then the creek. More than half this parcel is on the other side of the road," she said. "Behind us."

She led us along a soggy path through a

meadow that ended in a flat, grassy area separated from the road by a grove of manzanita trees; in the center of the field was a madrone tree, its smooth, peeling red trunk glistening in the rain. "This is the home site. If you build a two-story house here by the tree, you'd have a 360-degree view from the top floor. You could watch the sun come up in the east and see the sunset in the west."

I squeezed Erin's hand, my stomach whirling. The whole area looked like a photo spread from *National Geographic*. No people or houses anywhere, just trees and mountains and wind and ridges. It was spectacular. There was no other word to describe it.

Erin smiled at me.

"If you want to build two houses," Stephanie was saying, "this is also the perfect parcel because both places would be completely private, on different sides of the road."

"Two houses?" I looked at Stephanie.

"The county allows two houses per parcel and an unlimited number of Class-K outbuildings. As long as they're not over 600 square feet, you can have as many as you want."

"I want this side of the parcel," Erin grinned, waving toward the view of the mountains.

"I want it," I laughed. "How 'bout we live together?"

"It's a deal." Erin put her arm around me.

We stood and inhaled the view from the home site.

"Another excellent thing about this parcel," Stephanie said, "is that it won't cost too much to develop because you're close to the road and the existing telephone and power lines. You don't have to go off the grid for electricity, and you wouldn't have to put in a long road. Roads aren't cheap."

"Where's the water?" Erin asked.

"The spring for this parcel is down where we just came from, but it can be pumped up to the home site."

"And the septic?"

I glanced at Erin, amazed by her apparent knowledge of building issues.

"That you'd have to put in yourselves. I don't know how well the soil percs here. But I can give you the name of a heavy equipment operator who we've used a lot at the wildlife preserve. He can give you an estimate."

My stomach tightened. Buying raw land was just the beginning of the process. We'd have to make a road and bring in electricity and install telephone lines and pump water from somewhere and build a sewer system. And that was all before we even had a house. No way I was ready to tackle all that, let alone pay for it. "How much did you say Liz is asking for the land?" I looked around to see who'd asked that question. Erin looked at me, eyes widening. Those were *my* words.

Stephanie patted Puppy Schnoodles, who'd returned, his pink tongue hanging like a drooping flag from his mouth. "She's asking exactly what she paid for the land ten years ago--$145,000. Her terms are flexible. If you can make a down payment now, you can pay off the balance in two or three years with no interest."

Wow. Even I knew those were good terms. I also knew you were never supposed to reveal to a seller how much you liked a place, but Stephanie already seemed more like a helpful friend than a real estate person. For that many acres and this incredible view in this incredible wilderness, the price was a bargain, a giveaway compared with the inflated properties we'd looked at in Marin and Sonoma counties.

Erin looked down the hill. "Can you show us Parcel 39? Gina and Lin told Jane we should be sure to look at it."

"Ah." Stephanie switched on the Blazer's ignition. "Parcel 39 is already spoken for." The tires of her SUV squished slowly through the mud on the ridge as we continued forward on the road. "Rod and Cindy have first dibs on it, and I don't show parcels that other buyers have expressed an interest in. But I'm happy to show you other parts of the ranch."

"You can't show us 39?" Erin pressed, disappointed.

"Sorry." Stephanie inhaled. "I'm happy to drive you by the land Gina and Lin are buying and take you down to see Outlet Creek."

"That's fine," Erin said. "But at least point out 39 to us."

As we bumped along the road, Stephanie pointed to the right.

"That's it. Parcel 39."

Erin gazed wistfully down below us at the long stretch of oak meadow. The parcel was all on the south side of the road--not divided in two pieces like Parcel 40. We lowered our windows and peered out.

"You'll like Rod and Cindy," Stephanie said, speeding up again.

"Rod and Cindy?" Stephanie had an interesting

way of talking about people we'd never met and places we'd never seen as if we already knew them. Would this be considered a continuity problem in the film business, I wondered?

"The couple buying 39. Rod's a dentist and Cindy's a tech writer from the Bay Area."

"Are they in escrow?" Erin squinted down the hill.

"Nothing's in escrow yet, not even the Emerald Chasm or Gina and Lin's parcels."

I blew air on my hands, trying to get warm. These real estate arrangements up at Cherry Creek seemed very informal. In the Bay Area, a house or a piece of land was either in escrow or it wasn't. People didn't have "dibs" on a property. They made an offer and papers were signed and the seller accepted or rejected the offer. Stephanie's approach--perhaps it was Liz's--was very casual.

Stephanie stopped, getting out to open a gate across the road on our left. All the land on the far side of this gate, she told us, belonged to Liz.

"If Rod and Cindy change their minds," Erin said softly. "We'd like to see 39."

"You never know." Stephanie lowered her voice. "If you don't mind, I'd like to ask *you* a question."

I swallowed.

"How well do you know Gina and Lin?'

"They're really Jane's friends." Erin turned to me.

"I'm in a writing group with them," I said. "They're wonderful writers. Extraordinary writers, really. Gina wrote a wonderful novel called *City of Hermits* in which Liz, or someone similar to Liz, is a main character."

"Really?" Stephanie stared at me in the back

window. "Do you know Liz?"

"Never met her," I said.

Stephanie seemed to relax, taking a long breath and smiling as she pointed to a meadow on the right that she said was part of Gina and Lin's land. I was about to ask why she wondered if we knew Liz but forgot because she said something else that caught my attention. "Ken and I call that knob over there Rattlesnake Mountain."

"Are there rattlesnakes here?" Snakes were not my strong suit.

Stephanie chuckled. "Not to worry. Snakes hibernate in the winter; you're safe today."

As we bumped and slid for several more miles down the dirt road, which narrowed and grew rougher, Stephanie began to use the same lingo that those women from the book reading in Ukiah did, referring to hard and soft corners--which, she explained, were boundary points--off the grid electricity, DC converters, and housing materials like cob and rammed earth and straw-bale. She said the power lines along the road by parcels 39 and 40 stopped before this leg of the road, so that she and Ken, and Gina and Lin, if they moved here, would have to install a solar power system with a generator for back up when there wasn't any sun. Stephanie was even thinking about creating a hydroelectric power system using a seasonal creek that was on their parcel.

"It's going to take a good power source to run a 5,000-square-foot house," she said.

"Five thousand square feet?" Erin sat up. I knew what she was thinking because I was thinking the same thing: Stephanie and Ken must be incredibly successful Hollywood moguls--screenwriters or directors or producers or something--if they were going to build a house that size.

"Twenty exotic birds need space."

"How many?" Erin gripped the armrest. "Did you say. . ."

"Twenty," Stephanie nodded. "Most are rescue birds. Our kids."

"You're brave," Erin laughed. "A friend of mine had one cockatiel, and the bird nearly broke up their marriage. Twenty birds must be. . ." Erin trailed off.

Stephanie said that Ken had taken a lot of abuse from the kids because many parrots are averse to one sex or the other, and their birds mainly favored females. I could certainly see why they liked Stephanie.

The road finally came to an end in a grassy meadow just above a wild, wide, foaming river that roared so loudly we had to shout to be heard. To our left, an old railroad bridge spanned the creek, and above it, in the treetops, was the road to the town of Covelo, 30 miles northeast.

"They've stopped running the trains between Willits and Covelo because they ran out of money, which is a good thing because the sparks from the trains caused so many fires in the summer," she shouted. "This part of the Outlet Creek, where Cherry Creek flows into it, used to be a nude swimming hole in the Seventies. A lot of the locals snicker if you say you live at Cherry Creek because they used to swim here naked as kids. You'll get used to it."

There she went again, talking as if we would be living here some day. "Brrr," I said. Ground water had leaked into my hiking boots and the rain had soaked through my jacket.

"I should probably take you back." Stephanie opened the car door. "I told Ken I'd be home before dark to feed the horses."

Chips and Puppy Schnoodles jumped onto the seat ahead of me; I clung to the door as the SUV bounced into a pothole just a few yards farther along, slid, then stopped, wheels spinning wildly in the mud.

This was not good.

Stephanie backed up and tried to go forward. The tires kept spinning. "The four-wheel drive on this car sucks," she said, shaking her head.

The heater didn't work very well either. I pulled my scarf tighter around my neck. Stephanie revved the engine again and stepped on the gas, but the wheels dug deeper into the mud, filling the car with the smell of gas.

Erin pushed open her door. "So Jane and I will push."

"We will?" I had a terrible low back and Erin's left shoulder was a mess.

"Do you mind?" Stephanie said. "It's a long walk back."

I groaned as I got out. But what choice did we have? Our dogs had been locked in the car for a long time already, and I had to be at work in the morning. Walking home in the dark with the bears and mountain lions, or spending the night by the creek in wet clothes in a heat-impaired car with Stephanie's special-needs dogs was not my idea of a good time. Erin and I planted our feet in the mud and pushed against the car's backside as Stephanie revved the engine. The wheels kept spinning.

Erin looked at me. "You're not trying hard enough."

"I am, too."

"Well, visualize the wheels engaging and the car moving forward. Got that?"

"Got it."

"Okay, then." Erin yelled to Stephanie. "Now!"

I looked at Erin.

"Visualize, Jane!" she yelled.

"Say when," Stephanie shouted.

"When!" Erin called.

I pushed as if my life depended on it, which it did, as the mud from the tires sprayed my jeans. The car went nowhere. I resigned myself to the long hike back in the dark when, miraculously, the SUV pitched slowly forward.

"Yes!" Erin yelled. Stephanie drove a few feet ahead, to a flatter, firmer spot in the road, where we jumped into the car.

"Thanks," Stephanie said. "You've just had your official welcome to life at Cherry Creek."

Twenty minutes later, numb from the cold and covered in mud, we pulled over on top of the ridge to take one last look at the vast view from Parcel 40.

"Look! Over there," Stephanie cried. "I haven't seen the elk in months." A dozen enormous, furry, deer-like animals grazed below us in the waning light.

We admired them for a moment and rolled up the windows.

"What do you think?" Stephanie said.

"Amazing," I croaked, longing for dry clothes and our down jackets.

"It's fantastic," Erin said.

"Is there any heat?" My teeth chattered.

Stephanie turned up the dial, sending a blast of more cold air into the back seat.

I hugged my torso and watched my breath turn to vapor. "Is anyone else interested in Parcel 40?"

"You're the first." She glanced at me in the rearview mirror. "If you want it, I won't show it to anybody else. It's yours."

"Wow." I took a long breath.

Erin said nothing, staring straight ahead.

Stephanie turned to look at me.

"Don't show it to anybody else," I swallowed.

Erin swirled around in disbelief. I had complained the entire way up here about the rain and the desolate hills and the impossibility of buying anything so far from home, and now I had said I was interested in a wet, windy wasteland in the middle of nowhere.

"Good," Stephanie nodded. "You'll be very happy here."

"We could make a down payment of $35,000," I continued. "And when I sell my house in Mill Valley in a couple of years, we can pay off the balance. How does that sound?"

"Sounds great. Liz will be delighted."

Erin coughed. "Not to throw a damper on things, but I think before we go too far we should come back when it's not raining and walk the property lines. And I'd still like to see Parcel 39."

"Sure," Stephanie said. "Just tell me when."

"My schedule's back at the car," Erin said, rubbing her hands. "I'll see if I can get someone to cover for me next weekend."

On the way back to the gate, we scrutinized every tree and stump and bush with new interest.

When we finally reached our car, Luna and Woody, deliriously happy to see us, dragged us on their leashes through the bushes by the swollen creek next to the road, tails wagging furiously as they sniffed for bears and mountain lions and coyotes. We made a tentative date with Stephanie for the following Saturday.

In stunned silence, we changed into dry clothes at the rest area just past the gate and headed south.

"I don't believe you," Erin said.

"It would be like owning our very own national park," I whispered. "After we pay off the land, maybe we'd have enough left to build a little cabin."

Erin popped open a vanilla cream soda. "You'd be willing to plunk down your money and buy Parcel 40, just like that?"

"If Gina and Lin are buying land there, we'd have friends. We'd know people. That's my biggest fear--to be all alone out in the boondocks."

"We'd have a community," Erin nodded.

"A community," I echoed.

Driving through the dark, we reviewed everything we'd seen and heard at Cherry Creek: the trees and mountains; the remote hillsides; the elk; the no-pot sign; Stephanie and Ken's exotic birds; the strange references to Liz and the horse murderers; the dead caretaker; the huge, roaring creek; getting stuck in the mud and having to push out the big SUV.

As Erin chattered happily about what we could build on the land, on the top of the hill by the big madrone tree, slow waves of panic began to rise around my throat. Should it be a two-story house with a 360-degree view, she was saying, or something simple, like a yurt or a stick-frame cabin? She'd check to see if the hospital in Willits had an OB-GYN department and needed nurses. I nearly choked on the tea from the thermos. What had we done? What had *I* done? We now had "dibs" on Parcel 40. What if Stephanie sold it to someone else and we lost it? What if we actually bought it? I could hear the thunderous rumble of doors opening and closing and lives changing. *Our* lives.

CHAPTER 5

ON THE BEAT

Rick, my best friend in the newsroom, was already at his computer when I got to work the next morning. He kept his head down and his fingers whirling across the keyboard, a sure sign he was answering his e-mail. Not even Rick wrote stories at that speed.

"You're here," I said. "What's the occasion?"

"Got to put in some face time," he muttered.

"Create the illusion I work here. Then I'm taking Vito to a two-day pet psychic workshop."

I turned on my computer, which backed up to his; while it warmed up, I separated the slats of the Venetian blinds next to my desk to check the nearly black sky--torrents of rain driven by howling winds were pooling in the back parking lot.

"They're going to teach ESP to you and a Jack Russell terrier? Didn't know that was possible."

"No one does," he said, lifting an orange from a paper sack balanced on a mountain of papers. "That's why it's a fantastic story."

Rick was the *enfant terrible* of the newsroom; he cranked out so many articles each week that the editors tolerated his frequent references to their shortcomings.

"Are you free Saturday night?" He stopped typing and sucked an orange slice. "We're having a Bad Movie Monday martini party Saturday."

"Thanks," I said. "We've got plans, but I appreciate the invite. What's the movie?"

"*Stop! Or My Mom Will Shoot* with Sly Stallone and Estelle Getty. Sly says it's the worst film he ever made." Rick pushed his bangs off his forehead and studied me. "Why can't you come? Too busy running naked in the cemetery with the Year to Live gals?"

I inhaled, hoping I sounded casual. "Erin and I are taking another look at some land up in Mendocino County."

"What?" He tossed me an orange. "Marin County isn't dead enough for you?" Rick hated the suburbs, particularly the suburban tract town of Novato, where the newspaper and I both lived.

"I like hills and trees and birds and green

things," I said, uncorking my thermos of Red Zinger tea and scanning my e-mail. "Besides, we're just looking."

"Looking at what?" Becky, the home and garden editor and my other best friend at the paper, hooked her raincoat on the hat rack by the art department, booted up her computer and opened today's paper. "What are you doing here, Rick?"

"I work here, in case you hadn't noticed," Rick growled, pulling out his asthma inhaler and taking a snort. "In the time it takes Jane to write one of her lame editorials, I can write four stories. Plus, I write more profiles than anyone in Features and write a TV column six days a week that's been syndicated in 17 papers. That's what I'm doing here, Becky. Got it?"

"Touchy, touchy," Becky smiled, unfazed. The queen of multitasking, she was now listening to her phone messages, reading her home and garden column and riffling through the day's wire stories. "Seven inches of rain expected in Northern California in the next twenty-four hours," she announced, clicking away. "'Brad Pitt files a restraining order against a beautiful teenager who stalked him.' 'Monica Lewinsky has successful interview with House prosecutors.'" She leaned back in her chair and shook her head. "If I read another word about that woman and that no-good president of ours, I think I'll. . ."

"No right-wing diatribes," Rick warned, lofting an orange peel into the trashcan by the sports department. Sports never came in until lunchtime. "Save them for Mr. Toby."

Mr. Toby was the ill-tempered gray schnauzer

whom Becky and Alan, her college sweetheart and spouse, both devout Christians from Wisconsin, adored. Becky had raised three children while working at the paper and could write and edit stories while kibitzing with us and talking to Alan about what she was making him for dinner that night. Prim, unexpected and politically right of Rush Limbaugh, she was an acquired taste that Rick and I had definitely acquired. He kept a computer file of her most memorable musings that he called "Planet Becky: Where Nice People Say Nice Things About Nice People." His most recent "Planet Becky" entry was: "Dogs just love you. They don't care how much money you make."

"Jane's moving to Mendocino County," Rick said, hooking another orange peel over Becky's head. Reporters loved to break stories, particularly ones that involved their friends, even if they weren't true.

"That's not true, Rick," I protested.

Becky stopped typing. "Why Mendocino County?"

"We looked at some land north of Willits yesterday," I said. "We kind of liked it, but we're not moving anywhere.

"Willits is the home of the Skunk Train," Becky said, scanning a story she was editing. "Built in the 1890s to carry logs from the Mendocino coast sawmills. Nicknamed the Skunk Train because people said you could smell the gas engines long before you could see the train." She glanced over at me. "By the way, Jane, they just closed a munitions factory in Willits that leaked chromium-6 into a downtown creek. Might be a good story for you if you're headed up that way. I'd let you do something for Features if you want. Or you could do a travel piece about Covelo--that's also Mendocino County. The Yankee Army rounded up all the Pomo and Miwok and other Indian tribes from Northern California and drove them there like animals. It's right up your alley, with the diversity theme, Jane."

"You know so much, sounds like you should write it," I said. "Mike's already giving me grief about my UFO story."

"She's reading it off the Internet," Rick hissed.

"That's not true, Rick." Becky leaned around her computer. "Our son's fifth grade class took a field trip on the Skunk Train. It's quite a ways north, Jane. You'd have to quit the paper."

"The rats are deserting the ship," Rick sighed.

I laughed. "All we saw was raw land. There isn't a house or anything on it. Just trees and grass 16 miles north of Willits."

"That's almost in Laytonville then," Becky said. "Home of Wavy Gravy, the old hippie who runs Camp Winnarainbow."

"Go, Winnarainbow!" Rick chortled.

"It's a clown camp for kids," Becky said. "He has classes for adults, too. Maybe Jane can become a clown. Or a back-to-the-lander. Mendocino's where half San Francisco's hippies had their communes and grew pot."

"Being a clown's pretty similar to writing editorials," Rick said. "Jane might be good."

"I like writing editorials." I swallowed some Red Zinger tea and studied my day's assignments. "It's just. . ."

"If you like writing editorials for this paper, you're brain-dead."

"Be nice, Rick," Becky cautioned.

Truth be told, I was starting to hate writing editorials although I loved the newsroom and Rick and Becky and my other pals in Features. I'd gone to work for the paper four years before, desperate for a regular paycheck and a break from teaching English at schools that closed soon after I was hired. There weren't any desks near my boss, the paper's editor, so they put me at an empty computer in Features. We were a little universe of tranquility a few dozen yards away from the faster pace of the city desk, with its blaring police scanner, twice-daily news meetings and grumpy, just-the-facts, man, editors. But I was frustrated. Writing all day and working on my novel at night and weekends was wearing me out.

"If you leave, Jane, who would I talk to?" Becky said. "Wait until I retire." She and Alan had recently bought a condominium near Tucson and planned to move there, playing golf until they expired.

"You'll leave before me," I said, trying to think of an opener for tomorrow's editorial on why a local school board should stand up to a parent group demanding that a film on gay families be dumped from the family life curriculum.

"That reminds me," said Becky, who no doubt went to church with some of the parents leading the charge against the film. "I have to call HR about my pension plan. Those people upstairs treat my pension as if it's *their* money."

"Capitalist pigs," Rick shot.

"Oh, I have no problem with capitalists," Becky said. "But since I've worked at this company my entire adult life, you'd think they could show a little human kindness. Whatever happened to human kindness? And on the topic of human kindness. . ." Becky lowered her voice to a whisper and glanced furtively at me. "Have you noticed that Paul and Tricia are taking very long lunches together these days?" She was referring to the handsome entertainment writer and the editor of the paper's weekend magazine. "Do they really think that if she comes in from lunch five minutes after he does, we won't know they're an item?"

"By the way they pour over those page proofs," I smirked, "you'd think they were reading the Kama Sutra or. . ."

"Scoop!"

I sat up straight, clicked tomorrow's editorial back onto my screen, and faced forward. It was Pam, the Features editor, who liked me on some days and despised me on others. Pam had taken to calling me Scoop as a little joke that amused her immensely because, as an editorial writer who'd taught English before joining the paper's staff, I never had scoops and never broke any news, which was one reason why I was tired of my job. Lately, Pam had been offering me unsolicited tips on how to succeed in the newspaper business.

"Scoop," she said. "Have I told you that if you want your boss to promote you, you've got to look busy? If you don't look busy, your boss won't think you're working hard enough. Got that?"

"Sure," I said, pondering tomorrow's other editorial on the unsightly weeds along the median strips in our town, one of my boss's pet peeves. "That makes a lot of sense."

"Another thing, Scoop." She was spooning the last bite of fruit yogurt from a container. "Never leave the office before your boss. You can leave as soon as he's gone, but never before, and be sure you don't run into him in the parking lot."

"But my boss works till eight every night," I said. "I'd never get out of here."

"Think about it, Scoop," she said, dropping the yogurt carton into the trash bin in Sports where Rick had been tossing orange peels. "You'll save yourself a lot of grief if you take my advice."

"Thanks," I said, rolling my eyes at Becky, who was listening to this exchange with a furrowed brow.

"Don't worry about her," Becky said when Pam drifted over to the city desk. "She's taking that seminar on effective management and thinks she's mentoring you. Plus. . ." Becky lowered her voice. "She's still mad that I'm letting you write the UFO story. She thinks it's all bogus. I do, too, but it's a good story."

"The guy has videos to back it up," I protested. "It's legitimate." A Czech sailor had shown up at the paper a couple of weeks before claiming to have been visited by dozens of UFOs while sailing from Hawaii to San Francisco with a Navajo Indian on a 40-foot sailboat. No reporter would touch the story or believed his fuzzy videos, but I found the tale riveting and persuaded Becky to let me write about it for Features. I'd been calling UFO experts around the country and had accumulated some juicy tidbits about Area 51 and the U.S. government's suppression of UFO sightings.

"Jane!"

I ducked for cover. This time it was Mike, my boss, standing by his office door a football field away. "Got a minute?" It was an order, not a question. Was he all steamed up about UFOs, too?

I reached for my pen and a legal pad.

"What a rude bastard!" Rick flipped a finger at Mike's back. "Why can't the frigging executive editor call you on the phone or e-mail you or come to your desk like all the other editors? What an asshole. Editors are assholes."

"I heard that," Becky clucked.

"You know he's an asshole," Rick said. "He thinks he's fucking H. L. Mencken because he worked for *The Baltimore Sun* for a couple of years.

"It was quite a bit longer than that," Becky chided. "But I'll agree he has poor social skills. He's better than the Black Widow. Wouldn't you agree?"

"Oh, Jesus," Rick moaned. "That bitch fired half the newsroom."

As Rick and Becky reminisced about the Black Widow's brutal regime, I trudged past the empty desks in Sports trying to guess which of my recent editorials Mike was going to complain about. There was yesterday's hospital piece on the emergency room scandal, and Saturday's wishy-washy hand-slap of the Air Force for leaving a toxic plume of MTBE at the mothballed military base nearby, and today's quickie urging the socialist doctor from Belvedere to get rid of his roosters, whose crowing was bothering the residents of one of the county's most exclusive enclaves. No one had called me at home to query any facts, but then an alarming number of mistakes got by our copy desk. Readers, on the other hand, caught everything. One tiny slip and by 7 a.m. every phone in the newsroom was ringing.

A handful of curious reporters watched as I

entered Mike's office, a place everyone tried to avoid. He didn't look up, just continued marking the front page of the day's paper with his famous red grease pencil. It was a good sign, I thought, that he wasn't attacking the editorial page.

"God damn copy desk!" His eyes narrowed and his face turned the same color red as the pack of Marlboros in his shirt pocket. He leapt from his chair and steamed off to the managing editor's office. Through the glass, I could see him toss the paper onto her desk and cross his arms. I, meanwhile, wracked my brain for something diverting to say to Mike about Baltimore, where I had also grown up. "How 'bout them O's?" only worked so many times.

"Siddown." Mike sank back into his chair.

I hesitated. "Which chair?" There were papers piled on every seat in his office.

"Move those," he said, pointing to the stack of *Wall Street Journals* to my right. I reached down, about to place them onto another stack.

"Not there, for Christ's sake," he yelled. "Those are sister papers from other cities. Put the *Journals* on the floor."

Settled at last, I tried not to stare at the scar on Mike's lip that he'd acquired, according to Rick and Becky, when a bullet fired by a mugger in Baltimore grazed his face and landed in his wife's head. She'd died that night, they said, as the killer disappeared into the darkness.

"I've been wanting to run a police log for a long time," Mike began, pinging a rubber band against his Orioles coffee mug. "Readers love those things. Like the little old lady who calls the cops every time the neighbor's cat shits in her front yard, or the 5150 who swears there's a dead man walking around his attic. Funny stuff like that. You know what I mean?"

"Sure," I said. I rarely read cop logs myself, but I was delighted that apparently I hadn't been summoned to discuss a problem with one of my editorials.

"Well?" He watched me with his piercing brown eyes.

"People love those things," I stalled, hoping to catch his drift.

"Do you want the job?"

"What job?"

"Writing the cop log," he said, sucking on an unlit cigarette. "How many cups of that herbal tea did you drink this morning?" His chair yelped for oil as he leaned back. "You told me you wanted to work part time so you can write the great American novel, and this is your chance. The job is 30 hours a week. If you get inspired, you might become the next P.D James or Elmore Leonard."

The beginning of a smile crept across my lips. "So I'd leave the editorial page and do the cops log, part time?"

"For the city desk. You'd be a reporter."

"And I'd work four days, not five?"

"As long as you get your work done."

"And have Friday off?" I held my breath. That would mean three days in a row to write. The paper never let anyone go part-time. But Mike was right in front of me telling me I could. "And I'd be a reporter?"

"You don't think I'd make you a news assistant, do you?" He gulped some coffee. "You won a first for the paper last year. I'm going to take care of you. You'll be a reporter with full benefits."

"Wow," I said. I wasn't really a cops kind of person, but I could learn if it meant a job where I could stop pretending I agreed with the paper's editorial positions.

"I want to call it 'On the Beat,'" Mike was saying. "You visit three or four police stations a day, talk to the desk sergeants, flip through the logs, and bring back the best items from around the county. If you find a trend developing, like some con artist hustling seniors out of their Social Security checks or a gang of kids flattening tires, you turn it into a story. Of course, the big crime stuff, the breaking news, will still go to the police reporter. But the log would be one hundred percent your deal." He looked at me with his penetrating eyes.

I swallowed. Rick would give me untold grief when he heard about this. If writing editorials was purgatory, he'd say working for the city desk was hell.

"Can I have a day to think it over?"

"Sure." Mike puffed on his unlit Marlboro. "You're not insulted?"

"Insulted?"

"You might think it's beneath you."

Clearly, he had no idea how much I had come to dislike writing editorials. I hadn't either until that morning. I sat up. "If I were paranoid," I said, clearing my throat. "I might think you're kind of eager to get me off the editorial page. You have someone in mind for my job?"

Mike peered through the window at Brad, a tall, redheaded, veteran reporter who had started with the paper as a newsboy, gone to journalism school at Berkeley and had covered every beat in the newsroom during his tenure at the paper. He, Becky, and Sandy, the recently divorced office manager who dashed off daily letters to Doctor Laura about her ex-husband's infidelity, were the only Republicans in the newsroom.

"Keep this to yourself," Mike rasped. "I've been working on Brad for a while now. He's burnt out on beat reporting and knows everybody in the county. The edit page is a perfect fit for him."

"Good choice," I nodded. Brad knew so much about the county that before I'd even reached my desk in the morning he'd stop me to let me know how lame and misguided my day's editorials were. "He'd be great," I said.

"If he'll take it." Mike opened his office door.

"So when would this happen?"

He chewed his scarred lip. "End of next month. Two months at the latest. I've got paperwork three-feet high to fill out for those HR Nazis upstairs, and then I've got to lean on Brad." He turned. "You'll let me know tomorrow?"

"First thing," I said, getting up to leave.

"Do me one favor, Jane," Mike said softly.

"Sure, Mike." My heart was in my throat.

"No more UFO stories, okay? Pam's giving me hell for okaying it."

I nodded. "But Becky said. . ."

"Becky ran it by me, and I said okay. But now Pam's all bent out of shape. Thinks it's bogus, which I don't doubt."

"It's a good story, Mike. You'll be happy with it."

Mike rolled his eyes. "Just make sure it's not a one-source story, okay? Get someone on the record who's not a kook."

"I've already interviewed an ex-Air Force pilot. And. . ."

Mike wasn't listening. He was storming back to the managing editor's office with his grease pencil.

Brad was on the phone when I passed his desk, but he winked at me, just to be sure that I knew that he knew before I knew what Mike had talked to me about. *Please, Brad*, I prayed. *Be foolish enough to take my job so I can run around to police departments hunting for quirky "On the Beat" items.*

Back in Features, Rick was walking the dog with his Day-Glo pink yoyo while Becky was deep in conversation with Alan over some new kibble that had upset Mr. Toby's tummy. Paul had arrived and was tête-à-tête with Tricia.

"So?" Rick hovered next to my desk in his stocking feet and his yoyo. "What did Mike want?"

"Just some editorial series he's cooked up," I lied. "Nothing important."

"Did you tell him you're moving to the country?"

"Who's moving to the country?" Paul blinked the soulful brown eyes that had launched a thousand ships.

"Not me," I said.

"So what's the editorial blitz?" Rick smelled a rat.

"Um. . ." I hesitated. "Single-payer health-care coverage--a bunch of pro-con pieces and editorials." It wasn't a total lie. Mike had mentioned a few weeks ago that he wanted to do an editorial blitz on health insurance.

"And what does the esteemed editorial board think about single-payer health insurance?" Rick snarled.

"They hate it," I said, searching my wallet for pay phone change. "Too expensive. Brings us menacingly close to socialism. But we're keeping an open mind."

"Idiots," Rick reddened. "The U.S. is the only advanced industrialized nation in the world with no national health insurance, and this paper loves it."

I headed down the back staircase. I couldn't call Erin about the cops job with the entire cast of Features listening in, so I had to use the pay phone in the lobby. "Any requests from the vending machines?" I said to throw Rick off the scent.

"Food that drops is very bad for you," he said, patting his stomach. "I've gone 47 days without dropping a single dime in the evil machines."

"You're a wonder," I said, skipping down the stairs. The coast was clear. No one using the pay phone, and the receptionist in the lobby was too busy on her headphones trying to arrange childcare for her daughter to notice me.

"Hey," I said to Erin. "Guess what?"

"The paper is flooding?"

"Mike offered me a job writing a police log for the city desk. I'll be a reporter. Thirty hours a week with benefits. I can take Fridays off."

"Wow!" she said. "What did you say?"

"Told him I'd think about it," I whispered. "I'm in the lobby. Can't really talk."

"Come home early tonight. I'll take you out to Chinese food and you can tell me everything."

I cartwheeled back up to the newsroom with a decoy root beer from the vending machine in my hand. It was too good to be true. Land in the country and a new job in just 24 hours, all because I'd committed to this idea of living as if I were going to die. Which, of course, I was.

CHAPTER 6

HORSES MAKE A LANDSCAPE MORE BEAUTIFUL

Erin, Stephanie and I were pressed into the front seat of an all-terrain vehicle that she called the Mule, bouncing down Parcel 39 on a brilliant sunny day in early May, on our fifth visit to Cherry Creek.

We'd decided to buy Parcel 40. Max, Liz's lawyer, had received our down payment and signed land purchase agreement, but he'd never cashed the check or sent us any paper work. Stephanie had assured us that the deal was all a go, but we'd cajoled her into showing us Parcel 39 that spring morning because the dentist and his wife did not yet own it.

The driveway--a bumpy Jeep trail--cut through an open meadow, switching back through some oak and bay and madrone trees, then traversing more green fields. A jackrabbit broke from cover and zigzagged ahead of us.

Off to the right Liz's wild horses were grazing on the hillside. I counted six--all geldings, Stephanie said. There were three chestnuts, a tall black horse with a white blaze, and two adorable fuzzy black ones, not much bigger than ponies.

"I'm in heaven," I laughed. "It's an episode from 'Spin and Marty' on *The Mickey Mouse Club*."

"Stephanie's too young to remember Spin and Marty." Erin pulled my 'Niners baseball cap over my eyes.

Stephanie was negotiating a particularly tricky turn. "*The Mickey Mouse Club* was directed by Francis D. Lyon, with Tim Considine as Spin and David Stollery as Marty."

"Wow!" Erin said, slack-jawed. "How'd you know that?"

Stephanie switched off the Mule where the road came to an abrupt end, near a giant rock covered in lichen and shaded by a bay laurel tree. "You accumulate a lot of show biz trivia when you live in Hollywood with a film director." She pointed to her right. "Shall we hike to the home site across the meadow?"

We followed Stephanie for several hundred yards along a horse trail that crossed a steep hillside and opened onto a wide meadow rimmed by tall oak trees. One of the oaks dipped and curved, its trunk forming a dramatic, graceful U, a few feet above the ground. The soil beneath it was bare because the wild horses liked to scratch their flanks against the trunk and rest there in the cool shade of the tree, Stephanie said.

She looked up and back in the direction we'd come from. "It's a long way to bring electricity down from the PG&E lines up on the road, about half a mile, but at least you'd be close to the developed spring, over where we left the Mule."

We both turned from the crooked oak to the view in front of us. The sloping meadow descended gradually into a wooded canyon, and beyond that was the same series of ridges we saw from the top of Parcel 40. The first ridge was part of Cherry Creek but accessed from another gate off the Covelo Road, Stephanie explained. The next was Shimmins Ridge, on the far side of the road. The mountains far to the east were part of the Mendocino National Forest.

Erin and I looked at each other, inhaling the smell of sun on wet grass. I was thinking of the three-story brick duplex in Baltimore where I'd grown up, on a busy street by a bus stop, with traffic roaring by day and night. That would never happen here. Parcel 39 was heaven--quiet, endless and private.

"Have the dentist and his wife sent you their down payment on this parcel?" Erin tried to sound calm, but she didn't fool me.

"Good question." Stephanie folded her arms in front of her chest. "Cindy would like 39, but there's a smaller, 40-acre parcel down by Cherry Creek that Rod prefers."

I was shredding a Kleenex in my hand. "We're...in love with this parcel. I know we've put money down on 40, but Liz hasn't cashed our check. What if we switched? It's the same price, right?"

"Could we do that?" Erin nodded. "If the dentist can't decide?"

"I can write you a new check today," I said, taking a breath.

"Well. . ." Stephanie cocked her head to one side. "I haven't wanted to pressure them, but it's been over five months. I could call Rod and Cindy and tell them you're very interested in this parcel and give them a couple of weeks to make up their minds. If they say 'No,' the parcel would be yours."

We drove home in a swoon.

"It's so open," Erin said dreamily as we passed the ghostly, abandoned brick hotel at the second stoplight in Willits. "That meadow by the crooked oak is perfect for a house and a garden and an orchard--maybe even a pond down below."

"Our Xanadu."

"San Simeon," Erin laughed. "We could build a rammed earth house like your cousin Anne's in Sonoma." Erin had become an expert in alternative building materials since our first trip to Cherry Creek.

I took a breath. "Are we getting ahead of ourselves?"

"Oh, why not?" She bit down on a peanut butter pretzel. "Imagine hiking for an hour and still being on our own property, with the house on that open meadow, away from the road, and miles of hills and wildflowers and little seasonal creeks and trees and silence between us and the world."

"It'll be more expensive to develop than 40," I said giddily. "A lot farther from the road and the PG&E poles and telephone lines."

Erin squeezed my hand. "We'll make it work. First, we have to get it. And I think we will. I can see us there. Let's visualize it being ours."

Erin excelled at seeing positive outcomes to situations that left me dog paddling desperately in a murky limbo of doubt and uncertainty. So while she slept like a baby that night, I tossed and turned to images of the dentist and his wife chasing us off Parcel 39 with a giant, jagged toothbrush, pushing us all the way back to the noisy street where I grew up.

Stephanie called in the morning as I was getting dressed for work.

"Good news," she said. I waved to Erin to pick up the other phone. "Parcel 39 is yours. Rod and Cindy have decided to buy the 40-acre parcel down on Cherry Creek.

"Are they angry at us?" I asked.

"Not at all. They're looking forward to meeting you."

Erin and I danced around my office like *Saturday Night Live* cheerleaders. "We did it, we did it, oh, yes, we really did it," we chanted.

By the next weekend, we'd sent newly signed land purchase agreement papers to Max in Los Angeles and bought a beautiful blue tent, two green canvas camping chairs, a Coleman stove, and sleeping bags. Our life off the grid was about to begin. *Spin and Marty, here we come.*

CHAPTER 7

CONSIDER YOURSELF AT HOME

We'd barely erected our tent, when Stephanie brought over a man named Doug, a slender, wiry guy with leathery skin who played the violin for the Ukiah Symphony. He owned a fleet of earth-moving machines he could use to make a road across the hillside so we could drive the last leg to the flat, open meadow near the twisted oak.

"How much would a road across the meadow

cost?" Erin asked.

Doug pushed his baseball cap up on his head and gazed out at the hillside, chewing his lip. "Depends how much rock I hit. The more rock I hit, the more time it takes." He wiped his forehead with a blue bandana; his face was tanned and grooved from years of bouncing around on a bulldozer in the blazing Mendocino sun. "I won't really know until get in there with the Cat. Shouldn't take me more than a week."

"How much does a week cost?"

"Depends what I find. If I have to dynamite it could be more."

"Dynamite?" My eyes widened.

"Might have to. Depends on the rock. There's a lot of rock in the lower part of that meadow."

"Can you show us exactly where the road would go?" Erin looked skeptical.

"Can't say exactly until I get out there on the Cat. I'll try to make it as straight across the hill as I can. All depends on what I find."

Doug drove off with Stephanie in his battered Volvo, leaving us to contemplate the project in our green camp chairs that we'd dragged over to the crooked oak for shade.

"Hard to know how much anything will cost," I said, slugging down some vanilla cream soda.

"Everything seems to depend on something else." Erin pulled burrs from Woody's ears. The two dachshunds, with their silky, floor-length hair, weren't designed for the country. Even sheared as close as we could go, their hair was a constant tangle of foxtails and burrs.

"I'm sure we can work something out," Erin consoled. "Stephanie says his rates are fair and his work is good."

I squinted across at the hillside and tried to imagine a road running through the beautiful meadow instead of a horse trail. "So you feel okay building a road before we own the land?"

Erin tilted back in her chair. "If Liz is happy that we're buying the land, and Stephanie says it's okay, I think we're fine. The sale's going to happen, it's just a matter of time. So, why not put in the road? Even if we never build a cabin or a house here, having a road would give us the option. Imagine pitching our tent under these oaks."

"Have you ever hired a bulldozer before?" I said, knowing full well she hadn't.

"Relax," Erin laughed. "You're driving me nuts with your negativity. Change the tape, okay?"

"But Deb said. . ."

"Is Deb buying the land?"

"She's a lawyer."

"Well, lawyers are paid to be skeptical."

My friend Deb, who was an attorney, had gone silent when I called her from work and mentioned that we were thinking about putting in a road and possibly a pond--Doug said that would be easy-- on land we didn't quite own.

"What do you mean you don't quite own it?" I pictured her scowling into the telephone. "You either own it or you don't."

"Then I guess we don't."

"But," she sputtered, "what if the owner changes her mind? If she's as wealthy as you say, she's probably quixotic and does whatever she pleases. She could sell the land out from under you. She could sue you for destruction of her property. You've got to have something in writing."

I inhaled. I guess to a lawyer like Deb it must have sounded like kind of an unusual arrangement. "We sent in a land purchase agreement months ago, but Liz hasn't signed it or returned it to us or cashed our check."

"What if she changes her mind?"

"Stephanie says Liz is thrilled we're buying the land, and the reason her lawyer hasn't gotten back to us is because he's in a trial or something."

I glanced over at Rick. He had just hung up on his wife and was way too angry to eavesdrop on my chat with Deb. Becky was eyeing me curiously. Even though she was interviewing a beekeeper for the home and garden section, she was a great multi-tasker and could easily track two conversations at once.

"And who is this Stephanie?" Deb was saying?

"She's Liz's caretaker. She's very friendly and…"

"She's the caretaker?"

"She's very nice. And really smart." I looked down to avoid seeing Becky's raised eyebrows. "She's really more than a caretaker. She and her husband are from Hollywood. They worked in the film industry doing. . ." I paused. I wasn't sure what they did, but they did something.

"Does she have a real estate license?"

"She's just a person," I swallowed. "A very nice, knowledgeable and trustworthy person."

"You're vulnerable here, Jane," Deb said, clicking away on her computer keyboard. "If she were a licensed agent from a reputable firm, I could call her manager and insist this Liz or her lawyer complete and return the paperwork. But this is. . ."

"Informal," I said, doodling dollar signs on a yellow Post-It note. "Listen, none of the other buyers have their paperwork either. Not the dentist and his wife or even Gina and Lin, and Gina's known Liz for years."

"Well, Jane," she said soberly. "I hope for your sake it all works out. If you'd like, I can write a letter to Liz's lawyer on your behalf."

"Thank you," I said. "Erin visualizes it all coming through effortlessly."

"Glad to hear it," she said. "You can call if you need me."

Back at the tent site, we'd become aware of the fact that the waxy bushes that splashed the golden pastures by our campsite with green swatches of color were poison oak, into which Woody and Luna perpetually plunged in search of gophers and quail and who knew what else. Their coats were always loaded with poison oak oil, which they smeared on us when they snuggled down next to us in bed at night.

Erin was desperately allergic to poison oak. The night of Doug the bulldozer guy's visit, she toweled off the dogs, painting herself with a protective layer of calamine lotion while I inspected our bedding for rattlesnakes before we went turned in. I had never seen a rattlesnake except in the zoo, but Stephanie had warned us that there were lots of them at Cherry Creek and that they were particularly fond of the terrain on our parcel--open, south-facing meadows with rocky outcroppings and oak groves. I remembered a hiking buddy from college telling me that snakes love to sunbathe on big, hot rocks, like the one a few feet from our tent, so I was more hyper vigilant than usual--not the best frame of mind to be in at bedtime.

The sky that night was so full of stars that we opened the flap of the tent dome to gaze at them from our sleeping bags.

"So beautiful," Erin said.

I extinguished our newly acquired battery-powered lantern. "Do you think any bears will visit?"

"Gina and Lin say the bears here are afraid of people," Erin said sleepily. "We're not in Yellowstone. These bears aren't used to tourists and garbage and cars."

"How do you know?"

"Take a Benadryl," she said, turning over.

"Good idea," I said. "Where is it?"

"In the car. Good night."

I didn't want to put on my shoes and rummage through the car in the dark, exposing myself to lurking bears and other predators. So no Benadryl for me.

Erin was soon snoring, while I inserted my earplugs to drown out the deafening chorus of crickets and frogs, breeze rippling through the tent flaps. *This is the life,* I told myself, trying, as suggested by Erin, to see my cup as half full. *We are out here on our very own land*--well, on land that was almost ours—*with gorgeous, undulating ridges and a sky full of stars and no traffic noise to disturb our reverie.*

An unearthly scream burst from the hill above our tent.

I sat up. "Did you hear that?"

"I'm asleep," Erin groaned through her Benadryl haze.

Soon there were more blood-curdling screams followed by short, excited yips.

"What was that?" I clutched her arm.

"Coyotes," she said, covering her head with a pillow.

"They sound way too close." My grip tightened.

"Coyotes don't attack people," were her last words. I snuggled closer, but she was asleep again in seconds, oblivious to my terror. I peered up through the dome praying the coyotes would be distracted by a jackrabbit or gopher or whatever they preyed upon. *This is the life*, I told myself again, returning to my litany of positive things about owning, nearly owning, land in the country. *I'm the luckiest person in the world to be lying in this well ventilated, brand new tent with my beloved next to me and. . .*

Another hideous shriek. They were closing in.

It doesn't get any better than this, I repeated single-mindedly. *We're being serenaded by coyotes in our very own tent on our very own--* almost--*land.*

Hours later, Erin rolled over and smiled as the sun came over the hill in front of us. "How'd you sleep?"

"I didn't," I said, body stiff as a board, eyes swollen, head throbbing with fatigue.

"Too bad."

"I know *you* slept because your snoring harmonized perfectly with the coyotes' howling."

She laughed and unzipped the tent flap. Fog crouched in the valley below us, turning the ridgeline peaks into islands in an ocean of white. Jays and goldfinches and woodpeckers and towhees dipped down to drink from the natural spring just below us. The air was cool and unbelievably fresh. Too bad I felt like I'd been run over by a truck. I found our tea mugs and the kettle, while Erin produced gorgeous blueberry pancakes on the Coleman stove. Content at last, I sat next to Erin in a green canvas chair eating a breakfast Spin and Marty would have died for.

By 10 a.m., the sun had come over the ridge, scorching our campsite because the poison oak wasn't tall enough to provide protective shade. So we took a picnic down to the swimming hole at Outlet Creek, the same spot where we'd been stranded with Stephanie on that first day at Cherry Creek. Paddling upstream through a series of deep, wide pools, the sky clear and azure above us, I felt fatigue give way to pleasure at our grand scheme of purchasing our very own national park. Willows blanketed both sides of the creek, and a red-tailed hawk circled above us. I squeezed Erin's hand as we floated back toward the sandy beach. "This is fun," I said.

She smiled. "You're not suffering too much out here in the middle of nowhere?"

"I think I'm actually happy," I said, treading water.

Erin kissed my cheek. "Take a picture of this feeling with every cell in your body so you remember it when you're back at home wringing your hands about how much the land is going to cost and how far from civilization it is and how this will be the end of life as you know it. Okay?

"Okay." I clicked my mental camera.

"Promise?"

"The photo's on it's way to the lab."

One morning in August, Gina and Lin came over for Erin's now famous blueberry pancakes. Their land was just down the road from us, but we'd hardly seen them that summer at Cherry Creek. They'd mentioned that they camped on their land without a tent because they'd hidden it in some bushes near the creek and never been able to find it again.

"Is everything okay with Liz?" Erin asked Gina. We still didn't have any paperwork from her or Max.

"It's all fine," Gina said. "We don't know what's taking so long, but it's all happening. Rod and Cindy are up this weekend. Want to meet them?"

Rod and Cindy, the dentist and his wife, had now settled into their 40-acre parcel right on Cherry Creek, not far from Liz's cabin. I was nervous about seeing them. "Suppose they hate us?" I said.

"Don't be silly," Lin said. "They don't hate you. They love their parcel."

I looked at Erin.

"Why not?" she shrugged. "It's too hot to stay here in the sun."

Rod was a handsome, powerful, bearded man in his fifties, who was, at that moment, clearing a manzanita grove with a Bobcat. Cindy--tall and fair and pink--was watering some skinny redwood saplings they'd recently planted by the road. Near the creek was a long white mobile home that they called a fifth wheel.

"Welcome to Serendipity Ranch," Rod said, giving us all bear hugs.

We sat in their green Costco camp chairs that

were just like ours, in the shade next to the creek, sipping their deliciously cold sodas.

Cindy was pulling burrs from her dog's ears. Our dogs, who hated all big dogs, were in the car, which was parked in the shade. "Have any of you heard from Max or Liz?"

Lin and Gina shook their heads.

"We haven't either," Erin said.

"Stephanie says it's all going forward," Cindy said. "So Rod's clearing brush and, as you can see. . ." She pointed to Rod's little bulldozer and the trailer and a lovely, arched, redwood bridge across the creek that Rod had nearly completed. "We're making ourselves at home."

"We plan to build a road over to the crooked oak and a pond and eventually a cabin," Erin said. "Stephanie's carpenter friend Kerry is going to help us with the cabin."

"He is?" I stared at Erin.

"Lucky you," Cindy said wistfully.

"By the way," Rod said with a wink. "We're very happy with our parcel, so no worries about stealing Parcel 39 out from under us."

Erin laughed. "It's really okay?"

Rod laughed. "We love being by the creek, don't we, Cindy?"

Cindy smiled less enthusiastically. "It's home now."

"Cool," Erin said. "So everybody's happy."

❧

We weren't prepared for the giant, gaping gash slashing through what had days before been our glorious, grassy meadow. It was late one Friday afternoon in August when we arrived, red dust spinning in whirlwinds as Doug gouged his Caterpillar deeper into the hillside, tearing out the final stretch of road to the home site. The roar was so loud that he didn't hear us approach or see us as he pulled rods and levers, swiveling around in his chair, alternating between the shovel on the front end and the menacing digger claws in the back. When he finally spotted us, he turned off the engine; the silence was deafening.

"Thought I'd have to dynamite the last leg," he said, standing up on the rig, baseball cap in hand, pointing to the hillside beside us. "Found a lot of rock." He shook out his legs, wiping his forehead on his dusty T-shirt, nodding at our shocked expressions. "It always looks bad the first time you see it. But you'll get used to it. By next year, if you seed along the road and put straw down to stop erosion during the rainy season, the grass will grow, and you'll forget it ever looked like this."

"It's so. . ." Erin paused, shaking her head.

"Ugly," I gulped.

"Just for now. Not forever," Doug said in his hoarse, dust-coated bass. "Got to have a road if you want to get a vehicle over to your home site."

"What kind of seed should we plant?" Erin was already moving forward.

"Rye or barley will work. Something fast-growing. Get it down at Mendocino Ag Supply in Ukiah. Cover it with straw, and you'll be fine." He hoisted himself back up into his torn leather seat. "You still want a pond? I can do a soil test next week. If I find enough clay, I'll start right away. Too much rock and it won't hold water."

"Do we still want a pond?" I bleated, looking at Erin as I imagined the destruction that project would create.

"Absolutely," Erin said. "We'd like it down there." Erin pointed to a spot below the meadow, where two hills came together, creating a swale.

"Okay," Doug said, switching on the massive engine. "No problem. If you're going to stick around--" he was shouting now, above the roar of the Cat. "Don't come too close because I can't hear you, and I can't see you very well when I'm on this rig."

We watched the Cat claw a few more chunks of the hillside on its hulking march toward our home site, then headed for the creek.

"Just think," I said, paddling next to Erin in a deep pool down at Outlet Creek. We were looking up behind us at the enormous rocky cliff on Liz's spectacular, last-remaining parcel. "If that development behind our house in Marin gets approved, we'll hear bulldozers like Doug's for months. And trucks carrying dirt, and cement mixers, and hammers and everything else."

"We'll move up here if that happens," Erin smiled, pulling a piece of river weed from my cheek.

"Move up here?"

"I know you're scared. But it's all going to be okay. Liz and her lawyer will sign the paperwork, and the land will be ours, and the rain will come, and the grass will grow, and the road will look beautiful, and we'll feel like it's always been there, and you'll be happy."

"It's so shocking."

"Focus on the end result. When it's finished we'll be able to pitch our tent by the twisted oak, in the shade, and we won't be so blazing hot when we camp, and it'll be the beginning of our homestead. And maybe we'll even have our own little cabin by the spring."

I swallowed. "We don't even have title to the place yet."

She kissed my wet cheek. "I love you, you know. We're in this together. Does that help?"

Erin's pager went off the next morning while we were cooking sausages. The phone number on the tiny screen was her daughter's in New Mexico. Jiwan was three months pregnant and had started spotting a few days before, an ominous sign that worried Erin. "She knows how hard it is for us to call. She wouldn't page me if it weren't important."

We gulped down breakfast and drove as fast as we could to Liz's cabin, where Ken and Stephanie lived and had a telephone land line. Neither one answered when we knocked on their front door.

"What do we do?" Erin said. "Their cars are here."

"Go in, I guess. I don't think they'll mind."

Erin knocked again and entered, while I walked around the side of the house, looking out at the valley and the ridge beyond, toward Rod and Cindy's compound. I could just make out the metal roof of their RV.

"Hello? Ken? Ken?"

I jumped about a foot. Whose voice was that?

I followed the sound around to the back of the house and saw that the speaker was a brilliant red macaw, staring at me from a perch. Stephanie was a few steps away feeding the other birds in giant outdoor cages.

"Oh, Jesus, Jane," she said, dropping a metal plate of chopped vegetables, fruit, and nuts. "You scared me."

"I'm so sorry," I said. "We got a page from Erin's daughter, and we need to use your phone. She's pregnant, and it's kind of an emergency."

"Not a problem." Stephanie glanced at the door. "The door's unlocked."

I nodded. "She's inside already. Can I help you feed the birds?"

Stephanie shook her head. "Not unless you're prepared to lose an eye or a piece of your cheek. They're a little finicky."

I was riveted to the site of the big red macaws and white cockatoos, whose eyes followed my every move as Stephanie cooed and chattered with them.

"Have you heard from Liz?" I asked.

She coughed. "Liz and I aren't speaking at the moment."

"Not speaking?" I stared at her.

"Liz is not an easy person to deal with." She turned. "Let me rephrase that. She's impossible."

"Wow," I swallowed, thinking of Doug and his yellow Cat tearing through our meadow. Liz's meadow. "Is our deal still on?"

"Oh, yes. No worries about that."

I was dying to ask what Liz was doing that was so impossible, but Stephanie didn't seem to want to discuss it. "So I guess the Labor Day party you and Liz are throwing for the new owners is off?" Stephanie had been planning a weekend of activities for new buyers and old owners, culminating in a culinary extravaganza of roasted emu by the creek.

"Oh, it's on. We're having a luau and Hawaiian dancers from San Francisco."

"Even with the. . .problems?"

"Stop it, Schnoodles!" Stephanie yelled. One of the birds had lunged at the Australian shepherd, who looked startled. "Leave the bird alone."

"Jane?" Erin's stricken voice sent all the birds into an alarmed frenzy. "Jiwan miscarried. She was having twins. One of them. . ." Her lip trembled, and she blinked away tears. "Aborted naturally. The other one is fine."

"I'm sorry." I wrapped my arms around her.

"Twins would have been hard," she said bravely. In seconds she was sobbing.

❧

Erin flew to New Mexico to lend moral support to her daughter, leaving me in charge of the land purchase and bulldozing activities.

Stephanie called often. She said that Doug, the bulldozer guy, had finished the new leg of road to the home site and nearly completed the pond, where he'd found a lot of rock--not good for ponds--that he'd covered over with clay he'd found when he was digging. He'd mentioned, she said casually, that the top part of our driveway, the old ranch road, was too steep to pass a California Department of Forestry fire inspection, and we'd need a CDF permit if we ever built a house and wanted to insure it.

"You have to make a more gradual entry road, and you should do it now, while Doug has his equipment here," Stephanie said.

I took a deep breath. "A new entry road? Why didn't he tell us that weeks ago?"

She laughed. "Doug thinks of things as he goes along."

"I wonder how much a new entry will cost." His bill was mounting up faster than flies on road kill.

"He'll be fair, and he works fast."

Easy for her to say.

"One other thing."

I held my breath.

"About Bill."

"Bill?"

"He's the wonderful gay guy from San Francisco buying one of the two parcels above yours, and another parcel below yours."

I waited, heart in my throat.

"He'd like an easement to use your driveway so he can take his all-terrain vehicle down to the creek on his land below yours. He's fabulous. Camps here nearly every weekend with his friend Alan. You'll love them. He says you can swim in the creek any time in exchange for giving him an easement down your road and permission to build a little spur road across your land for his ATV."

I nearly fell out of my chair. "We're buying land in the middle of nowhere so we don't hear cars and see other people. Why would we want someone's ATV coming down our driveway?"

"I know, I know," Stephanie clucked sympathetically. "I told him not to ask you until he meets you, and you have a chance to see how nice he is at the Labor Day picnic. But he begged me to say something. He's a super guy. I know you'll like him."

I put down the phone. Would saying "no" alienate our new neighbor and create ill will? Was that more important than the quiet and privacy we were seeking on the land? What if this Bill was a partier and had dozens of friends from the Castro who'd want bacchanals at the creek and would roar down our not-even-finished road on our not-even-purchased parcel?

I talked to Erin and called Stephanie back. "Tell him we're sorry, but we crave privacy."

Stephanie called two days later. "I have good news and bad news."

I looked at my watch. I had an hour to take the dogs for a walk, shower and drive to work. "I'll take the bad first."

"The spot we found for the new upper entrance to your road is on Bob's property."

I swallowed. "Who's Bob?"

"Bill's friend. He owns the old Whitaker Ranch headquarters parcel on Cherry Creek Road, and he's also buying two of Liz's parcels, including one that's right above yours and next to Bill's. He says he won't give you an easement to build your entry road on his land unless you give Bill an easement to use your driveway to get to his lower parcel."

My stomach coiled.

"Don't panic," Stephanie comforted.

"Why not?"

"Bob doesn't own the land yet. You might be able to persuade Max, Liz's lawyer, to give you an easement for your new entry road before the title changes to Bob."

"That is a stupendous idea," I said. "Meantime, what do we tell Doug about building the new entry road?"

Stephanie lowered her voice. "Between you and me, I'd just go ahead and tell Doug to build it. Bob doesn't own the land yet, and what can he or Max do if the road is already in? They're not going to make you take it out."

"I should talk to Erin about that."

"Well, when you do," Stephanie said, "ask her about something else."

"Oh?" I shook my head as the dogs wagged their tails eagerly, waiting for their walk.

"Doug said today that most of your driveway, not the new part but the old part, badly needs ditches and culverts and grading and gravel in spots, and you should think about having him make those improvements while his equipment is here."

"How much would that be?"

"I can't really say. But better now than later. He'll be quick."

I inhaled. "Is there anything else? Can you hold while I find my smelling salts?"

Stephanie laughed. "As a matter of fact, Doug did mention that the new road across the pasture to your home site will be impassable this winter-- too soft and muddy from all the work he's done. I thought you should know because. . ."

"But Erin wants to build a cabin there this winter," I said, head spinning. "If we can't get a vehicle there, we can't build a cabin."

"Exactly," Stephanie said. "That's why I wanted you to know. But there is a solution."

I tried to visualize my dwindling savings account as half full and forget that Deb now referred to the land as "Futcher's Folly."

"If Doug brings in his water truck," Stephanie was saying, "and he wets the road down now and compacts the dirt and brings in gravel, it will be passable. But. . ." she paused. "That's very. . ."

"Expensive," I finished.

"Well, yes. It's much cheaper and easier to let

the rain compress the road naturally over the winter. But until it dries out in the late spring, he doesn't think you'll be able to drive on it."

"But we were hoping your contractor friend Kerry might build us a cabin that our set-designer friend Douglas has offered to draft plans for."

"Unless Kerry can *fly* his truck over to your house, that won't be possible."

I glanced at the calendar. "What I'd really like is to get my paperwork signed and back from Liz and her lawyer."

"Oh, you will, you will," she said. "No worries."

"You're speaking to Liz?"

"Oh, no," she said. "I probably never will again." She paused. "I've quit. I'm no longer the caretaker."

I stood up, sat down and stood up again, which way over-excited the dogs.

"Ken still works for her momentarily, but we're moving to Jay's guest cottage."

"Jay?"

"You know Jay. He lives in the house that Kerry built. He also has a guest cottage that he's offered us temporarily."

Now, I really felt dizzy. This was all so sudden. What if Liz changed her mind about Erin and me now that she and Stephanie had some sort of dispute? Would she turn on us, too?

"It's going to be a big change for Ken and me and the kids," Stephanie was saying.

"The kids?"

"The birds."

"Of course," I said. "The birds."

"Technically, Ken's still working for Liz, but I don't think he'll stay much beyond this week. This whole thing is affecting my health."

"I'm sorry." Panic was affecting my health. In fact, it was cutting off circulation to my brain. We'd never met Liz, never even spoken to her on the phone. All our assurances about the land came through Stephanie, who had now quit and might never talk to Liz again. I could see Deb rolling her eyes. "But you still think our land sale will go through?"

"Oh, yes. More than ever. Liz needs the money for her new animal shelter in Sonoma County, and she wants out of here."

I said goodbye and phoned Erin, who was making pancakes for her daughter and son-in-law.

"What should I tell Kerry, the carpenter?" I said, trying to keep Luna and Woody from chewing up their leashes.

"Tell him we can't built the cabin," she said. "No road means no truck, no materials, no cabin."

I called Kerry, explaining that it would not be possible for him to build a cabin for us this winter because of the road. "I'm so sorry," I said. "But we're running out of money. We've blown our budget on the road."

There was a long, ominous pause; I waited for the assault. "What you city people have to understand," he growled, "is that land in the country is very complicated and costly to develop. Buying the land itself is just the beginning. You need infrastructure--roads, electrical lines and poles, telephone lines and poles, water, springs, wells, septic. All those things cost money. You city people are clueless,"

Tell me about it, I thought, apologizing profusely for not hiring him to build a cabin that I couldn't afford on land I didn't own using a road that wouldn't be passable. I counted the hours until Erin returned as I looked down at the dogs, now profoundly agitated that their promised walk had been sacrificed to the depressing perils of developing rural property. Owning--or almost owning—raw land in the country was a lot like owning dogs, I realized, as I gazed into Luna and Woody's disappointed brown eyes. The initial purchase was only a nibble in the budget compared to the chomp of maintaining and civilizing them--from food and vet bills to bulldozers and buildings.

CHAPTER 8

BREAKING THE NEWS

My good friend Marny had a mournful and pleasantly pessimistic personality, which is why Erin dubbed the two of us "the Funmeisters."

My other closest friend, Nanette, and my beloved Cousin Anne, in San Francisco--had taken news of the pending land purchase in stride. But I dreaded telling Marny because I was sure she would see it as a very bad turn of events. Marny was a psychotherapist--kind, patient, and accepting of all kinds of crazy, neurotic behavior. She could listen for days—years, even--to any sort of problem I had, from alpha female control issues with Erin to deadlines at work or rejection slips from publishers. Marny always managed to reframe my fears, insecurities and shortcomings as charming eccentricities, even strengths.

But change a date with Marny, and she could let fly the full force of her righteous indignation. I was not good with disapproval, hers or anyone else's. But if she viewed my news about the country property as a threat to our friendship, which I feared she would, I had to be ready for an atomic reaction. That's why I hadn't told her sooner that we'd made an offer on the land and had installed two road extensions as well as a cavernous hole below the home site that we hoped by next spring, with the help of winter rains and runoff, would be a pond.

As I drove across the bridge over the blue calm of San Francisco Bay to Point Richmond, where we were meeting for dinner that summer night, I pondered how to tell her my news without upsetting her unduly. Simply saying that buying the land made me happy would not work. She knew me too well to believe that a mere real estate acquisition could lift my chronic gloom. Trying to tempt her with the prospect of camping at Cherry Creek was a non-starter because I'd never known her to willingly spend a night in a sleeping bag, without running water, heat or a toilet, in the 20 years we'd been friends. To vow that the land would not disrupt our lunch and dinner dates wasn't true either, since Erin, and, alas, I, too, now fantasized building a house there one day--and sooner than later. Since I was 50 and Erin 48, we couldn't afford to waste time lest those rickety disks in my low back and the stenosis in her cervical spine got worse. Wait too long and we'd be shuffling on walkers to the pond and the onion patch.

I'd just have to tell Marny the truth. Which was? Well, that in a lot of ways, the land was a dream come true. We could afford it, for one thing. Plus, when we hiked through the hills, spotting wildflowers we'd never seen before or gazing up at the stars at night, we felt free and alive and didn't bicker so much about her family's demands on her time or my tortured love of writing. Another thing was that we'd have friends around and potential community at Cherry Creek. Gina and Lin had recently formed a collective with six other women from the Bay Area and had invited us to join them. Although we declined, having fallen in love with our land--not to mention having bulldozed the heck out of it--we were thrilled that Swallowtail Ranch, as they called their place, would bring smart, fun, sympathetic women from the Bay Area to live down the road from us.

Still, I didn't want to lose one of my dearest friends over this vague but intense longing to live in the country. I didn't have much family. My only sibling, my older sister, who lived in West Virginia in a school bus with dozens of cats, had refused to speak to me for years. My father was nearly 90 and a continent away. Marny *was* my family. She'd coaxed me through relationship break-ups and innumerable smaller disasters. If she got angry at me tonight, I tried to persuade myself, it came from her fear of losing me, just as I was terrified of losing her. We were the Funmeisters, after all, and neither of us saw change as a delightful prospect. The key to the evening's smooth passage, I told myself, was reassuring Marny that no matter where I lived or what life changes I made with Erin, she and I would stay close and connected.

Marny was seated at a table in the red brick Victorian hotel where we often met for dinner. She was reading patient notes, a Vodka Collins in her hand. I glanced at her soulful brown eyes as she stood up, smiling. Instead of a hug, we touched our pinky fingers in solidarity, the greeting that we'd created over the years for reasons long forgotten.

"Hot off the press," I said, handing her a copy of my UFO story, which had finally run in the paper.

"Here's mine," she said, sliding me a new journal article she written on lesbian polyamory.

When we'd both scanned the other's latest opus, I took a deep breath and cleared my throat. "So," I said, "it turns out Erin and I are buying that land in the country we looked at."

Her penetrating eyes narrowed, nostrils flaring. "That land of Liz's?"

Somehow Marny, in her vast network of friends, clients and colleagues, knew Liz slightly, never saying exactly how, which could mean Liz had been one of her psychotherapy client. That would be weird.

"I thought this might be coming." She swigged her drink- shaking her head. I would have grabbed her glass and slugged down the vodka myself had not the stern faces of Bill W. and Dr. Bob been staring down at me from my frontal lobe.

"I don't like the sound of this," she glared.

"The sound of what?" I gripped the table to brace for her assault. "It's a bunch of bare land. We don't even own it yet. Liz's lawyer hasn't sent our papers back."

"Bare land," she said, running her hands through her short, wavy brown hair. "That's how it always starts."

"How what starts?" I swallowed.

"I know all about land in the country. Have you forgotten my 10 years with Ann?"

"Ann was before my time."

"Ann owned land in Mendocino County that was supposed to be for her occasional weekend getaways. She ended up spending more time up in that geodesic dome with her chickens and goats that she did with me. You won't like it, Janie. You'll hurt your back chopping wood, and Erin will want animals and probably a wallaby, and you'll come to the Bay Area less and less often and we'll never see each other."

This was going to be worse than I thought. "A wallaby?" I gulped.

Her nose twitched. "A wallaby, a kangaroo, some Australian marsupial. Ann's neighbors had one that was always escaping and eating her tomatoes." She sipped her vodka. "It's a metaphor anyway."

"Metaphor for what?"

"The insanity of it all."

"But we're not going to have livestock, and we don't even own it yet, and we haven't made any decisions about if or when or whether we'll ever live there."

"I know how it goes," she continued, eyebrows

raised scornfully. "First a tent, then a cabin, then you quit your job and build a house, and then you're gone. It will never be the same, Janie."

I felt tears building behind my eyes as the man and woman at the next table, elbow-deep in a bucket of steamed clams, stared at us curiously.

Marny pushed her salad plate away. "You know it's true, Janie."

"I'm not going to disappear," I said. "I'm not moving anywhere. I'm still right here." I pinched her forearm. "See? That's me. Everything's okay."

She snatched her arm away and put down her drink. "This is Erin's idea, isn't it?"

I chewed my lip. "It's both our ideas. It came from the Year to Live group."

"But it's more hers than yours, isn't it?" Her eyes bore through me.

"Well," I said, fingering my glass of ginger ale. "She's taken more of a leadership role in the plan, but I like the land, too. . ." I felt my voice trailing off. "I am a little worried about it all."

"You should be worried," she scowled. "You'll move up there, and you'll be too busy working on the garden or fencing the wallaby to write, and you'll get lonely and wish you'd never left. It's a bad idea, Janie."

"Wow," I said, shredding the napkin in my lap, the Funmeister inside fearing that everything she said was absolutely true. She was voicing all my deepest misgivings about this whole country thing--the loneliness, the isolation, the danger of falling into catatonic depression, of being too old and stiff to do the hard work raw land required.

"If we ever did move there," I managed to croak, "it wouldn't be for years, and you and I would still talk on the phone and have e-mail. And get together for visits. And if the world falls apart in January because of Y2K disasters, you and Susan can come up to the land and raise your own food and have a safe place to live. We can have a tent city."

"That's quite touching, Janie, but the world's not going to fall apart. That's media hype." Marny's nostrils flared.

"Well, if it does come to an end," I inhaled quickly, trying to make the best of it, "you can stay with us."

"That's wonderful, Janie," she said, shaking her head. "But the handwriting is on the wall. I'll never see you again."

"You haven't exactly been that available yourself," I shot back, reaching recklessly for a comeback. Was I getting myself into more hot water? "Not since Susan moved in."

"What?" She stared at me. "Susan moved next door, not *in*."

"What's the difference? You're always busy now." I crunched on a piece of ice, hoping my argument had gained traction with Marny, who'd always insisted that friends should never take a back seat to partners or lovers.

"That's not true." She put down her fork. "I'm not always busy."

"We used to have breakfast every single week, and you can't do that anymore. . ."

"Because my office hours changed."

"And you're never free on weeknights."

"I see clients at night."

"But you're busy on weekends, too, so. . ."

"I often have Saturday night free. . ."

"But you won't make dates with me and Erin together, so Saturday night doesn't work for me."

"It's not the same, Janie. We can't talk as intimately if Erin and Susan are there."

"But you see my point, don't you?"

"I'm always available for lunch on Thursdays. You're the one who changed that."

"But I have a job now, Marny," I said, wiping my tears. "And you're almost an hour away. It would take my entire lunch hour just to get to Berkeley."

The couple at the next table had stopped eating entirely in order to catch every word of our conversation. "Please, don't be too hard on me about this land thing. I can't stand to have you mad at me, and I'm very confused about it all. None of this is intended to hurt you. Can you be a little bit nicer to me? You're hurting my feelings."

Marny blinked, and a dram of compassion softened her face. "Well," she said, her furrowed brow relaxing ever so slightly, "I guess this is something you just have to do."

"It's not the worst thing in the world," I said. "You and Susan can come up any time and camp with us. I'd love that. Maybe you'll fall in love with the place. Liz has more parcels she's selling. You could. . ."

"Don't be ludicrous, Janie," she said, pitching her fork into some iceberg lettuce.

"Look." I pulled some photographs from my backpack. "These are the wild horses, and that's Stephanie on the ridge above our. . ."

"You're not in love with her, are you?"

"No!"

"That's good."

"She's Liz's caretaker, and she's been very kind

to us. That's the crooked oak right next to the. . ." I stopped myself from saying, "our future home site."

"Very nice, Janie," she said, glancing at the snapshots. "But I'll get melanoma from the sun and so will you." Marny drank the last of her vodka. "Still, if this is what you really want, and you're not just being bamboozled into it. . ."

"I'm not being bamboozled," I said. "We figured out we both wanted a place in the country. You're in a Year to Live Group now, too, so you know how important it is to identify your life's priorities. And it's incredibly beautiful there. You like beauty."

"Beauty's not the point. Ann's place was beautiful."

"And you didn't like it even a little?"

"I went up there because I had to if I wanted to have sex with her." She looked at me miserably. "The handwriting's on the wall, Janie."

"I love you, you know," I stammered. The couple at the next table had practically moved in with us. "You know how important you are to me, don't you?" Tears leaked down my cheeks.

Marny looked chastened. "You're important to me, too. That's why I'm upset." She wiped something from her eye. "If this is what you really want to do, I'm sure I'll adapt."

"That's the terrible thing," I blurted. "I don't know if I really want to do it or not. But whenever we're up there, I feel happy. And Erin and I get along better. And Ruby says it's a good investment even if we never build a cabin or a house or anything on the land."

"Ruby, the astrologer?" Her nostrils flared again. "You told *her* about this land before me?"

"She was easier to make a date with," I said, hoping for a laugh.

"That's a low blow, Janie." Marny slung her briefcase over her shoulder. "There's no point in discussing this anymore."

I took a breath, feeling desperate. "I don't want to lose you, Marny."

"Don't be silly," she said outside, clicking the remote lock on her car door. "You won't lose me."

I broke with our pinky-finger tradition and gave her a hug, which she accepted with stiff resignation

I drove home bereft and confused. Would my dear friend be perpetually angry with me? Was I giving up some important part of myself, of my independence, by entertaining the notion that one day Erin and I might call Cherry Creek our home?

Was Erin exercising undue influence over me?

No, I realized suddenly, thinking of the vast expanses of wilderness at Cherry Creek. It wasn't Erin. It was the land. The land had done this to me. Like William Butler Yeats' "Stolen Child," I was being drawn away from the life that I knew. The mountains, the silence, the air, the wild horses, the howling coyotes, the deepening pleasure and freedom I felt on the land were irresistible.

All the way home, as I thought of Marny and of how much I loved and valued her, that Yeats' poem reverberated in my head:

Come away, O human child!
To the waters and the wild
With a faery, hand in hand,
For the world's more full of weeping than you can understand.

CHAPTER 9

SHOCK TREATMENT

My father was passionate about medicine, women, astronomy, sailing, the Ivy League, world peace and his family. Several things about Dad drove me nuts, particularly his flirting with women and his fondness for the lecture format. He used that format during mandatory childhood "nature walks," in which, armed with field guides, specimen jars and binoculars, he set out to teach my sister, my mother and me the Latin names of every animal, vegetable, mineral or celestial body we had the misfortune to encounter. Although his pedagogical technique brewed simmering resentments in my sister and me toward all scientific endeavors, some vestigial love of nature managed to survive in both of us. My sister now lived wild in the mountains of West Virginia, and I was camping under the stars as often as Erin and I could get up to Cherry Creek.

Dad's defects not withstanding, I was crazy about him. He could be very funny, particularly between his first drink and second drink.

We were having cocktails at that very moment at his life care community outside Baltimore, in the apartment of Mrs. B., the newer of his two girlfriends. Determined to present the land at Cherry Creek more persuasively to my father than I had to Marny, I was now showing him and Mrs. B. a dozen new photos I'd snapped of Parcel 39.

Dad pointed to a shot of Stephanie and Puppy Schnoodles standing next to the Mule. "Who's the busty blond?"

"Stephanie, the caretaker,"I hissed. "Don't talk about her that way."

He winked at Mrs. B. "Janie has asked me never to refer to women's mammaries in her presence."

"She's quite right," said Mrs. B., who was tall, erect and pencil-thin, with perfectly coifed, naturally brown hair.

Dad rattled the ice in his glass. Mrs. B. took the hint and made him another drink after passing us a silver tray of cream cheese, caviar and crackers and refilling my ginger ale glass.

"You know, Mrs. B.," Dad smiled expansively,

as the bourbon hit his bloodstream, "Janie bought this land from an heiress who lives in Los Angeles. The heiress is fond of the ladies, I gather, as is Janie."

"As are you," Mrs. B. offered with false gaiety.

Dad took a closer look at two of the photos with a portable magnifying glass he kept in his pocket. "Looks like you have *odocoileus hemionus* on your land, Janie, and some *corvi corax*." He looked expectantly at me.

"Mule deer and ravens," Mrs. B. said, winking at me.

"Go to the head of the class!" Dad kissed her flushed cheek and finished his bourbon. "Your Wellesley education has paid off."

Tapping his pocket, into which Mrs. B. had placed her lunch roll in a Baggie for Dad to eat at breakfast, my father hurried me off to our next engagement--dinner at the main lodge with Mrs. R., his other beloved. Petite, patrician and silver-haired, Mrs. R. was the wife of an American spy who decades earlier had overthrown the democratically elected leader of a Middle Eastern country, replacing him with a nasty despot. Mrs. R. lived in Washington, D.C., but Dad had met her in Nantucket soon after my mother's death in Philadelphia in 1985 and had been rendezvousing with her regularly since then. A man who'd always played by the rules, my father justified his involvement with a married woman by explaining somewhat clinically to all interested parties that Mr. R. was mentally and physically "impaired" from an old war injury and a botched surgical procedure to correct it that had left him unable to fulfill his "spousal duties."

Dad had enjoyed his arrangement with Mrs. R. for years, but since leaving his house in Philadelphia and moving to his life care community in Baltimore, he was in a bit of a pickle. He was still fond of Mrs. R., but she had a husband. And Mrs. B., who lived in his community, had none. Mrs. B. had gradually taken over the number one position, and she did not like Dad popping over to Washington to see Mrs. R. or heading up with the spymaster's wife to his fishing club in the Poconos. When Mr. R. became too ill for Mrs. R. to care for by herself, Dad urged her to move to his life care community, which she did. Mr. R. was now parked in a room in the nursing wing a few doors away from Dad's sister, my Aunt Gwen. To his dismay, Mrs. R. herself had been assigned a garden apartment two doors away from Mrs. B.

"How's Mrs. R. handling all this?" I said to Dad, as several people on electric scooters whizzed past us toward dining room.

"Hard to say." He took in a deep breath. "She had a series of shock treatments not long ago and seems much improved."

"Shock treatments?" I stopped, moving aside to let a bent man with a walker pass.

"Her depression is unrelated to the change in our. . .status. Mrs. R.'s mother was clinically depressed, and Mrs. R. was raised by an aunt. A very sad childhood took its toll."

"Is she okay? After the treatments?"

He swallowed. "A little memory loss initially, but she's not as blue as she was and she has a new...friend. A urologist who lives in the B complex. He's wheelchair-bound but good company."

I digested this new information as we walked through the automatic sliding glass doors to the main lobby and dining room.

Mrs. R. was waiting for us and was looking great, beautiful in fact, in a bright blue suit, her cheeks flushed, her white hair short and stylish, a smile lighting her face as she spotted my father. I kissed her, surprised that Dad didn't. Once seated, he quickly handed her my photographs of the land, which she examined with interest.

"I think your dear papa is worried that you'll be too isolated on your land," she said, her edelweiss blue eyes moving from a photograph of Erin and me to the wild horses. "Like your sister and her cats."

My father winced, and I sighed. My sister, who hadn't spoken to either of us in years, lived with dozens of cats in hermit-like isolation.

I told Mrs. R. not to worry, describing our weekend gatherings with Cherry Creek neighbors and friends from the Bay Area who'd come camping with us. I didn't dare tell Dad that despite our expanding encampment on the land--we now had a plastic storage shed, a chain saw and a weed trimmer--we'd still not opened escrow and had no paperwork to show we owned Parcel 39 at Cherry Creek.

Mrs. R. glanced wistfully at my father. "You can feel isolated anywhere, of course, not just the country." She lowered her voice, leaning forward. "I take it you've met her? The new one?"

I nodded, rearranging the salt and pepper packets as I tried to think what to say.

Mrs. R. inhaled. "And? What did you think?"

I tapped my knife on the white tablecloth.

"She's okay." In fact, I liked her a lot, but I didn't want Mrs. R. to feel worse.

"She's a Republican, you know." Mrs. R. wiped something from her eye.

"I guess there are a few nice ones."

"I suppose." She glanced at my father, who was studying the menu. "Still, I'm a bit shocked." She pushed a lifeless tomato around her salad plate.

Dad emptied four creamers and six sugar packets into his cup and set about stirring his tea.

"I'm sorry about what's happened, Mrs. R.," I whispered, feeling horribly inadequate. I liked Mrs. R. She was fun and a little Bohemian, buying most of her clothes at garage sales, going to foreign and indie films regularly and even carrying a placard with my father and me in the gay pride March on Washington in 1987. But clearly, she was no longer Dad's main squeeze. It looked as if Mrs. R. had become one of his social rehabilitation projects, like my aunt in the nursing wing upstairs. He'd lost his spark for her, and she was devastated.

"Dad says *you* have a new friend?" I said, hoping to change the subject.

She smiled. "Oh, yes. Nice man. Another doctor." She sighed as she looked out over the room of white-haired elders, their canes, walkers and electric Scooters parked at their tables. "I knew your father would be swamped with widows on the prowl when he moved here. But Mrs. B.? A Republican? And so quickly. They've put me into an apartment right next to her. He won't even take me to the Poconos anymore because he says this place is a fishbowl, which it is, and people will talk and think badly of me--which I don't give a hoot about--because I have husband upstairs in the nursing wing."

"I'm so sorry."

Mrs. R. managed to smile at the student waitress, then looked back at me. "She's put her foot down, and he goes along with it."

In silence, the three of us watched an elderly woman hobble across the room with a walker, wave to Dad--who smiled and waved back--and shuffle out of the dining room.

"It's unnatural, don't you think, Janie? So many old people living in one place?"

"You're not so old."

"Do me a favor, my friend," she said, touching my hand. "Don't get too old. There's nothing they can do with us, and nothing for us to do. I tried to start a chapter of the Euthanasia Society here so like-minded souls can end it all when we've had enough, but the Quakers who run this place don't believe in the right to die. I think we should be able call it quits when we're ready, don't your."

Looking up, my father said quickly: "Mrs. R.'s on 100 milligrams of Wellbutrin three times a day and Zanex for anxiety. We'll increase the dose when we see what she can tolerate."

"She's not your patient, Dad," I said, turning back to Mrs. R. "I have a friend in California who's an M.D. and she's promised to help me get a lethal dose of something when I'm ready to go."

"I wish I had a friend like that." She looked meaningfully at my father.

"You mustn't keep skipping tennis, Mrs. R.," Dad said, spooning his butterscotch sundae.

"I don't feel like playing tennis, and. . ."

"Particularly when you're down," he continued. "Exercise releases endorphins and triggers neurotransmitters that elevate one's mood."

"Not my mood." Mrs. R. opened her handbag, removing an amber-colored plastic vial. "Nevertheless, I shall down my endorphins."

My father put down his spoon and straightened. "Janie, the management's concern about self-deliverance, or rational suicide, as they call it--and Mrs. R. and I have been over this--is whether or not the decision to take one's own life can ever be really rational. If the decision is based on persistent, irreversible suffering then it's not likely to be made on entirely non-emotional grounds and may be subject to cognitive distortions. Is it rational to solve a problem in life by ending life itself? Most people intending such a suicide would presumably prefer to be alive, just not under the current circumstances. That could indicate some ambivalence about any so-called *rational* decision to take one's own life."

"So you think if someone kills themself because they're depressed, it's not rational?" I said, dizzied by his heady response to Mrs. R.'s heartfelt admission. "What if the person is terminally ill and fully competent? Would you deny them that right?"

"Who wouldn't be depressed if they're in unremitting pain with a hopeless diagnosis?" sighed Mrs. R. "Speaking of which. . ." She looked at her watch. "It's been lovely, Janie, but I must go and see my dear husband before the goon squad upstairs puts him down for the night. Will you come swimming with me tomorrow morning in the heated pool, before all the old ladies arrive for physical therapy?"

"I'd love to," I said.

The three of us rode the elevator in silence to

the nursing floor, where Mrs. R. turned left, toward her husband's room, and Dad and I went right to see his sister, my Aunt Gwen, who was slumped in a wheelchair, chin resting on her pale white hand, her faded muumuu house dress riding up her legs. Her television blared *Jeopardy* although her eyes were closed.

"Good evening, sister." Dad kissed her cheek and switched the TV to cable news. "Look who's here."

Gwen looked but didn't seem to see me.

"Janie came all the way from California. She has pictures to show of the property she's bought in Mendocino County."

"Hi, Auntie," I gulped, shaken as always to see my favorite aunt, once so pretty and affectionate and tastefully dressed, curled up painfully in her wheel chair in a house dress, her white hair straggly and unkempt, her fingernails long yellow tapers.

"Janie, show Gwen your photographs."

I handed her the snapshots, which fell from her hand, landing on the floor. Dad scooped them up, holding each before her, one by one.

"Janie made the down payment with the money you've given her each year at Christmas," he said, speaking very loudly.

"Thank you very, very much, Gwen." I touched her hand.

She pulled her fingers away; her eyes were small and frightened behind her thick glasses. "Can't hear a word you're saying."

"Where's your hearing aid, Gwen?" Opening the top drawer of her dresser, he extracted a little skin-colored plastic thing that shrieked as he placed it in her ear. My aunt groaned.

"Can you hear me now, Gwen?" Dad yelled. "Look at the photographs. The attractive woman with the ample. . ." He stopped himself. Had he actually remembered that his sister, once "amply endowed" herself, had breast cancer and a horrendous bilateral radical mastectomy three decades earlier? "The handsome young woman," he continued, "with the long blond tresses works for the heiress who sold Janie the land."

Gwen stared at him.

"Exciting, isn't it? Janie has her very own ranch."

Gwen's eyes narrowed.

"How do you feel today, sister?"

A male nurse stuck his head in the door. "I'll come back later, Miss F. I see your brother's visiting."

"Who was that?" my aunt asked.

"Angel, the night nurse," Dad said. "You know him. He was stationed at the 8th Field Hospital at Nha Trang. The only U.S. Army hospital in Vietnam until April 1965."

"No privacy here at all," Gwen mumbled. "They come in and out whenever they please."

"You feeling alright?" Dad yelled. "Still taking your Prozac?"

"You don't have to shout."

"How do you feel?" he shouted.

After a long pause, she said, "Bored."

"What's that?"

"Bored," Gwen repeated.

"You're bored?" Dad looked incredulous. "Have you read the paper today? The Orioles have a new pitcher from Cleveland. Traded two fielders to get him. Shall I turn on the game?"

She stared at him as he surfed the channels looking for baseball. "Janie, tell Gwen about your land."

I cleared my throat and began, as ordered. "We're buying 160 acres in Mendocino County. Up in the mountains, an hour from the Pacific Ocean. I made the down payment with the money you've given me at Christmas the last few years, and I'll pay off the rest when I sell my house in Mill Valley. So it's your land, in a way. I wish you could come see it."

"What money?" she said, eyes narrowing like one of those experimental monkeys made enraged by electrodes stimulating the anger portion of their brains.

"The Christmas gifts from you. The $10,000!" I was shouting so loudly that every employee and resident on the floor no doubt heard about my aunt's generous gifts. "Thank you very, very much."

"Ten thousand dollars?"

Dad patted her hand. The distributions she had made to my sister and me and our two cousins had been his idea. The stock market was soaring, and my aunt was earning far more than she spent. "It's money your financial advisor said you didn't need, Gwen. Lowers your taxes to give it away."

"I haven't a clue what you're talking about," she said.

Dad pulled a tiny bourbon bottle from his pocket. "Would you like a drink?"

Suddenly, my aunt sat up, her gnarled fingers unfurling like a pincer claw to grip the plastic cup into which my father was pouring the amber liquid.

In one smooth motion she drew the cup to her lips and swigged all of the bourbon, letting the cup drop to the floor.

"Tell Gwen about the bears at Cherry Creek," Dad said, retrieving the cup and stuffing the empty split in his pocket.

"Dad, she's not interested in the land and she can't hear me."

"Tell her about the heiress. She has her hearing aids in."

I tried again. "The land belongs to this woman who started a wildlife preserve, and she's now. . ."

"Can't hear you!" rasped my aunt.

I turned to my father. "I can't shout any louder."

"Try again, Janie," he said eagerly. "I know she's happy to see you."

In desperation, I free-associated about the howling coyotes and the wild horses and Woody and Luna's mad dashes after the horses and our blue tent and the Coleman stove and camp chairs and pancakes for breakfast and skinny dipping in the creek. Satisfied at last, Dad settled into his chair and watched the Orioles. I moved on to the bears and the campfires at night with the Cherry Creek Irregulars, the unique group of new neighbors we were getting to know.

"I think we're going to build a cabin next year," I told Gwen.

"A cabin?" Dad looked up. "You won't live there, will you?"

I shook my head. "Just for camping."

"You might feel isolated."

"It's a weekend place," I said. "To get away from the newsroom."

"Don't go too far away from the newsroom,"

Dad said, his brow wrinkling. He loved the fact that I worked for a paper and finally had a real job. I'd freelanced for years and had turned to him many times for financial help when the assignments didn't come. "She's switched to the police beat, Gwen," he yelled. "Left editorials."

"Not exactly the police beat yet," I said. Mike was still undecided about what kind of items to put in "On the Beat," so it still wasn't a daily column. In the meantime, I was writing briefs and calendar announcements and occasional features for Becky. "Anyway, I'm not quitting, Gwen. No plans for that."

"Quit what?" Her beady eyes were locked on mine.

"I'm not quitting my job!" I shouted.

"Didn't know you had a job. No one tells me anything." She looked longingly at the pocket of Dad's jacket, where he'd placed the empty bourbon split alongside his dinner roll from Mrs. B.

"A good visit," Dad said, minutes later, as we took the back stairs down to the lobby, setting off the patient alarm and inhaling baked turkey and broccoli fumes that lingered in the air from dinner.

I couldn't wait to fly home to Erin, the dogs and the mountains of Mendocino County. After a week with Dad in the stifling suburbs of Baltimore, living on the land had never looked so good.

CHAPTER 10

JANE ACRES

At the paper one morning, Rick belted out a song he'd just written, a parody of the *Green Acres* theme music:

Oh, Jane, Willits is no place to be--
Outhouses, no 'lectricity
No neighbors for five miles around
Erin could kill ya and nobody'd hear a sound.

My buddies in Features applauded as Rick kept on singing.

At her desk is where we wish she'd stay
Writing stories and 10 briefs a day
Country livin' is no place for Jane
The air is fresh but the rednecks such a pain.

"I think I'll go visit some police departments," I laughed, tossing a reporter's notebook into my backpack.

My desk was the last place I wanted to be these days because Mike still hadn't made up his mind if he actually wanted to run the police log or not. Some days it appeared and some days it didn't. Meanwhile, the city editor had me typing up dozens of "In Your Town" news briefs from around the county. It was torture. It made tracking 5150s-- police code for the arrest of someone crazy--seem like nirvana. Graffiti tagging, spousal abuse, drunk and disorderly, shoplifting, and animal nuisance had become specialties of mine as I traversed the county in search of minor criminal activities I hoped Mike would find amusing. It could have been worse. I could have been stuck at my desk writing editorials exhorting the county's coyotes to stay up in the hills where they belonged instead of eating people's household pets, which they'd been doing all summer.

Another problem was that Pam, the former Features editor, now promoted to managing editor, seemed serious about her threat to move my desk away from where I'd been sitting next to Rick and across from Becky to a spot beside the city editor, who was coming unhinged since signing a six-figure book contract with a New York publisher to write the true story of her traumatic childhood. My new seat would be inches away from her, right next to the police scanner, which blared loud, crackly police and fire calls day and night.

Pam was convinced that now that I worked for the city desk, I needed to be closer to the world of fast-paced, daily-deadline news. She thought I'd grown too attached to Rick and Becky and my quiet desk by the window in Features and should have more contact--and closer supervision--from the news department.

"I've been writing editorials on daily deadlines for years," I pleaded. "I'll write fast. I'll be good. Don't make me move."

"Scoop," she said. "You've been hiding out with your pals here for too long. Feature writers work at a more leisurely pace. We're grooming you for the fast lane." She winked at me, which meant she wasn't grooming me for anything at all. In fact, she hoped to retard my progress at the paper because I'd fled the editorial page and had dared to write the UFO story she disapproved of.

"But I'm only. . ." I glanced over at the city desk, "only 129 feet away from the fast lane."

"That's too far, Scoop. I want you next to the scanner, ready to dash out on a moment's notice to cover fires and car wrecks and. . .well. . ." She tapered off, hurrying to the art department, where a graphic designer was waving a page proof for her approval.

I looked glumly at the few city reporters actually in the newsroom that morning. No one seemed poised to rush off on any breaking assignments. The business writer was eating a bag of microwave popcorn as she read the morning's paper; the court reporter was commiserating on the San Francisco Giants' recent string of baseball losses with Brad, my replacement as editorial writer; the education reporter was hiding in the library stacks behind a nine-foot pile of old newspapers kvetching with the librarian about our management's new plan to train reporters how to write more stories more quickly without wasting precious time gathering the facts.

"Pam's moving me to the city desk," I told Rick, who was busy sending out e-mails to other newspapers hoping they'd pick up his satirical syndicated television guide called "The TV Guy."

He leaned around his computer to make eye contact. "She's moving you to the city desk? That's out of the question."

I looked at him miserably. "She wants to put me right next to the city editor and the police scanner so I can learn how to cover breaking news."

"Complete bullshit," he said, face reddening as he rolled off the new, blue, ergonomic orthopedic yoga ball he'd persuaded HR to buy for him. "We've got to nip this in the bud." He made a beeline for Pam, who was plotting the World Series coverage with the sports editor.

"What's this I hear about your moving Jane to the city desk?" he roared, still wearing his Spandex shorts and shirt from riding his bike to work from San Francisco. "That's unacceptable."

Pam stepped back three feet, her nose twitching ominously. "Get out of those tights and take a shower, my friend. Contrary to popular opinion, Jane is not your employee, nor does she work in Features. She works for the city desk, and I want her there with her colleagues not in outer space writing woo-woo stories for Becky."

I knew it. She was still mad about the UFOs.

"Why does it matter where she sits?" he said.

"She can write mediocre stories anywhere. She's one of us, and we don't want her to move."

I flinched. *Mediocre stories*?

Pam squinted at me. "Scoop, did you enlist Rick to fight your battle for you?"

"No," I croaked.

"Move her and terrible things will happen," Rick warned. "Becky will retire. Morale will sink. I'll start coming in late."

"Now there's breaking news," she laughed, squaring her shoulders, checking her watch and folding her arms in front of her. "I'll give you 30 seconds to make your final arguments. What have you got?"

Rick picked up a Bolo Bat from the sports editor's desk and bounced the ball against the paddle. "It's ridiculous to think she'll write any better sitting next to the police scanner than she will sitting next to me. I give her her best ideas. For Christ's sake, it's inhumane to put her by that maniac of a city editor."

Pam smiled. It was common knowledge that she and city editor were not currently speaking. She pushed her glasses up on her nose and looked pensively at Rick. "Tell you what, my friend. I'll make you and Scoop a deal. We won't put anybody else in her desk. We'll leave it empty, and in three months, if all goes well, she can move back to your little corner of insanity."

Rick zoomed the Bolo ball past Pam's knees and whacked it on the rebound. "If you're going to move her back in three months, save yourself some trouble and don't move her at all."

"That's my best offer," Pam said, retreating to her office. "If that's not good enough for your royal

Spandex, we'll hold Jane hostage on the city side indefinitely, and you can pine for her until you dress up again as a crocodile. . ."

"Alligator," he snorted.

"And interview folks at the pond in the Presidio."

"It was a great story," Rick said. "Readers never forgot it. A totally original take on the alligator-sighting stories."

"And who ever saw a reporter in an alligator suit they didn't like?" Flipping Rick the bird, she closed her office door as the cast of Features applauded him for the second time that morning. Rick raised his hand to mine for a high five.

"Did you hear that?" he gloated. "I got your exile down to three months. I'll keep chipping away until she agrees to two. You owe me lunch for that."

"Sure," I said. "What I want to know is how you get away with talking to her like that."

"I'm the best reporter in the newsroom," he shrugged imperiously. "And she knows it." He stuck out his tongue at the overwrought city editor, who was standing by the scanner trying to figure out what had just transpired between Rick and Pam. "Will you be able to survive next to Dragon Lady?"

"I guess so," I said, glancing at her dubiously.

"Then let's get back to writing 'A Gay in the Life Of.' We're halfway through Episode Two, the combined family barbecue."

To amuse ourselves, Rick and I collaborated periodically on a sitcom inspired by Cannon, the copy editor, whose boyfriend's parents were moving next door to Cannon's parents in the same mobile home park.

"Sorry," I said. "I've got to pack my stuff and start moving."

Becky, who had been quiet throughout Rick's discussion with Pam, looked up at me conspiratorially. "That management training course has turned her into a bully. She actually likes you. I know she does."

"She has a funny way of showing her affection," I sighed.

The senior feature writer, a grand dame who'd won dozens of reporting prizes and was so deaf she couldn't hear the alarms blare during newsroom fire drills, tapped Rick on the shoulder. "What's wrong, dear? I saw Pam give you the finger. You're not in trouble, are you, darling?"

"Pam's moving Jane to the city desk," Rick growled. "It's a stupid idea and I'm making sure it doesn't happen."

"But you're a feature writer."

"She's moving *Jane*!" Rick yelled. "Pam wants her over there by the psychopath."

"What idiots!" she said. "I'll never understand management." She lunged for her ringing telephone, the only one in the newsroom that flickered red and toned like a bell instead of emitting quiet electronic beeps. "Why, hello, darling," she boomed as always, her stentorian voice silencing even the librarian and education reporter, who were still deliberating in the stacks. "Sweetheart, of course I'm busy. I'm always busy. Absolutely ridiculous. What can I do for you?"

From what I could make out, the publicist on the other end of the line wanted her to interview a Russian about a cookbook.

"My dear, everyone's cooking these days," she was saying, her aristocratic baritone ricocheting from editorial to city and back to Features. "I myself have always cooked, but many people haven't. Yes, do send me a fax. If it's *that* Russian, the one I knew in Shanghai when I worked for the daily there, please send him a kiss from me. Adore to help. Wonderful." She slammed down the receiver. "Dreadful woman," she rumbled in a whisper so loud the whole newsroom went silent again. "Wants me to interview a Russian about a cook book. I'll tell her no, of course. Damn publicists think they own the paper."

A few minutes later, Becky cleared her throat and quietly approached the senior feature writer's desk, a fax in her hand. I was sure I heard Becky say that the publicist in question had been offering the senior writer an interview with Alexander Solzhenitsyn, who had a new book coming out, possibly his last, since he wasn't well.

"Oh, for goodness sakes," she said, reaching for her phone. "Why didn't she say so?"

Becky rolled her eyes at me and returned to scanning the wires. I finished packing my cardboard box and trudged over to my new desk by the scanner.

"We won't forget you," Rick called. "*At your desk is where we wish you'd stay,*" he sang. "*I'll e-mail 'Planet Becky' updates every day.*"

CHAPTER 11

EUREKA!

We hadn't received anything in writing from Max, Liz's Beverly Hills lawyer, since sending him our signed land purchase agreement for Parcel 39

in May. It was now October. We had commissioned a nasty-looking hole in the ground that Doug promised would be a pond after the winter rains, and paid for two frightening red gashes across our hillsides--a new, gently sloping entry at the top of the driveway and the leg over to the home site. We'd acquired all sorts of gear and equipment: a special portable bag bed for Woody and Luna, and poison-oak eradication weapons for me, including a hideously expensive "natural" herbicide, long and thick protective gloves, a pump spray can with wand, masks, goggles, and a white, Ghost-busters jump suit. To top it off, we now drove the two-and-a-half hour trek to Cherry Creek in Erin's all-wheel-drive Subaru station wagon that easily navigated the tortuous six miles of dirt road between the highway and our tent, and to our neighbor Jay's house, the social hub of a small group of city slickers who now owned, or nearly owned, rural property at Cherry Creek.

We'd met Jay through Stephanie, and we loved him. He was a little older than us, gay, funny, smart and a telecommuter to his job with a travel services company in Miami. A warm and welcoming host in his spanking new, grown-up house built by Kerry, the contractor, Jay had electricity, hot and cold running water, a telephone landline and an Internet connection. Nobody's cell phones worked there yet, but that was coming. We now spent most of our Saturday nights at Jay's dining room table feasting on potluck dishes with our new friends: Stephanie and Ken, still living in Jay's guest cabin after the rift with Liz; the dentist and his wife--Rod and Cindy, who were had begun building a massive bridge across the creek on their parcel; and Mike and Robin, the former L.A. cop and his wife, who were holed up in their tiny shed cabin mainlining Diet Pepsi while they waited for their endlessly delayed manufactured home to be delivered. Occasionally, Kerry and his literary agent wife, Nancy, came. They were buying a parcel with Bill, the guy from San Francisco who "had dibs" on parcels above and below ours.

I think it was Robin, a dedicated former Girl Scout, who had dubbed our little group the Cherry Creek Irregulars. We amused ourselves endlessly with heartwarming stories of incompetence and disaster in our attempts to develop our rural properties—a feat that was turning out to be more challenging than we'd anticipated. One of our biggest concerns was the fact that eight of us still didn't own our land. We'd ripped it, gouged it and torn it apart with bulldozers, but we didn't have deeds or titles.

One day, without warning, Max, Liz's lawyer, called us at home. He said that he and Liz had hired a title company to proceed with the sale of the parcels. Number 39 would be ours by the end of the year, he promised. Our hearts soared.

Just one other thing, he added. "I have to charge you an additional $10,000."

I sank into my chair. I'd cleaned out my aunt's Christmas fund money. I could rob my meager 401K, but I'd pay a penalty fee for doing it.

"The law requires nonprofits to charge interest on land-sale loans," Max said coolly. "Since title to the land is held by Liz's nonprofit wildlife foundation, we have to charge the minimum-required interest rate."

"But, Max," I protested. "You accepted our offer

nine months ago and never mentioned interest. How can change the terms now? That's unethical."

"I have to," he snarled. "It's the law."

"Why didn't you tell us about the law nine months ago?"

"What's he saying?" Erin whispered.

I tightened my grip on the phone. "We have an agreement, Max."

"Liz never signed it," he said. "If you don't want the land, I have several other interested parties."

Oh, Jesus. My chest tightened. He was threatening to dump us. Our worst nightmare. Erin grabbed my sleeve and flashed me a "time-out" sign.

"Max," I said. "Let me call you right back."

I told Erin what Max had said. We stared at each other. "What do you think?" I swallowed.

"I didn't know our deal was considered a loan," she said.

I scratched my head. "Stephanie never called it a loan, but I guess that's what it is. Liz is like carrying the paper, only there is no paper, which is part of the problem." I wasn't sure what paper was, but it sounded good. "I wonder who these other interested parties are."

"Don't go there," Erin warned. "It's our land. We'll lump that tax in with the balloon payment in three years. By that time you'll have sold your house in Mill Valley. I say we go ahead."

"Could be Bill," I mused. "He's already buying the land above and below us. And he has deep pockets."

Erin scribbled a dollar sign on our message pad and seemed to gain strength from some hidden place within. "We're not backing out now. I've got savings. You've got your aunt."

I chewed my lip. "We're still getting a good deal. But it's just so. . ."

"Frustrating," Erin finished. She was dialing Gina and Lin, then Rod and Cindy. Max had told all of us the same thing; we all had to pay an interest fee he had neglected to mention in earlier conversations. We were relieved that this wasn't just a plot he'd hatched to wrench our beloved 39 away from us and sell it to someone else.

"Max," Erin said on the phone. "We'll pay the $10,000. Send us the paper work."

"Fine," he said, hanging up.

Stephanie didn't know anything about this latest development. She and Ken and their 20 birds and three dogs and two cats and four horses had closed escrow and were waiting for Liz to reimburse her for the hours she'd spent helping Liz sell more than a dozen parcels. Then they'd build their house above the Emerald Chasm.

"I'm having to sue Liz for monies owed and emotional damages," Stephanie confided.

"Wow," Erin said. "Are you okay?"

"I'm a wreck. I have nightmares, vomiting, diarrhea, lack of focus and panic attacks from dealing with all her emotional harassment and my financial loss."

"I'm sorry."

"We'll be okay. We've got the horses at Jay's, fenced off, and the big kids are outside in their cages. My little Roo-bird is inside with his mommy." Suddenly, she spoke in a low, slow tone that often meant trouble. "I've heard through the grapevine that Liz may send a private investigator out to question you and the other buyers about the transactions."

"A private eye?" I said, jaw dropping.

"She's trying to prove that I did nothing to help sell her property. Be forewarned: If someone comes to your house, you don't have to speak to them."

Maybe the planets were in retrograde because I was feeling emotionally damaged myself. My editor in New York had called to say my new manuscript was deeply flawed and needed work. The story was a downer, she said. If I rewrote it, and she liked it, she'd publish it. But not until I'd made the characters more likable.

I felt terrible. I'd killed myself on nights and weekends trying to write the thing, and she was right. The novel was depressing. My writing group had told me the same thing. But when would I have time to rewrite the book? I was exhausted at night from my job at the paper, and weekends at Cherry Creek spraying poison oak and hanging out with the Irregulars were far more diverting than trying to put a smiley face on my tale of death and betrayal in the Hamptons. Had the land hijacked my writing career as well as my savings? A year ago, publishing the novel was close to the top of my bucket list. Now I could hardly stand to think about it. The pond and the roads and the extra 10 grand I needed to scrounge up for Liz were zapping my energy for my grand literary ambitions. Adding insult to injury, Doug called to say the wild horses were trampling the pond levee and could destroy the whole thing if we didn't fence it fast.

On our next trip to the land, Kerry, aided by Erin and me, dragged T-posts around the parched earth by the pond in record heat, erecting a solar-electric fence. The next day, we cooled off at the creek, in Liz's swimming hole down past the Emerald Chasm. We were skinny dipping in one of the secluded pools when we saw a man and a woman on the far bank dragging lounge chairs to the edge of the water. Two enormous Doberman Pinschers sat next to them, growling. We smiled and waved nervously, but the owners ignored us.

"Those are the pot growers," Erin said quietly, muting her voice so it wouldn't carry across the water. "Stephanie thinks they have a bunch of plants on the bank behind their house and says not to mess with them or their dogs.

"Pot growers? Right here?"

"Right here in River City," Erin laughed.

Liz's lawyer called us in early December. "You close escrow on Friday," Max said without a hello. "Here's the number of the title company in Santa Rosa. Set up an appointment with this lady and be there Friday."

"Such a warm and fuzzy guy," Erin laughed as we floated up to the title company that Friday afternoon.

A ditzy blond woman wearing a powder blue knit pants suit, false eyelashes and White Diamonds perfume, cooed over Woody and Luna, nearly forgetting to process our paperwork as she brought out endless snapshots of her two manicured Maltese. But when we left her office, we were dizzy with happiness and relief. The land was ours. The paper work was signed. We held title to Parcel 39.

"You should forget that rewriting that depressing novel," Erin said, squeezing me tight. "Why not look forward instead of back? Write about Cherry Creek. It's a lot more fun."

We roared north to our homestead in Mendocino County and a celebratory party with the Irregulars. The long wait was over. And maybe Erin was right. I would scrap that book and embrace the rural life.

CHAPTER 12

BEAT CHANGE

The newsroom had been gearing up for Y2K for months, as editors panted for more stories on how Marin County and the world were preparing for what some forecasters said would be technological Armageddon. No one had a clue what would really happen when the world's computer systems rolled over from the year 1999 to 2000, but, it was mid-December, and keyboards at the paper from Biz to Editorial were clicking out copy. Would airplanes fall from the sky at 12:01 a.m. on New Year's Day? Would worldwide energy, telecommunications and financial grids collapse? Would banks fail or lock customers out as panicked investors withdrew their money? Would the football, basketball, ice hockey and ski seasons come to an inglorious end as the world collapsed? Could televangelists make out like bandits as guilty followers attempted to reserve their places in heaven? Marny loved me again, but she wasn't buying any of the Armageddon hype. The world was not going to end and she did not need to keep dozens of containers of gas in her garage, ready to flee in her car to Cherry Creek if the shit hit the fan. The shit wasn't going to hit the fan. Not on Y2K, she insisted.

She was in the minority. Target, Home Depot and local hardware stores reported runs on generators, candles, lanterns and wood stoves. Firearms and open-pollinated non-hybrid seeds were also in demand because householders needed to be able to grow their own food if grocery stores and transportation systems were crippled. Law enforcement agencies were investigating gangs and paramilitary groups rumored to be planning to use the Y2K crisis as a cover for robberies and other crimes. The California National Guard was poised to deploy near large cities, particularly Los Angeles.

Rick, Becky and I were sick of Y2K.

"Going to ride out New Year's up on the land?" Rick smirked, tossing me an orange. I had survived my three-month ordeal in exile and was back in Features.

"Nope," I said. "We're staying close to home.

Going to a lesbian dance in the recreation room of an apartment complex two minutes from our house."

"Sounds exciting," he laughed. "Sparkling cider and lights out at 10 p.m.?"

"Listen to this, you guys," Becky said, reading from the wires. "A group of psychologists has created a diagnosis called Millennium Dysfunctional Disorder--the inability to function as a result of fears about Y2K transition. Want to localize it, Rick?" Becky looked at him with her brown puppy dog eyes.

"I'm localizing two ridiculous Y2K stories already. Ask Jane. She's not doing anything now that Mike murdered 'Off the Beat.'"

"That's not true," I wailed. "I've got my hands full with the story on emergency room preparations."

My life at the paper had changed. Mike had pulled the police log because the paper's management feared lawsuits from suspects named in log items who had not been formally charged. He was sure they'd change their minds when they saw the light, but, in the meantime, I was off the hook and had a new beat covering healthcare, which I was loving. If they revived "On the Beat," the police reporter would write the log, which made a lot more sense.

"Are you panicked about Y2K?" Becky looked at me thoughtfully.

"No. But I'm having trouble sleeping. It's more buyers' remorse than Y2K. Got any remedies?"

"Try martinis," Rick offered. "Or that green stuff they grow in the Emerald Triangle."

"Bill W. wouldn't approve," I said. "When I start

worrying at 3 a.m., I read this book I ordered off the Web called *Genocide and Vendetta*. It's a history of the military and economic persecution of the Native American tribes of Mendocino and Northern California."

"I told you about those round-ups, Jane, when you first looked at that land." Becky rolled her eyes. "You should write a story about it."

"There's a new book out on concentration camps," Rick said, tapping his keyboard. "Here. It's called *Remnants of Auschwitz*, by Giorgio Agamben. I'll send you the link. That should relax you."

"Erin won't let me turn the light on," I continued, unperturbed. "So I burrow under the covers with my headlamp and read about the Yankee round-ups and massacres and enslavement of California Indians in the 1850s and '60s, and eventually I fall asleep."

"I've got a copy of *Mein Kampf* I'll let you borrow," Rick laughed. "That might help."

"I interviewed the author of that Auschwitz book," Becky said, still reading the wires. "He wrote a book called *The Man Without Content*. He says art has exhausted its spiritual vocation."

"Not to change the subject," Rick said. "But it's time for some 'Planet Becky.' You missed several entries that were added when you were in exile." He chuckled to himself. "Here's a good one: 'I'm so darn sleepy. Somebody tell me some gossip to wake me up.'"

"Speaking of which," I whispered, glancing up to be sure the coast was clear. "Paul and Tricia aren't taking long lunches anymore. Do we know what happened?"

Rick went silent. Becky dashed me off an interoffice e-mail. "Tricia did something bad. I don't know what it was," she wrote. "But Paul's not speaking to her."

I e-mailed Rick, who wrote me that he didn't know what was going on, but that he thought Paul and Tricia might have split up--which meant he knew they had split up but that Rick had been sworn to secrecy by Paul. Rick also said he thought that Paul might have a new girlfriend, and that Tricia might have had one too many glasses of chardonnay one night and called Paul's wife and told her that not only had she and Paul been having an affair, but that Paul was now involved with someone else.

I e-mailed this news to Becky--everything except the part about Paul having a new girlfriend, which I knew would upset her. A good thing, too. She e-mailed me back that she was relieved her two colleagues were no longer cheating on their spouses.

"Listen to this 'Becky' item, Jane," Rick snorted. "'You can't get ahead without going to these management training meetings and stabbing somebody in the back. That's one of the first lessons about rising to the top that you ought to know.'"

Becky stopped typing and looked up. "Did I say that?"

Rick nodded.

"Must have been when Pam was trying to train Jane how to succeed in business."

"Listen to this entry," Rick grinned. "'As someone who has worked since she was 16, I can say that the boss is generally wrong. It's one of life's little lessons. That's why it's important never to become a boss. But nine times out of 10 you should just shut your mouth and do whatever they tell you to do. Provided they don't tell you to shoot someone.'"

I laughed and slugged down some herb tea. How could anything ever really bug me, even Y2K and my jitters about buying land in the country, when I got to work ten feet from Rick and Planet Becky herself?

CHAPTER 13

LABOR PAINS

My heart kicked against my ribs as a shrill ring brought me upright and fumbling for the light. Erin knocked over a water glass reaching for the phone and groaned. Middle-of-the-night calls were regular occurrences when she'd practiced midwifery. But she'd closed her practice. My father in Baltimore was healthy; Erin's mother in Santa Rosa was holding her own. And the world had survived Y2K with barely a hitch. No reporters had been summoned from their beds to the newsroom on New Year's Eve. Life continued blandly on. So who was this?

"Hi, honey." Erin spoke in her rock-steady, compassionate midwife's voice, as if she'd been awake for hours. "When did you say your water broke?"

Uh-oh. It was Jiwan, her daughter. The baby wasn't due for another five weeks.

"I'll get there as soon as I can," she was saying, her voice strong and loving. "Sounds like we're going to have a baby."

The magic words. "We're going to have a baby." That's what Erin always said to laboring mothers no matter what the hour or how tired she was.

Signing off, she yanked a suitcase from the upper shelf of her closet and turned on the shower. "Jiwan's water broke. Can you make me some tea and toast and get on the computer? Find me a direct flight from San Francisco to Albuquerque on Southwest?" She glanced at the clock. It was 4 a.m. "I think I can make that eight o'clock flight. My credit card's in my purse."

"Is Jiwan okay?"

She inhaled. "I wish she were going to term, but. . ." She trailed of, closing the shower door behind her.

"It is what it is," I finished. That's what she always said when options seemed limited and the situation out of her control.

"Should I book you a return?" I shouted over the torrent of water, zipping up a fleece sweater and heading for the kitchen. The plan had always been for her to stay for three weeks after the baby's birth to help her daughter and son-in-law.

But so far nothing about this pregnancy was going according to plan. Erin had been on the phone with Jiwan several times a day since she was put on bed rest to avoid an early delivery.

"Book my return for three weeks from today, whenever that is. Southwest doesn't charge if I have to stay longer."

Longer? That didn't sound good. Could I survive a month without Erin, handling Xanadu by myself?

I put on the kettle, booted up my computer, gave up because my dial-up was so slow and called Southwest. Yes, there was a flight at 8 a.m. and yes, there was a seat. As Erin packed, I pondered what I needed to do: cancel our Valentine's Day dinner reservation for that night; decide who I'd celebrate my birthday with in two weeks; call our friend Douglas to see if he still wanted to drive with me to Cherry Creek on the weekend to explore the home site and design us a little house.

I placed an apprehensive Luna and a groggy Woody on the back seat of the car, gathered their leashes, dressed for our morning hike and roared down the freeway with Erin, in hot pursuit of the airport shuttle bus all the way from Larkspur to Mill Valley. Luna, to whom suitcases always meant the horror of abandonment, lay trembling into Erin's arms, while Woody lay curled in the back seat, oblivious to the drama. Despite the cold, steady drizzle in Marin and the winter weather she was about to encounter in New Mexico, Erin was dressed like a ray of Southwest sunshine, in a wide-brimmed straw hat, white linen pants, a beige cotton sweater and her multicolored hand-woven blue wool jacket we'd bought her last year in Santa Fe.

"Don't forget to call Stephanie and tell her that Bob has agreed to a land-swap agreement so we've solved the problem of our driveway entrance being on his land," Erin said, brushing her hair as we drove. "And confirm with Douglas about this weekend to be sure he's driving up with you to see the land. And you may as well ask Kerry if he wants to bid on Douglas's cabin sketch when it's ready and give us a sketch of his own. Let's cross our fingers we can afford what Douglas comes up with. Take pictures of the road so I can see how the new leg to the home site is holding up in the rain, and be sure to check the pond to see if it's holding water. Take the camera, of course, and…"

"Stop!" I begged. "Just one command at a time. I don't do well with more."

"They're not commands." Erin scowled at me. "What's the matter?" I must have looked stricken. "Are you angry?"

"Happy Valentine's Day."

"Oh, sweetie. Of course. I'm so sorry." She kissed my cheek. "Happy Valentine's Day."

"I know you're worried about Jiwan and the baby, but there's a lot going on with the land, and I'm nervous,"

"Of course, you are. I'll make it up to you when I get home." She scratched Luna's ears. "I'll take you out anywhere you want to go. The Buckeye, Casa Madrona, Stars. You name it."

"Your present's on the back seat," I said, holding back tears.

She reached behind her for the heart-shaped box of Mrs. See's chocolates I'd bought, sniffing the box longingly. "Thank you, Valentine. I'll take them to New Mexico. My card for you is sitting in my desk unsigned with a silly present that I never wrapped. Whoa!" she yelled, as I swerved down the exit ramp to Mill Valley and blasted into the parking lot, screeching to a halt next to the airport bus.

Erin pounded on the driver's window while I hauled her suitcase from the trunk.

The bus door shot open and up she went, suitcase in hand.

"I love you," she called.

"Love you, too," I waved, forcing a smile.

The driver whooshed the door closed and the airport bus disappeared up the freeway. Back in the car, I saw my Valentine's card for Erin and the unopened chocolates sitting forgotten on the seat. A tight, sad, familiar feeling gripped my chest as I headed home. I wanted to cry, to pound my fists against something. Why? What was I feeling? I looked at Luna, who was trembling next to me in the seat where Erin had been sitting. Uh-oh, I thought. This is not good. I was feeling just like my little dog. Scared and abandoned. And worse, a gnawing resentment of Erin's love for her daughter was trying to set up camp in my heart. Forget it, I told myself. Nip those feelings in the bud. Jiwan is Erin's child. She's having a baby and she needs her mother. Rip out those jealous tent stakes right this minute. Turn this unexpected schedule change around. See the cup as half full. Enjoy your three weeks alone. Write something new. Have a birthday party with Marny and Nanette and Cousin Anne. Take Rick to lunch. Call your father. Most of all, figure out why you bought 160 acres in northern Mendocino County and what you're going to do with them.

CHAPTER 14

THIS LITTLE PIGGY

Erin's granddaughter was not born at home, as Jiwan and her husband had hoped, but in a New Mexico hospital. Sarib Jot Khalsa was a healthy, beautiful girl, who tipped the scales at four pounds fifteen ounces. Her mother was sore and exhausted. The proud papa was bushed. And Erin, who had been at her daughter's side throughout the ordeal, was up to her ears in cooking, cleaning, and helping the young parents adjust to their new life.

And this little piggy went weep, weep, weep all the way home. Sometime during Erin's absence, I foolishly decided to open my closet door and read through the manuscript of my novel, a terrible mistake. I'd intended to write a riveting yarn about a life-changing séance with a dying woman and had ended up with a vitriolic diatribe.

Wobbly and blue, I looked forward to the day trip with Douglas to see our land. It would be just the ticket to get me out of my gloom. Douglas and I rarely spent time together alone, without our more extraverted spouses, so burgers and malted milkshakes with him at the Bluebird Cafe in Hopland, along with his thoughtful questions about our vision for the land, lifted me. The seasonal creeks were gushing down the hillsides on Parcel 39, and the pale green moss on the twisted, leafless oaks gave the landscape a haunted look. There'd been a small mudslide on the new leg of road to our home site, but in all other respects, the road was solid and hard. I'd left the Subaru at the top of our driveway, but we could easily have driven over it to the crooked oak. Douglas was awed by the beauty of the land, but on the drive home he couldn't hide his shock at how remote the place was. Like many of our friends, I think he'd visualized our place on the coast, close to the charming, artsy village of Mendocino, where so many San Franciscans stole away to for romantic weekends.

How could he help but be disappointed by the town of Willits, which, on that rainy afternoon, looked more like a bedraggled stray dog that no one would willingly adopt as their own than a beguiling little purebred village that Erin had given up trying to convince me it was. Douglas asked if I thought we'd be comfortable living so far from friends and family and city life, posing all his questions as gently and diplomatically as he could. Was the possibility of having a garden and a gorgeous mountain view enough to make me happy? Were we serious about building a structure that committed us to such a faraway place? I tried to be upbeat, reminding myself that Douglas was a Broadway set designer whose livelihood depended on being able to hop on red-eye flights to New York for meetings with directors and scenery construction shops. He *had* to be part of the urban cultural sizzle. Small wonder his idea of a country place was the spectacular house he and Stephen now owned overlooking the ocean in the pricey Marin County resort of Stinson Beach, half an hour from San Francisco. I sank lower with each new question because his reservations mirrored my own. How had this wilderness thing happened? I needed Erin to explain it all to him and to me. But she had flown the coop to New Mexico.

Back at home, I dipped from melancholy to misery. I was a flop. Anybody could buy land in the country if they had some money. Anybody could work at a newspaper if they had half a brain and knew how to use spell check. But anybody could *not* write a good book. Anybody could *no*t be a successful artist, like Douglas, with his name on Broadway marquees and money in the bank from his successes. Living in the country had been on my bucket list in the Year to Live Group, yes. But what was so wonderful about being miles from neighbors, having to work all day in a garden, never hearing a fire engine roar by or traffic noises in bed at night? If I was going to write something terrific and keep working, I couldn't be going up to the country every weekend. This country thing was what Erin wanted, wasn't it?

Stop it, I kept telling myself. *Buying the land hasn't taken anything away from you. It's already added to your life and your relationship, providing us both with a beautiful, wild place of our own to camp and explore and share with good friends.*

But that half-full cup seemed forever beyond my reach. Life felt flat and depressing. I wanted inspiration. I needed Erin to *inspire* me to write something wonderful that made so much money we could travel or develop the land or do anything we wanted, like live in Paris or visit temples in India. If she would transform herself, stop watching *Seinfeld* and *Law and Order* on TV and become, well, yes, my muse, I would become more creative and productive, even bulldozing that pile of dispirited words in my closet into a fantastic yarn that flew off the bookstore shelves.

Erin wasn't extremely sympathetic when I called her in New Mexico to share my doubts and misgivings. She was knee-deep in diapers and dishes and cooking for the kids. She wanted *me* to boost *her* morale, and I came up short.

Marny and Nanette and Ruby, the astrologer, tried bolster me up. You're not a failure, they said. If your novel needs work, you'll rewrite it when you're ready. And if you're worried about spending so much time and money on the land, don't build *anything* there right now. Enjoy your tent. Make some new friends here, and spend more time with old ones. Take another Spanish class. Go to therapy to find out what will really make you happy.

Therapy. Right. I'd been to therapy. I'd been to therapy one, two, three, four, five, six different times in my life. Erin should go to therapy, I told myself, so *she* can be a better partner for me and make me a better writer. They all laughed when I told them this. Erin wasn't confused and depressed, they said. She's happy with your life together. She enjoys her children and grandchildren and she loves you and this land you've bought. Your unhappiness is your problem. Focus on making yourself happy. Exercise more. Maybe try Prozac or a little Celexa.

Erin returned, exhausted but happy. When I picked her up at the airport, she couldn't wait to see the dogs and sleep in our own bed and sip a beer (her daughter didn't drink) and sit down in front of the TV--which her daughter didn't have.

She called Jiwan in New Mexico the moment she walked in the door, which instantly reminded me for the millionth time that I didn't have these kinds of special bonds with children who needed and adored me, whose faces lit up when I phoned and who counted on me for advice and love and support. I tried to twitch away this nasty wave of jealousy and bury my Poor Pitiful Pearl doll.

"What's wrong?" Erin said, the dogs crawling over her, vying for space in her lap. "Are you upset about something?"

"No," I said. That was another thing. Why were the dogs always so glad to see her? I was the one who'd fed them and walked them and petted them the past month.

"Yes, you *are* upset." Her blue eyes studied me

suspiciously. "What is it?"

"I'm a failure," I said.

"You're not a failure."

"My novel is terrible."

She shrugged. "You'll rewrite it and make it better or start a new one. You've published other books. You know how to do it. You're a fine writer. You won a national journalism award. The paper's happy with the job you're doing on the healthcare beat. That's not failure."

"But that's how I feel."

Erin looked at me. "I know you're disappointed about your book. I understand that. But the editor said you needed to do a rewrite months ago. Why are you so depressed about it now?"

"I reread it."

"You're angry at me. I hear it in your voice." She picked up my hand and kissed it. "I went away for a month. . ."

"On Valentine's Day."

"Which I couldn't help because my daughter went into premature labor and. . ."

"You missed my birthday."

"Yes, and I missed your birthday, but you threw a party for yourself and had a lot of fun."

"I did."

"So what's the problem? How can I make you happy?"

"Stop watching TV."

She stared at me. "You'd be happy if I stopped watching TV?"

I nodded.

She emitted a long-suffering sigh. "What's my watching TV, which I know you think is low-class and slovenly, got to do with how *you* feel?"

"I want you to inspire me to greatness."

Erin's eyes widened as she leaned back against the couch, laughing so hard tears ran down her cheeks. Arms crossed, I watched in silence. Luna started to shake anxiously. Erin pinched my toe. "And this little piggy went wee, wee, wee all the way home."

"You're mocking me," I pouted.

"I'm sorry," she said, her laughter gone. "But you're hurting *my* feelings. I've just come home from a month away, and I'm thrilled to be here and to see you, and you're telling me you're not happy because I watch TV and don't inspire you to greatness."

"I know it doesn't sound. . ." I trailed off.

She looked at me hard. "You're jealous, aren't you?"

"I am not." I looked away.

"You're jealous of my relationship with my daughters and grandchildren, aren't you?"

"No," I reddened.

She was getting mad now. "So because I spent a month with my daughter, who had a very, very difficult birth, and had a tiny baby whose life was at risk, and who needed help getting back on her feet, you're mad and think I'm not enough for you?"

"Not exactly," I said guiltily, hating the person she was so accurately describing. Now, I'd managed to ruin Erin's good mood at being home, and she was pissed.

"So," she said, chewing her lip. "Let me get this straight. While I was changing diapers and cooking for Jiwan and washing dishes and cleaning the house and sleeping in a lumpy loft bed, you were here by yourself thinking of all the things that are wrong with me and our relationship, right? Because your book needs work, right?"

"No."

"What then?"

"I have buyer's remorse."

"What?" She stopped scratching Woody's ears and stared at me.

"You're taking me away from my friends and my life and culture and stimulation and dragging me off to the middle of nowhere."

She shook her head. "I'm dragging you to the middle of nowhere?"

"Yes."

"But we haven't gone anywhere. We live right here."

"But one day we will live there, I know it."

She was either going to slug me or start laughing again. "I hope we will someday, but you're right here right now and you've had nearly a month to revise your novel. And you didn't do it. Was that my fault?"

"I couldn't bear to look at it."

"And if I stop watching TV, and we don't go up to the land, you'll write a great novel?"

"It sounds stupid, I know."

"It does indeed." Erin slammed her beer down on the coffee table. "And because I left on Valentine's Day, and I was gone for your birthday, you got jealous and then angry with me."

I didn't answer.

"I'm right, aren't I?"

How could she have figured it all out so easily? I felt so dumb and selfish and transparent.

"You know what?" she said. "I do love my

daughters. I adore them. But my daughters are not my partners. You're my partner. I've chosen to spend my life with you." She leapt up and pulled open the garage door.

"What are you doing?"

"I'm packing," I said.

"You're leaving?" My heart began to pound. She really was mad.

"Yes." She pulled a duffel bag from off the shelf and began tossing clothes into it.

"Where are you going?"

"Same place that you are."

I looked at her. "Where's that?"

"There's only one cure for this sinkhole you've fallen into."

"Where?" I said. But I already knew.

"Cherry Creek."

"I thought we were staying home this weekend so you can rest."

"You and I need a trip to the country together more than I need to sleep in my own bed."

"What if it rains? The tent will might leak."

"Weather report says sunny and mild tomorrow."

I looked at her. She was serious.

"Hurry up. Get the dogs' leashes and bowls and the sleeping bags, and I'll pack the food."

And I did, and she did, and up the freeway we drove.

❧

The pond was a pond, full of beautiful, deep, luscious green water. The hills of Cherry Creek were sparkling green and inviting in the sun, alive with water cascading through the canyons. The wild iris and the tiny white popcorn flowers were popping up everywhere. It was so warm that we both jumped naked into pond. A baptism. A celebratory cleansing. We slept in the tent and cooked bacon and made pancakes on the Coleman stove in the morning and talked about where to build the cabin if we liked Douglas's design. My gloom lifted. The dogs ran up through the hills and wagged their tails and chased squirrels deliriously, digging for gophers and munching down what Erin called crappetizers-- deer and coyote poop.

Suddenly, it was clear to me that we hadn't made a mistake buying Parcel 39. We weren't crazy to want a cabin there and maybe some day a real house. The land was magic; the same hopeful message leaped from every green stem and budding oak branch and wisp of cloud: There is no pursuit more meaningful and important than falling in love with Earth and her abundance. That *is* success, and my life was about to lift into the stratosphere because of the land. I prayed I could hold on to that feeling, keep it inside me forever. No more self-doubts, no more looking back and seeing failure. I had everything I needed to be happy--a beautiful, loving partner and two crazy, sweet dogs, and close friends like Marny and Nanette and Cousin Anne. I had a job I loved that paid me to write. We had my house in Mill Valley and Erin's house in Novato, and now we owned 160 acres in the most beautiful place in the world. *Get a life, Jane,* I told myself. And she whispered back, "*Wee, wee, wee all the way home.*"

CHAPTER 15

WOODY COME BACK...

Douglas's plan for our cabin was fabulous--a one-room cedar studio with high ceilings, solar electricity, a tiny kitchen area, bathroom and shower, double-paned windows overlooking the mountains and a wrap-around deck. He named it the Outback Cottage, and we loved it. There was just one problem--the contractor's estimate to build it was more than $50,000.

We were shaken. We consulted Ruby, our

astrologer, the Tarot deck and our friends. Finally, we made our decision. For $4,100, a company in Sonoma would come up for the day to erect a 15-by-20-foot precut plywood shed with a metal roof. The same contractors had built Mike and Robin's tiny shed house, which they'd dubbed "the cabinette," and had wired, insulated and lived in for more than a year. They offered to do the same thing for us, wiring and insulating our shed, adding plywood walls and ceiling, building front and back decks, installing counters and laying a linoleum floor. We knew they could do it because Mike, who had learned basic construction skills in the army, had already cherried up their shed and built us a magnificent outhouse near our tent. We needed help, and they needed money.

The cabin was set to be constructed the Tuesday following Memorial Day, when the Irregulars were gathering at our place for a holiday potluck under the crooked oak. The day of the party was endlessly blue, the sun warm but not too hot. Everyone brought food, and we gorged at our new plastic picnic table on grilled chicken, baked beans, salad, and sinfully good brownies that Rod, a fantastic cook, had made from scratch. As we ate, we entertained ourselves, as usual on the latest rural-living crises.

Rod and Cindy chronicled the engineering and permitting challenges of converting a railroad flatcar into an automobile bridge across Cherry Creek at their home site. Robin, a former Girl Scout turned Deadhead turned born-again Catholic, told of the latest threatening letter she'd had to write the manufactured home company that still hadn't delivered their house. Stephanie and Ken reported on the status of the raucous menagerie of birds now living at Jay's guest cottage, as well as the three dogs and two cats. Jay himself, a world traveler whose long-term partner had died four years earlier, doubled us over laughing with the latest tales of his quest to find a suitable boyfriend among the lumberjacks, carpenters, waiters and cowboys he'd met in Mendocino County.

When the Irregulars headed home, promising to return the next day to watch our cabin go up, Erin began washing the lunch dishes on the picnic table with hot water from our solar shower bag. I let Woody and Luna out of the car, where they'd been stowed until Rod and Cindy left with their big dogs, whom our little dogs hated. After a quick walk, I put them inside their portable dog fence to keep them from heading off in search of the wild horses, which they sorely wanted to eat.

"I'm going to paint the outhouse," I announced. Erin's friends had given her money to build the outhouse for her birthday. Now that it was finished, constructed out of enormously heavy cement siding called Hardie board, it needed a coat of paint.

Erin frowned. "Isn't it late to start a project?"

"Nope," I said. "It's a perfect time." The early evening air was mild, the wind calm, and we had a couple more hours of light left before sundown. If I didn't paint the outhouse, I'd be forced to don my white jump suit and tear poison oak from around the base of our big oak trees, a thoroughly disagreeable task that Erin couldn't do because she was crazy allergic to poison oak.

"The dogs don't like being in a cage," Erin grumbled. She hadn't quite forgiven me for my lament in March that she didn't inspire me to greatness. She was also irritated that at today's picnic I'd polled the Irregulars on where they thought we should erect the new cabin. They'd all agreed that the place we'd picked, down the hill from the meadow, was a bad idea. As a result, we'd changed our plan and were going to have the contractor build the cabin close to the crooked oak, which would be cooler in the summer heat, more protected and closer to the outhouse. Erin resented what she considered my role in overturning a decision we'd already made and, I concluded, was taking out her feelings on me by trying to manage every move I made.

"The dogs have been cooped up in the car all day," she said, opening the cage. Woody and Luna charged over to the woodpile beyond the crooked oak to sniff for mice.

"Say three Hail Mary's and ask the Goddess for protection," I said. "Let's hope the woodpile keeps them busy."

I dragged the folding ladder over to the outhouse and began rolling primer on the roof. There was no crescent moon carved into the front door because Hardie board was notoriously brittle, making it difficult to cut, but other than that, we were well pleased. "Will you chase the dogs if they run away?" I called to Erin.

"What's the point of having all this land if the dogs are trapped in a little cage?" With a sigh, she set the clean skillet on the picnic table. "I'll retrieve them if they run away."

I poured more sea-foam green paint into the roller pan. "Do you promise?"

"When they're near you," Erin said, "you watch

them, and when they're near me, I'll watch them."
She dipped a plate into hot water.

"How can I watch them if I'm painting?"

She didn't answer, and for a while the dogs dug manically around the woodpile, barking wildly when they smelled prey.

I was happy. Glad to be outside on our land making our outhouse beautiful, pleased with our Irregulars party and our new friends, grateful we no longer had to lug a shovel into the bushes when nature called.

Just as I started to roll a second coat of paint on the roof, with darkness beginning to fall, the dogs began yelping from somewhere above us on the hill behind the tent.

I looked at Erin and scanned the hillside. "I thought you were watching them."

"They were closer to you the last time than to me." She looked up from the book she was now reading on solar electricity. "We were sharing custody, remember?"

"Luna! Woody!" I yelled, over and over again. Eventually, Luna trotted down the rocky, oak-covered hill, tail wagging, burrs all over her, oblivious to our panic. Woody was still howling somewhere above us.

I glanced at Erin and looked down at my paint-covered latex gloves. "Will you go look for him?"

"I need to start dinner."

"But I'm painting, and. . ." A blood-curdling yowl came from somewhere above us.

I dropped the roller, pulled off my latex gloves and started up the steep, rocky slope behind the tent.

"Hurry!" Erin called. "He's in trouble."

"I'm hurrying," I yelled back. Where was that crazy dog? Why hadn't we kept them in their cage? At the top of the hill, I scanned the field, which stretched for nearly a quarter of a mile to the far canyon. The field was eerily silent. I heard one choked Woody bark and froze. One hundred yards ahead, two thin, four-legged creatures stared at me. Woody dangled from one of the coyote's mouth.

"Stop it!" I yelled. "Put him down!" Waving my arms, I ran toward them, a universe away. "Woody!" I screamed. "Woody, come!"

"What is it? What's happening?" Erin called from below.

"It's coyotes!" I said. "Coyotes have Woody."

Her cry galvanized me; I was racing up a near-vertical slope, shale kicking off my heels. Surprised by my spurt of energy, the coyote dropped Woody's small body in the grass and disappeared into the far ravine.

"Woody!" I called, panicked and stumbling forward. How could I live with myself if we lost Woody, our dear little blind love child dog? Where was he? I scanned the high grass. Where was that willful little dog?

"Have you got him?" Erin called, only now cresting the hill.

Suddenly, I saw something black popping up through the grass. It was my boy, his little black head bobbing toward me as he hopped through the grass. Not only could he walk, he could run. "Woody, I'm here!" I yelled. "Over here!"

When I leaned down to pick him up, he tried to dodge me, barking fiercely, scared to death.

"It's me, Woody," I comforted, finally scooping

him into my arms. His heart was pounding against my racing heart as he panted furiously. There was blood on his neck, which was leaking into my hand. I couldn't look down, afraid of what I would see.

Erin was next to me now, stroking his head. "Sweet little baby boy."

"I'm afraid to look at his neck," I said, stumbling down the rocky hillside.

At the picnic table, I handed him to Erin, who'd found a towel and her glasses and had wrapped him up, holding him close as she parted the fur on his neck. "It's not too bad," she said at last. "He has some puncture wounds on the back of his neck and two small ones on his throat. But he's not bleeding much." She turned to me. "What did the coyotes look like?"

"Like dogs," I said. "Like tall German shepherds with long, skinny legs."

With the last remnants of warm water from the solar shower bag, we cleaned the small holes on Woody's neck, setting him down on the ground gently to see if he could walk. He took a few steps and collapsed pitifully.

I wiped away tears. "Shall we drive him to the all-night vet in Santa Rosa?"

"It's a holiday," Erin chewed her lip. "It'll cost an arm and a leg. Let's see how he does tonight, and in the morning we can take him to the vet in Laytonville if he's worse."

Legs still shaky, I put away the paint, gathering wood in the stone-lined fire pit we'd recently dug near the picnic table. After dinner, we took turns holding Woody, sitting under the stars, the fire glowing, the night cool, our knees still weak from fright.

"I think they were starting to shake him to death," I inhaled, stretching my legs in front of me.

Erin kissed Woody's ear. "They were going to eat you for dinner, little boy."

An owl hooted in the distance, and we both jumped when something rustled in the leaves behind us.

"We would never have forgiven ourselves if Woody had been killed," I said.

Erin nodded. "But what's the good of having all this land if they have to stay in a little cage?"

Erin had a new cell phone that got reception here, so I dialed Mike and Robin. "I'm sorry to call so late," I told Mike. "But Woody was captured by coyotes and I. . ." Emotion choked my throat.

"Coyotes got Woody? Is he okay?"

"We think he's okay," I said. "He's not bleeding, but he's still shaking. I was wondering if, after the cabin's up, before you put in the insulation or anything else, if you would build us a fenced back yard behind it so the dogs can be safe. I don't want to go through this ever again."

"Sure thing," Mike said. "We can talk about what materials you want to use tomorrow. Give Woody a hug. See you in the morning."

That night, Woody slept next to Erin on his new flannel camping bag; Luna lay between us on our sleeping bag. I kept remembering his agonized howl from the hill above us and seeing his long black torso dangling from the coyote's mouth.

All through the night, we checked on Woody. His heart was still pounding fast, and his breathing was shallow. He startled us once with a choked, nightmare bark, quickly falling back to sleep. We barely slept.

In the morning, Woody still couldn't walk and was frighteningly subdued. We decided that I would drive him to the vet in Laytonville, and Erin would stay behind to wait for the crew and oversee the construction of our new shed home. She'd made all the arrangements with the contractor, so it made sense. And she promised to document every step of construction with our camera.

With a heavy heart, I carried my little patient toward the vet's, putting him down for a moment to pee before we went in. Something miraculous happened. He could walk again, sprinting happily toward a gopher hole and starting to dig.

"Woody," I cried. "You're okay." I lifted him up and squeezed him against my chest. "You're okay, you naughty dog."

In the examining room, the vet inspected Woody quickly, said he didn't think anything was broken but that he needed to keep the little dachshund for several hours while he took X-rays, cleaned his wounds and gave him a full exam. So, that was it. I wouldn't get back in time to see the house go up. But at least little Woody was going to survive. On the grassy lawn of the vet's place, I wrote about the terrible event in my journal, then closed my eyes and thanked the goddess he'd survived. Later, in town, I bought a chocolate croissant and a decaf latte to celebrate.

When Woody emerged from the back room, he pranced out, head high, tail wagging. The tension left in my throat and chest and shoulders dissolved. The coyotes hadn't broken any of his bones, the vet said, his limbs were all in tact, and his shock symptoms were gone. I hugged the doctor, paid my bill and pulled into the Chief hamburger stand, where the enormous painted Indian loomed over the parking lot. I bought a burger patty for Woody and French fries, cheeseburgers and shakes for whichever Irregulars were still on hand at the cabin raising.

As I bumped around the last switchback above our home site in the Subaru, I squinted down below at our new cabin, a plain, ungainly plywood shed that seemed to tower above the pier footings on which it sat, its front windows too close to the roof, the big Dutch door looking way more like a barn than a home.

Under the twisted oak, Erin, Mike, Robin, Rod, Cindy, Stephanie and Ken were sipping drinks from their coolers, the crew gone. The moment I opened the passenger door, Luna jumped into the seat to lick her bedraggled and subdued brother's ears; he managed one weary wag of his tail and melted into Erin's arms.

"Burgers, shakes and fries for all," I smiled, opening the take-out bags of food. "In honor of Woody's recovery and our new home."

"To Erin and Jane's new cabin," they cheered, raising their milkshakes.

"And to the Goddess for bringing us to Cherry Creek and for keeping our little Woody alive," Erin said.

Robin sipped her Diet Pepsi, confessing to the group that when I'd called last night, and she'd heard Mike say to me--"Coyotes took Woody?" she thought Mike meant Woody, their neighbor, who weighed about two hundred pounds and lived down the road from them. "I kept thinking, that was one heck of a big coyote."

That night, we slept in our new cabin on our new futon bed with Woody and Luna between us. We decided then and there to name our parcel Blind Dog Ranch. That way, no matter what happened to Woody out in the middle of nowhere, we'd always have his spirit close to us. How grateful and fortunate we felt that night to be able to close the front and back doors knowing that we were safe from coyotes, bears, snakes, skunks and things that go bump in the night. How grateful we felt that little Woody was alive and that soon we'd have a fenced yard instead of a cage where we could keep both dogs safe. After that, who knew? There were more adventures to come, but we'd dodged a big one. Hopefully, our good luck would continue.

CHAPTER 16

SSSNAKES

"Tell me about your mother," yawned the young psychotherapist my HMO had assigned me when I'd told them I was having trouble sleeping and could use some help learning to see my cup--and my rural property--as half full.

I knew she didn't really care about my mother, so I stared at two books on the shelf behind her-- the *Diagnostic and Statistical Manual of Mental Disorders* and *PDR Pharmacopoeia Pocket Dosing*

Guide. Dosing guide. What did this woman with her cleavage and short skirt know about dosing? She was a kid, really, a clinical psychology intern. She'd dozed off in several of our sessions, and I didn't want to interrupt her alpha state now because, she'd explained last time, when I offered to buy her a latte from the cart outside, she was riding in a 100-mile bicycle race for mesothelioma and rose very early each morning to train.

My silence jerked her awake, her eyes popping open with surprise to see me sitting across from her. "You were saying?" Clearly, she hadn't a clue what she'd just asked me.

"My mother didn't like the country," I said. "She grew up in Arkansas, in the Mississippi Delta. She couldn't wait to get out of the South and go to college in New York. She did have a flower garden in our back yard in Baltimore."

"Interesting," blinked the shrink. "Your condition may be genetic."

"What condition?"

"Alpinophobia." She scribbled something on a pad. "I'm referring you to a psychiatrist for evaluation."

"An evaluation for what?"

"Fear of mountains," she said. "It's relatively rare, but there are a number of documented cases." She scribbled a doctor's name on a pad, handing it to me. "I'm afraid our time is up."

Two weeks later, I was sitting across from a skinny, red-haired psychiatrist telling him about the rattlesnake Gina and Lin and Erin and I had seen slide under the cabin last weekend. I kept thinking about what a rattler could do to our little blind Woody and the ferocious, intrepid and single-minded Luna. Both of them loved digging under the cabin for mice. What if they came across a rattlesnake? There was a night's sleep gone just contemplating that scenario.

"I'm not convinced you have alpinophobia," said the psychiatrist, attacking a cobweb on the ceiling with a feather duster, then wiping his hands with a lemon-scented towelette from his briefcase. "More likely ophidiophobia." He was jotting something on a prescription pad.

"What?"

"Irrational fear of snakes."

"It's not irrational," I protested. "Our new land is crawling with snakes. Stephanie says they love our parcel. If I could just sleep through the night, I'd be. . ."

"We've had some success using Buspar to deal with these issues," he said, flicking a speck of dust off his desk. "I'd also like you to attend our anti-anxiety workshop on Wednesday afternoons." He glanced at the clock. "Our eight minutes is up."

I was feeling a little rushed. "My fear of rattlesnakes is reality-based," I said, picking up my backpack. "Mostly, I just can't sleep." There wasn't a chance that this guy could teach me how to see my cup as half full.

"Many phobias have some basis in reality." He wiped a coffee ring from his desktop. "In any case, you'll find out you're not alone. I'd like you to buy the book we use in the group at the hospital store."

"But I work on Wednesday afternoons. The Dragon Lady's taken a leave of absence to write her memoir, and Robert, the new city editor, won't like me drifting off to attend an anxiety class every Wednesday afternoon."

"Avoidance," he said, brushing a microscopic something from his tie. "Perfectly natural. Your fear won't subside until you face it. Try the support group and come back in a month. Don't use the Desyrel--the brand name for trazodone, a serotonin modulator--until you've taken the Buspar for two weeks." He rose, shaking my hand, then wiped his own hand on another small towel from his briefcase. "If these drugs aren't effective, I've got other tricks up my sleeve."

Wow, I thought. What a great healthcare story for the paper. Patient complains about insomnia and leaves doctor's office with an exotic cocktail of psychotropic drugs.

I dashed to the hospital bookstore.

"If you are one of the millions of Americans who suffer from obsessive-compulsive disease," began the book he wanted me to buy, "you've come to the right place. OCD means you may suffer from the persistent intrusion of unwanted thoughts accompanied by ritualistic actions."

Ritualistic actions?

Erin laughed when I told her about the psychiatrist and the OCD group. "I hope you're not going."

"If I left work for that long, Robert would go crazy. Anyway, we may have a cure for my insomnia. The shrink prescribed me that anti-anxiety drug that Teresa says all the nurses at her clinic take like candy when they're having a bad day."

"Buspar?" Erin rolled her eyes. "Where's the bottle? That stuff's horrible."

"If I'm OCD, maybe I need it."

"You're not OCD or alpinophobic or

ophiophobic. You're a wonderful, normal person. You had a setback with your writing, and you're going through menopause. You probably need more estrogen, which is why you've gotten your knickers in a knot over moving to the land, which we're not going to do anytime soon. Those are the reasons why you can't sleep. You've convinced yourself that something's wrong with you. There's nothing wrong with you."

"Why do I feel like such a failure? Why am I so scared that you're setting the agenda for both of us?"

She shook her head and sighed. "I'm not setting your agenda. I wish I could set your agenda. I'd wave my magic wand and get that damn book of yours published so you'd be happy and love me again, and then we'd start building a house, and I'd get a nursing job in Mendocino County."

"And the insomnia?"

"Every woman in her fifties that we know has insomnia!" she said, face reddening. "It's our age, Jane. It's our estrogen drying up. You are a wonderful person--smart and kind and a lot of fun when you're not taking life too seriously. You're having a rough patch right now, but you're not abnormally afraid of snakes or the country or mountains or me. You love the country. You're happy up on the land. Did you tell the shrinks that?"

"I may not have," I said, scooping up Luna, who was trembling.

"And let me tell you something else." She waited for me to look up. "I can be perfectly happy living here in Marin County with you forever. We have a good life, we have friends, and we have miles of public open space to hike in with the dogs. It's fine with me if we don't move anywhere. Do you understand?"

I nodded.

"I want to spend the rest of my life with you, you crazy lout. I love you. I want you to be happy. I don't know why you feel so worthless and unlovable. That's what you should be working on in therapy, not OCD or fear of snakes. Okay?"

"Okay," I croaked. "I love you, too."

"Glad to hear it," she said. "Now, where are those pills?"

I snuck out one of the sleeping pills and swallowed it quickly before handing her the two little bottles.

She flushed the Buspar and Desyrel down the toilet.

I didn't obsess about rattlesnakes that night because I was comatose from Desyrel. The next day at work, I catnapped through a phone interview with a man who'd raised a grapefruit the size of a basketball in his backyard garden.

CHAPTER 17

STEPHANIE'S VISITOR

Stephanie called. "Guess what happened to us last night?"

"Uh-oh." I signaled Erin to get on the other phone.

"We had a visitor."

"Your mother, right? From New Mexico?" Erin sat down next to me.

"Arizona. But I'm not talking about her."

"A rattlesnake?" I offered.

"We were marauded by a bear."

Stephanie was talking fast. She had been up in the loft of Jay's cabin with Roo-bird, her beloved bare-eyed cockatoo, just getting him down for the night, when her mother started yelling from downstairs that she'd heard something. This annoyed Stephanie because if anyone talked to her while she was putting Roo-bird to bed, he behaved very badly and wouldn't go to sleep for hours. Her mother kept insisting that something was on the front porch, bumping against the door, and she could have sworn it was a bear. Stephanie told her mother it couldn't a bear because there was no room for a bear to sit on their front porch. Roo-bird was shrieking by then, and all three dogs were inside barking at the door. Stephanie came down from the loft and looked out the window. Yes, there was indeed a bear, a great big California black bear holding a large bag of garbage, poached from the bin at the side of the cabin. He was turning circles like a circus performer, trying to sit on the front door stoop that was half his size. Her mom was screaming at her to lock the deadbolt before the weight of the bear broke through the door.

At this point the real circus was in the living room, where 10 birds screamed warning calls, three dogs barked, Stephanie was yelling at Ken, who refused to get out of bed, and her mother was in a complete panic. The bear gave up on the stoop, went around the cabin to the stairs and lumbered up to the back door and the closed bin of dry dog kibble on the deck.

"Did you let the dogs out?" Erin asked.

"I was afraid the bear might hurt them," she

said. So her mother banged on pots and pans and screamed at the bear through the window. But the bear couldn't have cared less. His head was planted in the tin bin as he tried to get at the kibble.

"What about the firearm?" I asked.

"What firearm?" Stephanie seemed surprised.

"You told me once that you have a little gun."

"Oh, that. That gun was another problem. It seems the gun was in a box somewhere."

They had dozens of boxes, Stephanie said, that they'd never opened since leaving L.A., and the gun was buried in one. Meantime, her mother was yelling, "Kill the bear, kill the bear!" And in the middle of all this, Stephanie and Ken got in a fight over why he hadn't taken the garbage to the dump in the first place. Plus, Stephanie was shouting to her mother, "We can't kill the bear. This is a wildlife refuge. And I can't find the pistol." In truth, she said, they wouldn't have wanted to kill the bear anyway.

"But if you'd found the gun," I said, "couldn't you have shot it into the air just to scare it?"

"Inside the house? Jay would have loved that. As it was, the place was complete chaos, with all the birds squawking and my mother banging on pots and the dogs barking.

"Then Jay called and wanted to know what the heck was going on down there because the noise was triggering his ligyrophobia."

"His what?" I said.

"His fear of noise. I was so desperate I let Chips out, and bless her heart, the dog ran to the back stairs barking from below and surprised the bear, who fell backwards, tumbling down the stairs with the kibble tin stuck to his head. He was stupefied by Chips, who began to herd the bear away from the house and down the mountainside while the other dogs and my mom cheered her on."

"Chips was the hero," I said.

Erin was laughing. I was thinking about my father's 12-gauge shotgun. He'd offered to give it to me several times, but I'd always refused because what was I going to do with a shotgun in the suburbs? But I could see I might need it soon at Cherry Creek.

"Are you afraid of the bear coming back?" Erin asked, while I pondered Jay's ligyrophobia. That was one diagnosis the two shrinks hadn't given me, although it was possible I had a little touch of it because I hated noise so much I slept with earplugs every night, and an eye mask, too. What was the term for fear of light, I wondered.

"I'm not afraid of the bear anymore," Stephanie was saying. "Now that I know Chips can herd it away."

Stephanie's mother, on the other hand, couldn't take the stress. The following evening when Ken was late returning from the Emerald Chasm, she wanted Stephanie to check to see if he needed help. Her mother's real dilemma was that she didn't want to leave the safety of the cabin *or* be left there alone in case the bear returned. At dusk, after an hour of agonizing over the decision, Stephanie persuaded her mother to drive with her to their parcel, promising her it would be completely safe and that her fears were unjustified. As they crossed the front yard, halfway between the car and the front door, they suddenly heard the thumping sound of the previous night's bear clambering down Jay's driveway. Her mom was caught like a deer in the headlights. Reacting like a cartoon character, she began moving first one way, then the other, then back again, unsure which direction was the quickest way to safety. Once in the house, she picked up the phone and changed her flight. She was leaving early the next morning.

"I don't think she will ever be back," Stephanie said wistfully.

The moral of the story, she said, was that Erin and I must never, ever leave food, garbage or anything else around our cabin that might interest a bear if we didn't want to send our company packing. We had actually learned this already the hard way. One day last summer we'd left a teakettle in our tent and headed home. Unbeknownst to us, bacon grease from the stove had splattered on the kettle, and the bear, smelling it, had ripped open our tent, digging his teeth into the metal. I thought it was the work of teenage punks with a BB gun, until Erin pointed out that not only were those were teeth marks on the kettle, but that there were no teenagers who lived at Cherry Creek.

"You were lucky" Stephanie said. "A bear ripped the door off the big refrigerator that Bob, the guy who owns the old original Whittaker homestead here, kept on his porch in his outdoor kitchen."

"Wow," we both said.

"But it wasn't a problem," Stephanie laughed. "He'd bought the fridge with an American Express Gold Card, so they gave him a new one because it was less than a year old. From that time on he scared the bears away by keeping Christian music playing loudly on his radio when he wasn't there. The sound of Debby Boone singing 'Be Thou My Vision' frightened the bears so much they never returned."

"Makes sense," Erin giggled. "That bears would be pagan." We laughed 'till we cried. Stephanie's story made me feel much better. Country life was fun and beautiful and all that cool stuff, but sometimes it was downright dangerous. Between the bears, the rattlers and coyotes, it was a miracle any of us ever slept.

CHAPTER 18

PONDIFICATING

We had to get ready fast. Fourteen women were coming to our land for summer solstice, and we wanted the place to be safe, hospitable and inviting. I donned goggles, gloves and the white jumpsuit, hoisted a two-gallon tank of eco-friendly chemicals onto my back and prepared to attack the wily green poison oak vines still strangling many of our oak trees. Erin weed-whacked the high grass around the pond and the cabin with our gas-powered, two-stroke weed eater, a maddeningly temperamental machine whose plastic trimming lines snagged constantly on rocks and fallen branches, causing the engine to sputter and die as the string retreated maddeningly inside its housing.

Marny and Nanette, both camping-averse, skipped the party, having visited with their partners for a day on Erin's birthday weekend. Awed by the land's beauty, Marny forgave me for buying the place and finally seemed to understand why the land exerted such a pull on me.

On Friday afternoon of the party, cars and coolers full of wine, sodas, beer and gourmet delicacies began to arrive with accompanying screams of shock and amazement at the beauty of our land and the ridiculously long, six-mile dirt road drive from the highway. Gina and Lin brought two of their Swallowtail Ranch land partners--Jane Hernandez, a vivacious, Cuban-American film producer from Berkeley, and her former partner, Kate, a musician, singer, acupuncturist, and physician assistant, who'd once been a night club and cafe performer in Fayetteville, Arkansas, and Tulsa and later made her living singing advertising jingles in Japan.

Janet and Holly, two smart, fun-loving goddesses from the newsroom who'd recently fallen in lust, arrived with a giant, inflatable air mattress that allowed them to spend so many hours in their tent processing their religious, cultural, class and personality differences that other campers took bets on how long their relationship would last.

Janet, who dubbed the spirited weekend

"Janestock," was an endearingly anxious Jew from Los Angeles. She'd brilliantly covered a sensational lesbian love-triangle murder in which a 67-year-old former art teacher bludgeoned to death her 71-year-old Mill Valley rival, whom she suspected of stealing away her lover. Holly, the paper's sports editor, was an outgoing, party-loving jock raised by fundamentalist Christians in North Carolina.

Relationship tips for the struggling new couple were provided by everyone at Janestock, including Sylvia and Sheryl, Jewish New Yorkers who were psychotherapeutically savvy, and Jane Lawton, who'd broken away from her Pentecostal Southern Indiana roots to come out as a lesbian in California. Jane's partner, Teresa, a lively, dramatic and mystically inclined nurse and astrologer, saw from a quick sun-moon-rising-sign assessment that Holly and Janet were star-crossed.

Stephanie left her new cabin above the Emerald Chasm to attend solstice dinner, as did Irregular Cindy, who told us that Rod had warned her on her way out the door not to forget that she had a husband when she attended our potluck and drumming circle around the campfire. Robin, apparently sensing pagan influences, stayed away.

For three days we ate, swam naked in the pond, skinny dipped at the Emerald Chasm, laughed, hiked and ate some more in the shade of the crooked oak, barbecuing everything from eggplant to enchiladas on a dilapidated propane grill we'd rescued from Rod and Cindy on its way to the dump.

Seeing our land through the eyes of new and old friends made me realize that I had not only adjusted to the snakes, bears and coyotes, I was now *addicted* to the rugged beauty of their habitats. The fact that the Janestock group was crazy about the land and had driven hours to come and see us, gave me hope that we wouldn't be all alone in the middle of nowhere if ever we made Cherry Creek our permanent home.

The pond, 20 feet at its deepest, was glorious for the Janestock weekend. Private and secluded, it was a delicious, mothering womb, a place where the Janestockers floated and paddled and laughed, light and mindless as beach balls.

There was just one small problem.

Water was rapidly disappearing. At first we thought it was going down because of evaporation from the sun. But soon after Janestock, the water level sank an alarming five feet. A pretty little stream that wasn't supposed to be there now ran from the base of the pond's dam through the lower meadow and far down the hill. This rare summer stream thrilled the wildlife but meant that our escape from the intense summer heat, which scorched us even in our insulated cabin, was draining away.

We called Doug, the bulldozer guy, to tell him the bad news.

"Ponds are tricky," he said laconically. "I hit some rock when I was digging yours, but I covered it with clay. Clay's what you want for a pond. Rock's bad. Water can leak out around it."

"Can you fix it?" The pond was a key to our paradise.

There was a long pause. "You could try dumping in some Bentonite."

"What's that?"

"Bentonite's a fine gray powdery clay that comes in 50-pound bags."

"How much do we need?"

"Hard to say," he drawled.

"How do you put it in?"

"Any way you can. The clay settles on the bottom and finds the leaky spots."

"Does it work?"

"You could try catfish."

"Catfish?"

"Catfish don't like leaks--threatens their survival--so they plug up the holes themselves."

"Does it work?" Erin asked skeptically.

"There's a fellow down in Redwood Valley I heard stocked his pond with catfish. Ended up with a heck of a lot of catfish, which can be annoying, but his pond is tight now."

We googled leaky ponds. A couple sites said Bentonite can work, but no one mentioned catfish.

"At least you can swim in yours," Gina said with her enigmatic smile one afternoon as we sipped iced tea under the crooked oak.

We stared at her. "You've got a problem with your pond at Swallowtail?"

"Only that it doesn't hold water," she laughed. Doug had built the Swallowtails' pond just after he'd made ours.

Gina sighed. All she and their partners had wanted, she said, was a small pond that would draw wildlife and was deep enough to cool off their collective in the summer. Now they had a cavernous crater—Doug had made it bigger than a football field--with a puddle in the middle. He'd hit a spring, which was probably why it didn't hold water.

Erin and I were surprised. Wouldn't finding a spring would be a good thing?

Lin shook her head. "Springs can be good if they feed into your pond, but this spring lets water out. We're going to have to fill it in."

"That whole giant thing?"

Erin touched my arm. "Don't get riled up. We're going to fix our pond."

Erin found an agricultural supply store in Ukiah that sold bags of Bentonite.

"We plan to use the stuff to fix our leaky pond," she told the clerk on the phone.

"Really?" said the clerk.

"Does it work?" she asked.

"I don't know. How many bags you want? They're 50 pounds each."

Doug hadn't said exactly how much we needed. But any amount was too much for our Subaru after we'd piled in with the dogs and all our gear. Even if there had been space, Erin and I couldn't lift 50 pounds, even together, so we'd never be able to unload the bags.

I called Mike. "Can you pick up as many bags of Bentonite as you can fit in your truck next time you visit Ukiah?"

"No problem," he said.

"The bags are heavy."

"Fifty pounds isn't bad," he said.

"Can you scatter them for us, too? We'll pay you, of course."

"Sure," he said affably. "I'll call you when it's done."

Mike was singing a different tune when he called a few days later. "That Bentonite is very nasty stuff," he said. "I put in 20 bags, and the powder got all my clothes and skin and hair. Even with a bandana over my mouth, it went down my throat. I won't be doing that again."

"I'm so sorry," I said, taking a deep breath. "Can you tell if it worked?"

"I put a stake at the water line yesterday," Mike said. "Next time you're up here, if the water's at the same level, you'll know it worked."

It was too dark to check the pond when we arrived at Cherry Creek the next weekend. But first thing in the morning, we raced down to check it out. Our hearts sank. The water was more than a foot lower than Mike's stick. The Bentonite was a failure.

We called Doug.

"You need a lot more than 20 bags," he said.

"Why didn't you tell us that?" Erin shook her head.

"Fixing a leaky pond isn't an exact science."

We were depressed. We loved that pond. We needed our pond so we could survive the hot summer days for years to come. As it was, with the sides so steep and the water falling so fast, we had to descend its slippery banks by lowering ourselves on a long rope tied to one of the boulders Doug had removed when he was excavating.

I called Mike, who was now making awnings for the front and back porches of our cabin. "I'm afraid we need more Bentonite," I said.

He groaned. "I promised Robin I wouldn't touch that stuff again."

"You don't have to dump it in the pond," I begged. "Could you pick up 20 more bags in your truck and drop them off? We'll put them in."

"Okay," Mike said. "As long as I'm not dumping the stuff."

"Thank you," I said. "You're the best."

"We need a truck," Erin said when I hung up. "Life would be much easier if we had a truck. Then we wouldn't be so dependent on Mike."

I made a truck the second item on our latest wish list, right after a pond that holds water.

The bags of Bentonite were neatly stacked beneath the oak tree above the pond when we arrived one early fall weekend. We sat at the pond's edge in the blazing sun, the dogs barking up in their fenced area behind the cabin, wondering how we were going to move the heavy bags from the foot of the oak tree to the water. The steep sides of the pond were more slippery than ever now that they were covered in a thick, sticky layer of Bentonite.

Erin had an idea. We would drag each bag onto a tarp and slide the tarp to the water's edge, where we'd slit the bag with a knife and scatter the powder.

Amazingly, we managed to slide the first sack down to the water's edge.

"Now what?" I said, fighting my nasty and unreasonable desire to blame Erin for this whole mess.

"We open the bag and spread it."

"Spread it how?"

"We scoop it out. Go get those plastic yogurt containers from the cabin."

Yogurt containers in hand, feet sinking into the mud, we managed to empty a bag of the fine white chalky powder into the pond as clouds of white dust headed straight for our mouths and noses.

The cloying powder rose off the water as the Bentonite hit the surface, turning the pond and the air above it milky white.

"Interesting stuff," Erin said.

"Only 19 bags to go," I whined.

After a break, we struggled in misery through five or six more bags, skin and nostrils and mouths clogged by the fine white powder. Luna, who we could now trust not to run away, watched curiously from the shade beneath the big rock, while the still-not-to-be-trusted Mr. Woody barked from the fenced yard above.

"We've got to get this stuff out into the middle so it can sink to the bottom and do some good," Erin said, standing up. "The only parts we're covering are the edges."

"I thought most of the rock was near the edge, right where we're dumping it." I was cranky enough to throttle a rattlesnake.

Erin surveyed the mess. "Doug said the leak could be on the bottom or on the far side, at the levy."

"I wonder how the pros do this," I said, oozing sarcasm. "Do you think they toss this stuff in with yogurt containers?"

Erin wiped her face on the sleeve of her blue work shirt. "They probably have a machine that blows it in."

"Shall we call Willits Rental?"

"Like *they're* going to have a Bentonite spray machine? I called ten stores just to find the Bentonite."

I called Willits Rental anyway. They'd never heard of a Bentonite spray machine.

Erin had a brainstorm. We could blow up the

plastic rowboat that my father had given me when he cleaned out his attic and use it to dump the Bentonite into the water.

Two hours later, even hotter and crankier, we'd blown up the boat. Now bare-breasted and covered in white powder, Erin volunteered to take the helm. By the time she and the Bentonite were at sea in the plastic craft, the boat was sagging badly. A bandana tied over her mouth, she paddled out to the center, scooping and tossing the powder with containers as she went. More great clouds of white dust hit the water, filled the air, then sank, somehow heading, we prayed, for the dreaded leaks. She paddled back to the shore, where, cursing and groaning and threatening to mutiny, I managed to load on two more bags.

By Sunday afternoon, we had dumped all 20 bags into the pond, our backs and shoulders screaming for mercy. Before heading home, we inserted a stake at the water line, as Mike had done, and crossed our fingers.

When we arrived next time, the pond was down another foot.

Erin called Doug. "We put two more tons of Bentonite into the pond last weekend, and it's already down another foot."

"Bentonite really doesn't work well if you throw it in," he told her.

"You're kidding." Her eyes opened wide. "Why didn't you tell us that to begin with?"

"It *can* work," he said. "But it works best if you drain the pond and mix the Bentonite into the soil."

"Drain the pond?" This was unbelievable.

"Do it in November, when the water's really low, and it's too cold to go swimming."

Who was he kidding? Like we knew how to drain a pond. "Isn't there a way to fix the leak with one of your bulldozers?"

"I can't take the Cat in there. I'll get stuck in the mud."

"So how do we drain the pond?" said Erin intrepidly, ready for action.

"Get a pump. It's not hard."

Where would we get a pump? And who was going to crawl around the bottom of our pond mixing the terrible white powder into the mud? There had to be an easier way to fix the leak.

We called another heavy equipment operator named Bud to come to our place and evaluate the pond. Bud was a handsome, big-boned, friendly man in his late fifties, with broad shoulders and huge hands. He wore jeans, a baseball cap and a blue stripped, zip-front engineer's work shirt. He said he could bring his excavator up and dig out the levy, going lower than the deepest part of the pond and creating a new keystone of clay that would keep any water from seeping out. But that would cost about $20,000, he said, and would have to be done when the pond was bone dry.

"Can't promise it'll work either," he added, sipping Erin's lemonade on the bench under the crooked oak. "Might be cheaper just to dig a new pond."

"Um. . ." I felt like crying.

"What are our other options?" Erin said bravely.

"You could install a plastic liner. They're not cheap, but you get a bunch of people, twenty or so for a pond that size, to help you spread the plastic into the hole, and a backhoe to make a flat ledge around the circumference so you can attach the plastic. Of course, with liners you run the risk of deer falling in and getting stuck and ripping the liner with their feet when they try to get out."

Erin poured more lemonade. For what seemed like hours, she laughed and chatted with Bud about everything, including the Whitaker family, who used to own Cherry Creek and invite Bud and his parents up to hunt, and the old vauxite mine they ran down by Outlet Creek. Depressed to see our entire Saturday draining down the pond hole, I donned my white jumpsuit and assaulted some poison oak.

"How come you're so charming with these contractors?" I asked Erin when Bud was gone. "That meeting took most of the day. Are you having as much fun as it seems like?"

"It was okay," she said. "And that's how you learn stuff." She looked down at the notes she'd taken on a yellow legal pad. "Today I learned that putting in a septic system takes a permit, which might be hard to get because the soil is so rocky here it might not perc, and if it doesn't perc, no permit."

"Perc?" I stared at her.

"Percolate. The ground has to be able to filter the waste. If it's too rocky, the waste runs right through. He also said that our driveway needs more grading, which he doesn't think Doug can do because he doesn't have the right machine. Plus..." She paused, waving her pad. "He gave me the number of a guy in Willits who needs work and can drain the pond for us and mix in the Bentonite."

"Way to go!" I gave her high fives.

"If that doesn't work." She stopped herself.

"Well, it will work."

At the next Irregulars dinner at Jay's, Rod and Cindy offered us the old pump and the PVC pipe they no longer used to bring creek water up to irrigate their lawn and redwood trees.

A new plan for the pond was in motion.

A few weeks later, Tony, the young guy Bud told us about, emptied the pond with Rod and Cindy's pump plugged into Tony's generator. He and a friend brought up 50 more bags of Bentonite. Erin stayed up at the cabin all week while they rented a motorized tiller to mix the Bentonite into the muck and a compressor machine to tamp the muck down. It was a horrible, dirty, slippery job, but by the end of the week, the two guys had sealed our pond with clay.

All we had to do was wait for the rain, then the summer, to see if it held water.

The leaky pond was bad, but it wasn't catastrophic. A catastrophic problem was the one that Liz, to whom we still owed $100,000, was having with her 36-year-old son, Drew, who had been arrested on suspicion of committing two rapes. A third victim alleged that he had drugged her with a   potent tranquilizer, raped her and videotaped the crime at his seaside home in Mussel Beach.

"Do you think this arrest could somehow screw up our deal with Liz?" I asked Stephanie. "We still owe her the balloon payment."

"No worries," she said. "Liz doesn't want any of her land back. I'm sure she's way too busy organizing Drew's defense. I wouldn't be surprised if she even sold Parcel 29, her land on Outlet Creek. She'll be far too distracted to come camp and swim."

"Do you think Drew would visit Cherry Creek for any reason?" I said nervously.

"No way," she clucked. "He's in jail and his bail is set at $10 million because he's a flight risk. If he does post bail, he'd need to be near his lawyers. Liz will hire the best criminal lawyers her money can buy."

Still engaged in her own legal battle with Liz, Stephanie confided that she'd hired a Ukiah attorney named Tim, who had, earlier in his career, been chief counsel for the People's Temple and Rev. Jim Jones, the megalomaniacal San Francisco community organizer and cult leader who had ordered his followers in Guyana, including Tim's son, to drink arsenic-laced Kool-Aid in 1977.

"The plot thickens," I said.

"Let's hope the Bentonite thickens," Erin laughed, switching on our solar-powered radio and tuning in KZYX&Z, the station that had become our link to civilization when we were on our land.

CHAPTER 19

KHARMACEUDICALS

The rains came and the pond filled and spring arrived, and then summer, and the pond still leaked as badly as before.

Leaky pond or not, I was happier than I'd been in a long time. I left my manuscript in the closet and felt uncharacteristically optimistic--sometimes for a minute or two, sometimes a few days--about the land at Cherry Creek and the happiness it could bring to our lives for years to come.

The success of Janestock and other gatherings on the land gave me confidence that our friends *would* visit us in the country if we lived there full time. In fact, when friends stayed with us at Blind Dog Ranch, we all seemed to laugh more, talk more and feel much more relaxed than we ever did in Marin, where we squeezed our socializing with friends into frenzied Saturday night dinners. At Cherry Creek, we all got used to the outhouse and the absence of electricity and dependable cell phone reception and computers. Without electronic distractions, time seemed to stretch out luxuriously, with hours to talk, eat, swim, hike and sit around the campfire under the stars, singing and sharing stories and listening to the wind in the trees and the howl of coyotes. We kept a tent pitched for friends like Jane and Teresa, our most regular campers, who always brought fabulous food to share and regaled us with nursing tales from Teresa's clinic and goofy corporate management stories from Jane's job as a human resources specialist at a huge American conglomerate.

The healthcare beat at the paper was keeping me busy and engaged thanks to rancorous fights between the community hospital administration and its publicly elected district board. But the office felt a little lonely now. Rick had a new baby and had adjusted shockingly well to fatherhood, filing most of his stories from home so he could look after his son while his wife went back to work.

More devastating was the fact that our beloved Becky had retired with Alan and Mr. Toby to their condo in Arizona, where Becky had blossomed into a freelance golf writer.

"Next week is the Phoenix Open," she e-mailed Rick and me, "and I have press credentials; I can even go in the locker room if I so desire. But I will not do so. However, I plan to go in the press tent to get food and sneak it out to Alan."

Instead of glancing across the aisle several hundred times a day at Becky's wide eyes and nervous smiles, I faced a pretty but painfully quiet new college grad, who rarely spoke with anyone except her fiancé, whom she called each day at 11 a.m. and at 5 p.m.

Weird wire stories and droll reports on the activities of Alan, Mr. Toby and her three kids no longer emanated from Becky's seat, which meant that Rick when actually showed up, we had to simulate her presence by revisiting old entries from his file of her funniest statements--"Planet Becky: Where nice people say nice things about nice people."

"'I always wanted to be a police officer,'" Rick read from the Planet log. "'But I could never do the pushups. I don't like guns, either; that would be another problem.'

"'A dog is only as loyal as his last walk,'" he continued, adding, "'I didn't even find out about the Sixties until the Seventies.'"

"Read that skiing one," I said. "I liked that one."

He clicked through his file. "Here it is. 'When I was skiing, all I could think about was saving my own life. I never bothered to worry about my children. It was every man for himself.'"

Rick kept scrolling. "Okay, here's one that came after you'd just told her that trying to manage our department, which she was doing that day, was like herding cats. And she said, 'I don't even like cats.'"

The trauma of losing Becky was offset by the excitement of my beat, particularly covering night hospital district board meetings, a gloves-off sideshow in which the district board and the administration hurled insults and threats at each other. Both sides would collar me in the hospital hallway before, during and after board meetings trying to cajole me into giving them the last word in the next day's paper.

One topic that came up a lot on my new beat was near to my heart--how to take care of Marin and the nation's growing senior population.

All of our friends had aging parents, and most of us had to juggle the demands of jobs, relationships and households to deal with their growing needs and vulnerabilities. My father, despite chronic atrial fibrillation, was still enjoying life in Baltimore in the company of Mrs. B. and Mrs. R., but Erin's mother, Maggi, who lived in Sonoma County, was in constant and excruciating shoulder and leg pain caused by cervical stenosis. The powerful painkillers she took made her wobbly and groggy, barely alleviating her pain. She could no longer leave her house without assistance, often calling Erin from floor of her house, where, having "slipped" off her bed, she stoically explained that she was "resting."

One Saturday summer morning at Cherry Creek, we were washing our breakfast dishes on the front porch of the cabin when we came up with a solution to Maggi's distress. We'd been listening on our solar-powered radio to a show called *Trading Time* on KZYX&Z, the listener-sponsored station that had become our link to our new community.

Trading Time was a one-hour local call-in program for listeners who had something to sell, trade, give away or buy. People advertised all kinds of stuff on the air, from goat poop and clunker cars to upright pianos and propane refrigerators. The only rules were that callers couldn't be commercial enterprises, sell more than five items or hawk anything illegal on the air.

Erin and I both did a double take that morning when a caller announced that he would give away medical marijuana to anyone with a doctor's prescription. Before the hosts could cut him off, he'd given out his phone number and his name-- Professor Ping-Pong of Willits.

"Did you hear that?" Erin shouted, scribbling down his number. "Mom's already got a doctor's prescription for pot. Could be a lot better for her than the Oramorph she's taking."

"Professor Ping-Pong?" I laughed. "What kind of name is that?"

"I don't know, but I'm calling him." She dialed her cell phone and bingo, he was on the line, listening to Erin describe her mother's pain and the troubling side effects of the narcotics she'd been prescribed. She assured him she had a letter from Maggi's doctor recommending she try medical marijuana as a palliative. In minutes, she was off the phone and smiling.

"I scored," she laughed. "We can get it next time we come if we bring Mom's letter from her doctor."

"What'd he sound like?" I said, turning down the radio. "If his name's Professor Ping-Pong, he's got to be a little weird."

"He was really nice," she said, dumping the breakfast dishes into our plastic tub as she hung the solar shower bag from the hook we'd placed on the ceiling of the cabin, over the counters Mike and Robin had installed. "He said what he has is leaf, not bud."

"What's leaf?" I'd never been much of a marijuana smoker because herb made me way too paranoid.

"Leaf is the plant's leaf, which is different from the bud. The bud's the part of the plant that people smoke. The leaf is what they trim off before they sell it. Buds have more resin and cannabinoids and THC, the chemical that makes you high, but the leaf is often used in remedies, and that's what we're getting."

"How'd you know all that?"

"He told me."

I called Marny when we got home. "We're getting some medicinal marijuana for Erin's mother next weekend. A guy named Professor Ping-Pong announced it on the radio. He's giving it away to people with prescriptions."

"Be careful, Janie," Marny said. "And write down what happens. Then call and tell me how it goes."

It was dark when we reached Professor Ping-Pong's house in Willits the next Friday night. His place was on a normal, tree-lined street, but it was kind of unusual, in a gated compound of buildings marked by an unlit neon sign advertising the dairy it apparently had been in a past life. We shook some sleigh bells on his gate, and eventually a bearded man wearing a knit cap and a woven Guatemalan vest appeared from the darkness.

Erin extended her hand. "I'm Erin. This is Jane, my partner."

"Nice to meet you, Professor Ping-Pong," I said, heart racing.

He nodded, scanned the street, then led us in to a building that must have been the old creamery shop, with a counter and some old soda fountain stools. It was dark and cool in there. We could just make out the outline of a young woman with long dark hair sitting at a table. She had a Greek goddess name--Hera or Demeter or Artemis or something.

Erin described her mother's bleak situation, then handed him the doctor's letter. Without speaking, the professor read and returned it.

"How's your mother going to take the marijuana?" he said at last.

"She likes brownies." Erin sighed. "Blondies more than brownies, actually. I thought I'd make her some."

"Your mother doesn't smoke pot?"

"She may have, but not in years. My stepfather used to smoke on the roof of our apartment in San Francisco, but I don't think Mom did."

He reached under the old store counter, producing a brown paper grocery bag. Inside it was a plastic bag that crinkled. "I'm giving you two pounds of leaf."

"Wow." Erin peered inside. "Thank you very much."

"You know how to make blondies?"

"Regular blondies but not pot blondies," Erin said, extracting a pad and pen from her purse.

Nodding, the professor wound a strand of his beard around his pointer finger. "You need to prepare the butter first. Put two pounds into a crock-pot along with about a quarter of the leaf and let it simmer overnight. Maybe 12 hours. Then strain the butter and make your brownies with the butter in the usual way. Freeze whatever butter you have left over and any of the brownies--blondies-- she doesn't need."

"I'll do that," Erin said. "Thank you very much."

"The leaf is potent when it's cooked and ingested, but edibles take longer to hit your bloodstream than pot you smoke. If she eats too many brownies thinking it's not working, she may feel higher than she wants to be, so ask her to be patient and wait an hour before eating a second or third."

"She loves sweets," Erin said. "I'll tell her to take one to start with."

We thanked the professor and tiptoed to the car, looking in both directions for narcs, spies, police or other nefarious characters.

"We did it!" Erin let out a deep breath as we drove away. "We got medical marijuana for Mom."

We gave each other high fives.

"Did you notice the way he scanned the shrubs outside and studied the doctor's letter?" I gulped, hands still shaking. "He thought we were narcs."

"He knew we weren't narcs," Erin said. "Two middle-aged women with graying hair? White hair in your case. Anyway, he wasn't selling it. He's such a believer he's giving it away. He's a hero, and brave."

I called Marny on the cell phone. "We got the po. . . We got the stuff for Erin's mother from Professor Ping-Pong," I whispered. "He lives in an old dairy and someone named Astraea or Atlanta was with him when he handed it over. He wore a little knit cap and eyed us suspiciously."

Marny hooted.

"Erin's going to make blondies for her mother. That's a brownie with butterscotch and light brown sugar instead of chocolate."

"I know what a blondie is, Janie. I hope it works."

"Be careful," Nanette warned, when I told her about the professor.

"Absolutely," I promised.

Following the professor's directions, Erin baked the blondies, eating half of one as a test. She got so high she could barely talk. Her mother ate five and didn't feel a thing. The pot didn't touch her pain, so she stuck with the Oramorph. Now Erin and I had a freezer full of pot butter and our first close encounter in the Emerald Triangle.

CHAPTER 20

NO TIME TO WASTE

We were drinking tea in bed at home with the dogs one morning when *The Today Show* went live with breaking news. A passenger jet had crashed into the World Trade Center. As flames and smoke engulfed one tower, a second jet hit Tower Two. Terrified workers and firefighters streamed out of the collapsing buildings amidst toxic clouds of smoke and ash that were blanketing Manhattan. News came of a third plane crashing into the

Pentagon and of a hijacked airliner going down near Pittsburgh. The explosions shocked and confused the world. Who was behind the assaults? Were there more to come? American airports closed down for days. My father, on his way from Baltimore to spend his ninetieth birthday with us, was stranded in Arkansas, where he'd stopped to visit a family farm.

George Bush, who was reading to schoolchildren during the attacks, promised to punish the perpetrators. But who were they? *Where* were they? Was this the work of a small group of individuals or an attack by a sovereign nation? The President and his cabinet began to sound the drums of war immediately, prepping the country for a retaliatory attack in the Middle East, probably on Iraq or Afghanistan. Everyone was edgy and frightened. The price of oil soared. Conversation in our neighborhood, at local food coops, and in the newsroom focused non-stop on safety and security. If war broke out in the Middle East, might it escalate into nuclear war? If oil supplies were limited, could Americans reduce our addiction to oil, learn to live on less, grow our own food, and develop sustainable local economies?

The nightmare triggered by the World Trade Center attacks dwarfed my fears of snakes and bears and the fear of becoming too isolated. Perhaps buying the land at Cherry Creek had not been an impulsive folly but a wise, even prescient act that could provide us with a place of escape in a catastrophe.

"If we're on the eve of destruction, the cabin could be a sort of retreat center," I said to Erin as we drove to Cherry Creek that Friday night after the attacks, desperate to be away from the addictive television news coverage airing nonstop on every channel. "Our friends can come and stay with us."

"Let's visualize good things happening not bad ones," Erin said calmly. Luna trembled in my lap. Woody was sleeping on the back seat.

"Good things like what?" I said.

"Like maybe this will be our inspiration to develop our water system at Cherry Creek and work on our infrastructure." She glanced over at me. "I love you, you know."

"I love you, too."

"Do you?" she said softly. "Or do you see me as the big, bad ogre taking you off to the country and away from the things you love?"

I chewed my lip. "I've got a bad personality."

"Stop it," she said, reaching for my hand. "We're trying to be more positive, remember?"

I called Nanette from Erin's cell phone, inviting her and her partner, Dee, to come live on our land if the Trade Center attacks triggered some sort of disaster or nuclear war.

"Thank you, Janie," she said. "That's very thoughtful. But I hope I don't survive a nuclear attack on San Francisco. I'd much rather be dead."

She had a point. "Will you save me some poison pills for when the time comes?"

"I'm working on it," she said. "Be safe."

I left a message on Marny's machine inviting her to come live with us in the country if things fell apart. She called back to thank us and said that for now she and Susan would take their chances in the Bay Area.

Erin edged into the carpool lane. It was

definitely time, she said, to develop a reliable source of fresh water and begin to consider when we wanted to build a house.

"A house?" My stomach roiled despite my resolution moments earlier to flush fear and negativity from my soul. "Can't we just boil pond water on the Coleman stove in the cabin?"

That wasn't enough, she insisted. We needed infrastructure: housing, plumbing, septic, solar electricity, and telephone lines.

I swallowed. "Lin told me that they closed off the road to Covelo during the Depression, and the place became nearly self-sufficient."

"That could be us," Erin said, tapping the steering wheel. "With fresh running water, we could have a garden and a safe food source."

"Could we possibly survive by ourselves?" I said as we sat in traffic in Santa Rosa. "What if we're cut off from civilization by a terrorist attack or the end of oil, and we're living at Cherry Creek on our own, with Jay and Ken and Stephanie and Mike and Robin and Rod and Cindy as neighbors? How do you think we'd fare? Who would you want on your survival team?"

Erin flashed a thumbs-up to the driver of a pick-up truck with an "Impeach Bush" sticker on the bumper and turned to me. "Well, let see. Jay hates all outdoor activity. Mike has great survival skills, but his cigarette smoking might get to us. Cindy and Rod. . ." She paused. "I'd definitely want Rod on our team. He knows carpentry and dentistry, and he's got a great sense of humor. Plus, he's a gourmet cook."

"Mike can shoot a gun if we have to fight off invaders trying to steal our water and vegetables and invade our house."

"That's a pleasant thought," Erin mused. "But if the only green things Mike and Robin eat are M&Ms, they may not be much help in the garden."

"Gina and Lin can teach us how to save seeds and raise livestock."

"Right," she said. "Those are skills we'll need."

By the time we reached our cabin, inhaling the clean mountain air and swooning over the sky full of stars, we had the beginnings of a survival plan. And by the end of the weekend, with Erin's cell phone and a dog-eared copy of the local phone book, we'd created an action plan. The Laytonville electrician who'd installed the propane heater in our cabin would work with a solar-electric installer and a plumber from Willits to create our water system. The plumber would haul in two, 3,000-gallon water storage tanks and place them 100 feet above our tapped spring. The two electricians would install solar-electric panels and a small pump to send the spring water up to the tanks. From the tanks the water would travel by gravity feed through PVC pipes to a hose bib right by the cabin.

Two months later, we had fresh spring water running to--but not inside--the cabin. Erin had arranged a meeting with a Willits architectural designer whose specialty was green building. We'd brainstorm with her our vision for a house we could live in for the rest of our lives. If Armageddon came, we'd be ready.

CHAPTER 21

CH, CH, CHANGES

"For everything you have missed," wrote Ralph Waldo Emerson, "you have gained something else, and for everything you gain, you lose something else."

We were losing, we were gaining.

Erin was becoming an expert in home construction, having read dozens of books and attended several contractors' trade shows in San Francisco with Stephanie. She had scheduled our first meeting with a Willits architectural designer who specialized in natural building materials. Erin had also launched a search for a contractor to build whatever house we came up with.

Saving ourselves, our families and our friends from Armageddon was going to take some money.

I was putting my house in Mill Valley up for sale.

The "chicken coop" was what one of the neighbors called my place, apparently built by some hippies in the Sixties who'd cobbled together a ramshackle structure on the parcel. It was a sunny, brown-shingled cottage close to a nature preserve on a narrow little street called Pixie Trail. The uneven pine floors, crooked doorframes and beach-white stained walls gave the place what I called charm. Others termed it "funky." Although I hadn't lived in the house for eight years, it was my mental escape hatch, the place where I'd always told myself I could flee to if Erin and I drove each other nuts.

"Are you sure you want to sell it?" Marny said when I told her I was putting it on the market.

"Of course, I'm not sure," I swallowed. "But we have to sell one of our houses to pay off the land and build a new house, and mine makes the most sense because it's too small for both of us to live in."

"When are you moving to the land?" she said without a trace of recrimination.

"This is just a first step." My voice quavered. "We have no idea when any of this will happen."

"Well, Janie." She was quiet for a long time. "I just hope you've discussed this with your astrologer."

I called Ruby, who said the alignment of planets

in my fourth house, related to home and hearth, and was favorable for selling my little cottage at a substantial profit. Housing prices were soaring in Marin and across the country, and she also saw positive influences on my second house, associated with money and finance.

A week after the "For Sale" sign went up, we had five offers on the chicken coop, all above the asking price. I panicked. I was still panicked six weeks later, when I signed the closing papers, moments before I was wheeled into the hospital for an emergency operation on my knee. My knee had swelled up like a balloon, because, I discovered quite a bit later, I had I'd been bitten by a Cherry Creek tick that had given me Lyme disease. That was the bad news. The good news was that we now had enough money to pay off the land and build a small house.

Stephanie called to congratulate us. "Guess what?" she said.

My stomach tightened. A "guess what?" from Stephanie could mean anything.

"Liz's son Drew has disappeared--in the middle of his trial."

I signaled to Erin to pick up the phone. "Where'd he go?"

"Nobody knows. The judge is continuing the trial without him."

"Poor Liz," Erin said, sipping her tea.

"She's going to lose the bail money if he doesn't return," Stephanie said.

"Maybe Liz helped him escape," I said, a thought popping into my head. "Maybe Drew is hiding at Cherry Creek."

"What?" Stephanie said. "No way."

"He knows the land," I offered. "Maybe he's down by the creek in a pup tent. Who would know?"

"He's left the country," Stephanie said confidently. "I'll bet you anything he's in Mexico."

At Cherry Creek the next weekend, someone sped by us at the gate in a big black pick-up.

"I think that was Liz's son," I whispered to Erin, craning around to check the license plate. "He looked like the picture in the paper."

"That's Bob," she laughed. "The guy who plays Christian music to scare the bears. Even if it was Drew, and it wasn't, we'd have nothing to fear because we're not surfer chicks and we don't hang out in beach bars. You don't even drink."

"I'm serious," I said, relieved but not convinced.

"So am I."

In February, the jury convicted Liz's son, in absentia, of 124 counts, including rape and the poisoning of three women. The verdicts carried a sentence of 124 years.

Drew had flown the coop, but Erin had found her man, a contractor named Tom Allen, a minor legend in our area for his craftsmanship, honesty, intelligence, humor and dedication. We'd known for some time that he'd built a neighbor's house at Cherry Creek, on Black Bear Road, and when they gave us a tour, we loved their place, a two-story stucco house with vine-covered redwood pergolas over the decks and a built-in stone oven that heated the entire home. Every detail, from window ledges and moldings to countertops and porch posts, was lovingly executed.

"You really think Tom Allen would build your house?" said Nancy, the architectural designer we'd hired to translate our primitive sketch for a south-facing ranch house into plans for a real home. "Tom Allen is in great demand, and he's expensive."

"We've got the money," Erin said airily.

Easy for her to say, I thought. But it was true. My poor Aunt Gwen had died in Baltimore, leaving me enough money to make our house more than the one-bedroom cottage we'd envisioned.

"And if he's really good," Erin continued, "we don't mind paying a little more."

I nodded nervously, wondering when I'd start to see my bank account as half full instead of half empty.

Erin now had a plan for our Xanadu, and I was, as usual, holding on for dear life. She'd decided that as soon as we'd snagged Tom Allen, we'd have him start our house in the summer, three months away. She would move to our cabin to watch and oversee construction. The following year, house complete, she'd land a nursing job somewhere in Mendocino County. She knew she'd find work because she'd already had a nibble from a small clinic in Laytonville, seven miles north of us.

Tom was finishing a house at a 10,000-acre elk-hunting resort called Shamrock Ranch, just north of Cherry Creek, and told us we could meet him there to drop our freshly minted architectural plans. The design was simple. Our bedroom and bathroom and my office would be on the east side of what Nancy called the "great room," and Erin's office, the guest bedroom, second bathroom and pantry would be on the west side. The house would face south, its 20-foot sliding glass doors opening on to a deck and the spectacular view of Shimmins Ridge. The metal roof would overhang enough to keep out the high, blazing summer sun and allow the low winter sun to come in. The exterior would be fire-resistant stucco—crucial in the wilderness--and the floors would be acid-washed concrete, the radiant heat built into them.

We loved the vintner's house Tom was building, as well as the twinkle in his eye, and begged him to say yes. He was friendly but noncommittal.

Erin called him every few weeks. Summer was fast approaching. She kept calling.

At last Tom got back to her. He'd be happy to build our house, he said, but he could not start it for another year. If we could wait, he was in.

Erin was bummed. In a year her disability insurance would be gone, and she'd have to return to work, sore shoulder or not. If she were working, she wouldn't be present to watch Tom hammer every nail, cut every board, drill every hole. I was thrilled. The longer the house took to build, the longer I could stay at the newspaper writing stories I enjoyed about medical issues that I thought mattered--the county's soaring breast cancer rate, the AIDS epidemic, the fight for control of the community hospital.

We told Tom we'd wait for him.

Becky e-mailed me from Arizona. "There's life after the newspaper. I'm living proof. When are you going to quit?"

"My dream is to work from Cherry Creek two days a week and work in the office two days," I replied.

"They won't let you do it," she wrote back.

"Rick does." I pressed "Send."

"Rick lives in San Francisco. That's a lot closer. I'd make a clean break if I were you."

A clean break. Did I have a clean break in me? The big changes I'd made in my life had often been messy and half-hearted. I was always one foot in and one foot out, haunted by doubts and clinging to the past. On good days, I was hopeful; on bad days I was J. Alfred Prufrock, afraid to eat a peach or wear my trousers rolled.

CHAPTER 22

DETOX

Determined to be in top form for her new job, whatever it might be, Erin left to spend three weeks in San Diego at a health and detox facility offering wheatgrass, raw vegetables, colonics and starvation.

I joined her for a week in hopes that a punishingly healthy regime might halt any inclination my joints might have to balloon up mysteriously, as my left knee had a few months earlier.

Erin met me at the airport. She looked great-- tan and strong and mellow.

"Too bad Debbie Reynolds won't be here," she said. "She taught yoga the first two weeks. Gina Rowlands was a hoot the first week. And Liza Minnelli is a regular."

All the movie stars were gone, and there were no distractions, which was unfortunate because I didn't adapt easily to deprivation or enjoy my twice-daily, self-administered wheat-grass enemas. My favorite activity was lounging listlessly in the Jacuzzi while Erin planned all aspects of our new life. That included the solar-electric system that would allow us to live untethered to Pacific Gas and Electric.

"If the sun's not out, and the solar panels don't charge the batteries enough, the batteries won't produce the energy we need," Erin shouted over the whirling jets. I gazed light-headed into the foaming water, dreaming of hamburgers. "Batteries are tricky and expensive. Are you with me?"

"Tricky," I said, jerking up.

"If they don't stay charged, they die, and they're very expensive to replace. So we'll need a generator to charge them when it's rainy or overcast, and I think the Honda 5,000 will work for us because it runs on propane and is powerful enough to run a whole house. If we buy the generator now, we can use it to power the cabin when I move."

"Are you really going to get a job up there?"

She stared at me. "Do you have a problem with that?"

"No," I said. "Just seems like it'll be hard

without running water or a bathroom. And won't you. . .miss me? I'll miss you."

"Of course, I'll miss you," she said, kissing my cheek. "But I'll be creating a new life for us. It's for the cause."

"But. . ." I sat up straight. What was I smelling? It was cooked food, like French fries. I squinted through the lattice at a figure in sweats carrying something under a towel.

"Hi, Brigit," Erin called, turning back to me. "Brigit's in my body-mind connection class. Lives in Dead Horse, Alaska, six months of the year and Spunky Puddle, Ohio, the other six." She sipped from her water bottle. "Anyway, the generator's expensive, but buying it now will make life at the cabin much easier."

"Alaska to Ohio's a long commute," I said, the smell of French fries eroding my brain.

Erin pinched my arm. "Are you listening to me? The generator's $6,000, but it's really a good one. Mike wired the cabin when he insulated it, so we'll have electricity inside when the generator's on. Another great feature is that you can turn it on from the cabin with a remote switch, so we don't have to go out in the rain at night and tug on a cord to start it. Isn't that cool?"

"I wonder where that smell is coming from."

She stared at me. "Don't think about food. It only makes things worse. Anyway, Willits Power sells them, and they'll do the maintenance, too."

"Is there a Burger King near here?"

"Drink some water." Erin handed me her water bottle. "You don't want to get dehydrated. The other thing we need to address is the cabin's roof. I've talked to the guy who worked for Jay, and he says he can take off the metal roof and put a layer of plywood on underneath it and then put the old roof back on. That way the roof won't be so noisy in the rain. And he'll build us a shed for the generator at the same time."

Whatever Brigit was eating, I wanted some of it. "I think I smell hamburgers and French fries," I said desperately.

"There's a Wendy's and a KFC down in the mall," she said, sipping her water. "Sometimes if the wind's in the right direction, you smell the fumes. Anyway, with the roof fixed, the acorns dropping from the oak trees won't sound like terrorist attacks, and Luna won't freak out."

"Terrorists?" I said weakly.

"We can't give her any more doggy Valium. It makes her so disoriented she's pitiful. But if we don't do something, I'll be sleep-deprived in the winter and so will she when she visits."

"Sure," I said, staring out past the trellis to the courtyard. "It might be a chicken sandwich from Popeye's. Do they have Popeye's in San Diego?"

"Shift your focus," Erin said, stepping out of the water. "Thinking about food makes you hungrier."

"Hello, ladies."

A slender, white-haired woman was hanging up her kimono and kicking off flip-flops. I recognized her from the opening night ceremony, when she'd testified that wheat grass and raw food had cured her rheumatoid arthritis.

"Hey, Diane," Erin smiled.

"Guess what?" the woman said to Erin as she slipped into the hot tub. "Brigit brought a bucket of fried chicken back to her room just now, and one of the teachers gave her a second warning. One more and she has to leave."

"Guess she hasn't learned to find the friend in her mirror," I said, spouting some of the dogma I'd learned that morning in self-esteem class.

"Find what?" the woman said.

"She doesn't love herself," Erin laughed.

"Well, no," Diane said. "Those toxins and saturated fats are terrible for her diabetes. But we're not here to judge, only to forgive." She turned to Erin. "You're from the Bay Area, aren't you?"

"Marin County," Erin nodded. "But we're building a house in Mendocino County."

"Wonderful," said Brigit.

"Off the grid," Erin added proudly.

"Off the grid?" Diane didn't understand.

"You know. Solar power. No PG&E. We'll buy solar panels and install them on the roof of our house in Novato first and have a grid inter-tie, and then we'll move the system up to Mendocino when our house is ready. It's solar-powered electricity with a generator back-up."

As Erin explained volts and wattage to Diane, I stretched out on my towel and drifted off into a light coma.

Sometime later, we shuffled back to our room, where Erin's cell phone was bleeping. She had a phone message from Stephanie. An American bounty hunter from Hawaii named Duane "Dog" Chapman had spotted Liz's son Drew surfing in Mexico, following him to a taco stand in Puerto Vallarta and throwing him into a van. Long before Drew and Mr. Dog reached the border, the Mexican government arrested Chapman for kidnapping a man. Drew was extradited to the

States and was now in federal prison serving out his 124-year sentence. He would not be making any surprise appearances at Cherry Creek.

CHAPTER 23

POURING IT ON

It was 5 p.m. I'd filed a story, shut down my computer, packed my briefcase and was about to roar up Highway 101 to Cherry Creek. Robert, the new city editor, had given me tomorrow off. In seconds, I'd be on my way north to witness what Tom had told us again and again was the most pivotal moment in home construction--the pour.

The pad had been bulldozed, flattened and compressed by winter rains. The stem walls were in; the plumber had laid down the radiant heat, water and sewer pipes, and the electrician's conduit tubes were snugly secure in masses of gravel and rebar that would keep the infrastructure level when the cement covered it for eternity.

The pour was the culmination of weeks of tedious but critical work by the crew--surveying the perimeter, building forms, and calculating room and wall measurements. Everything had to be perfect, Tom said, because cement was unforgiving, and we needed to be there. We'd know why when we witnessed this near-mystical moment in our home's construction.

There was just one problem. Erin, now living in the cabin and working at a healthcare clinic in Ukiah, had a mandatory, daylong staff meeting that she couldn't miss. Which left me.

I glanced at my watch, resolved to let the phone call go to voice mail, then picked up the receiver, thinking it might be Erin.

"Jane?"

I gulped. I'd recognize that baritone anywhere. It was Roger, the paper's publisher. A 5 p.m. call from the publisher, even this benign one, who'd actually visited me in the hospital when my knee swelled up, was never a good thing. His voice was unnaturally calm. "Can you come upstairs for a minute?"

I glanced involuntarily at Becky and found myself looking instead into the vacant eyes of the young editor who now occupied Becky's orbit.

"Hey," I said to Roger. "Is there any chance we could talk. . ." I looked at the calendar. "On Thursday?"

Long pause, which meant "no."

"I'm sitting here in the conference room with..." His mellow voice tapered off. "With seven folks from the hospital who'd like to talk to you about your story in yesterday's paper."

Shit, shit, triple shit. The hospital story. "I'll be right up," I said, grabbing a legal pad.

I'd known this call might be coming, but I'd hoped I'd be far from Dodge City when it did. My story yesterday had embarrassed the hospital because it reported the facts: The hospital had recently been cited by the California Department of Health Services for violating nearly a dozen safety codes, including a claim by one surgeon that the operating room staff supplied him with dirty scalpels.

A small sea of faces glared at me as I walked through the door of the publisher's conference room. At the far end of the table was the hospital's volatile, hotheaded female CEO, who also taught "Body Sculpting by Margaret" at a local gym. Seated around her were the hospital's public relations director, the medical and nursing directors, the president of the hospital board, the president of the hospital foundation, and the director of the ICU and the head of the ER. Batting for the paper, if not for me, were the executive editor, the managing editor, Robert, my boss, and Roger, who was bearded, handsome and extremely ill. The publisher had advanced, inoperable prostate cancer that had metastasized to his spine. He missed very little work despite excruciating pain that he managed with massive doses of painkillers and steroid drugs that sometimes slurred his speech and left his face puffy and flushed. Leaning back in his swivel chair, he stroked his beard.

The only empty seat at the table was in enemy territory, between the director of nursing and CEO Margaret. I slunk into it, careful not to tip over her bottle of Evian.

"Jane," Roger began. "Margaret has some concerns about your story on the state's findings about the hospital."

Taking her cue, the CEO held up yesterday's paper, pointing to my story with her tanned, perfectly sculpted red fingernail. "We're bleeding because of this story, Jane. Our patients are terrified. They think our intensive care unit is a dangerous place, which it's not. It's one of the safest, best-rated ICUs in the state." She pointed to a thick stack of letters on the table. "These are testimonials we've received from hundreds of grateful patients. I also have here our last joint hospital accreditation report and our own internal evaluation documenting our outstanding ICU outcomes and safety records. The DHS citation was a vicious and unfounded attack."

The hospital's PR director winced at the CEO's characterization of the state's report. Margaret had never gotten the hang of keeping her mouth shut, which was one reason why I enjoyed covering the hospital so much. She kept the beat lively. I glanced at the publisher, whose pupils seemed to roll behind his lids, leaving only the whites of his eyes visible.

"You've always been fair to the hospital in your coverage, Jane," Margaret continued. "But this story was extremely one-sided."

I cleared my throat and looked expectantly at my boss, Robert, the city editor. Surely he'd defend me. We'd been over every fact in the story at least three times. But he wouldn't make eye contact as he jotted something on a yellow legal pad.

The publisher held up a hand, stealing a quick peek at the CEO's cleavage before he spoke. "Was there anything in Jane's story that wasn't true? Were there factual errors? If so, we'd like to know what they are so we can run a correction."

Correction? My heart stopped. Correction was the most dreaded word in a reporter's lexicon. Corrections, and their even nastier siblings, retractions, ended careers in journalism. They meant somber meetings behind closed doors, unusual in newsrooms because there weren't any doors. Corrections and retractions were a death ray in the form of triplicate error reports that were filed in a locked drawer by the city editor's desk and in the perpetrator's personnel file. The forms described the error, the reason for it, and the exact wording of the correction that would run in the paper.

"There were no errors," Margaret said slowly.

"Thank you, Goddess," I mumbled to myself, letting out a breath.

"But the story was extremely biased. Jane interviewed many of the hospital's critics but didn't quote a single one of us."

The publisher looked at me. "Is that true?"

I glanced again at the city editor, still studying his notes. He wasn't going to step in.

"As Margaret knows," I began, making a mental note to let the air out of Robert's tires tonight, "I called her and the hospital's public relations officer as soon as I learned of the DHS complaint. Both of them declined to comment. So did every hospital physician and administrator I managed to reach on Monday. So we made the decision to go with what we had." I stared at the city editor, hoping he'd back me up. No luck. Still scribbling on his pad.

"Is that true, Margaret?" Roger leaned forward. "Jane called you and you wouldn't comment?"

Margaret tapped her vermillion fingernails against the polished cherry conference table. "The state's charges are completely off-the-wall. Absolutely unjustified. We opted not to dignify their findings with a comment."

Roger stared at her, stroking his beard. "Let me see if I have this right. You wouldn't comment on the story when Jane called you, and now you've assembled half the hospital brass here to complain that what she wrote was biased because it didn't contain your point of view? Am I missing something?"

Margaret's face turned the color of her fingernails. "We told her that we thought running any story on the DHS complaint was irresponsible and premature and came at a very bad time for us. We asked her to wait."

Roger's nostrils flared as his blue eyes lasered in on the CEO. "This is a news organization, Margaret," he began. "When this county's community hospital gets called on the carpet by the state for some extremely serious safety violations. . ."

"*Alleged* safety violations," Margaret interrupted.

"My point is that we are a newspaper, Margaret, not the hospital's house organ. We don't hold breaking stories because they clash with your timing." He paused to sip some water, grimacing as he swallowed. "You know how much I appreciate all that the hospital staff has done for me. They're miracle workers, as far as I'm concerned." He wiped something from his eye. Not quite miraculous enough, I was sure Roger and everyone in the room was thinking. "But these DHS findings are very serious. And they're news. If you've changed your mind now and want to tell your side of the story. . ."

I stopped breathing. *Please, Goddess*, I prayed. *Don't let her say she wants to tell her side of the story tonight. I'll never get to Cherry Creek.*

"I'm happy to give you space on the editorial page to respond," Roger continued. "And I know Jane will call you, as she always does, on any future stories she writes on this or any other hospital-related topic."

"Of course," I said, trying to contain my elation.

"So, dear friends. . ." Roger pushed back his chair, uncrossed his legs, eyes tightening with pain, and rose slowly, gripping the table for support. "If no one has anything else to say, let's adjourn." He extended his hand to the CEO. "I'd suggest that in the future, Margaret, the hospital or its spokespersons talk with reporters when they call you for comments on a story. Then you won't have to take your wonderful staff away from their important work to traipse up here to plead your case." He turned. "Thank you, Jane. Thank you, all. Have a good evening."

Was I hallucinating, or did Roger wink at me?

As the hospital troops waited for the elevator, I dashed down the back stairs to the parking lot, spotted Robert's car, opted not to molest it and jumped into my new truck. In minutes, I'd picked up Luna and Woody at home and was heading north on Highway 101.

I would miss all the hospital hullabaloo when we moved, I thought, as I sat in freeway traffic in Santa Rosa, amazed that I no longer thought of moving to Cherry Creek as an *if* but a *when*. I loved hospitals. When I was a kid, I'd raced with my sister around the wards of Johns Hopkins on weekends while my father saw patients or finished some report. My sister and I would tentatively touch the strange stigmatas on the giant marble feet of the statue of Jesus that loomed over the hospital's front lobby. I'd dreamed of becoming a doctor until I encountered my first college chemistry class.

But if Robert wouldn't let me telecommute from Mendocino County--and everyone assured me he wouldn't--my career as a medical writer would be over. Sure I could freelance. But would I want to? Didn't I want to write fiction again? Or were the facts becoming more interesting to me than my own invented tales?

I rolled into Cherry Creek a little after 10 p.m. It was so hot that Erin was in shorts and a tank top. After a hug, she switched on the remote control generator, now installed in its own shed a hundred yards away, and zapped my frozen Trader Joe's enchilada in the microwave. I couldn't stop talking about the tense meeting with the publisher and hospital staff.

We were so hot that night that we left the front door open, placing the wire gate across the threshold to keep the dogs in and bears, snakes and coyotes out.

At 4 a.m., Woody howled at something that rustled outside in the leaves. I woke again at 5, holding Erin tight. Was that a truck on the road somewhere above us?

"I think that's them," I whispered, kissing Erin's shoulder. "It's a cement truck come to make our dr. . ." I hesitated. "Our dream come true."

"It's not your dream, so much, is it?" Erin said softly. "Your dream is to work at a newspaper and write healthcare stories until you die from stress."

The roar of engines was coming closer. "It is kind of fun."

Erin sighed as we spied the first cement truck grinding down our driveway. "We can stop right now," she said. "If you've got cold feet, we can send the contractors home and you can stay at the paper forever."

"I want us to be together again," I said, firing up the teakettle on the Coleman stove. "It's weird living apart. The dogs and I are lonely without you."

"Really?"

"I want to do this," I said, returning to bed to squeeze her hand. "I want to build this house. And live this dream. I'm paying for it, aren't I?"

Mistake. Erin frowned. "I want you to do more than write checks, Jane. I want you to really *want* this place, and want me."

"I do," I protested, sneaking a caffeinated black tea bag into my cup. This was going to be a long day.

"Well," she smiled. "In that case, will you promise me, please, to try to enjoy today a little bit, for me? I want so much to stay, and I can't. This is our foundation, Jane," she said. "Our *foundation*."

"It's going to be rock solid."

"Is it rock solid now?" She was staring at me.

Fatigue was pulling me back down toward the mattress.

"Are we rock solid?"

"We're rock hard," I said, as screaming dogs and a fleet of spewing vehicles drowned my words.

In pajamas, tea mugs in hand, we stepped out on the cabin's plywood front porch that Mike and Robin had built two years ago now, and counted six pick-up trucks and two cement mixers, one with a crane the height of our tallest oak. Richard, the plumber, was conferring with Tom as they reviewed the house plans a final time with the cement contractor--a burly man with a droopy mustache, powerful shoulders and a sagging belly. The cement crew of six guys wore T-shirts, shorts and high, black rubber boots. It was 89 degrees at 6 a.m. and expected to hit 105 by noon.

All morning in the crippling heat, the cement circus did its tricks, as new trucks rumbled down the hill and empty ones departed. The crew worked shin-deep in cement, leveling and smoothing the gray muck that came surging out of a tube attached to the overhead crane. They flattened and pampered the cement with trowels, including a large electric one. Some complained that their feet were burning, because, Tom explained to me, the chemicals in the cement were acidic and would blister and crack their feet through their rubber boots if they stood in it for too long.

By 4 p.m., the surface of the foundation was neat and smooth, and the cement trucks were gone. Tom's crew of three hosed down the slab so the cement would dry slowly, a challenge in this heat wave. The slower it dried, the less likely it was to crack later on. Erin's job, Tom said, would be to hose down the slab twice a day for a week to keep it cool. He'd be back in the morning with rolls of burlap and plastic to hold in the moisture. In two weeks, when the slab was dry, he and the crew would start the start framing. From then on, he said, the house would go up quickly and start looking like a house.

So this is it, I thought, when everyone had gone and I gazed in blessed silence at the vast expanse of gray concrete in front of me. *Our foundation, the footprint of my new life with Erin, has been set in cement. This unnatural oblong sitting in our once pristine meadow is the floor of our home.* I still couldn't get my mind around the concept or the reality that we were building a house from scratch and that I was looking at its foundation.

As I loaded the car to drive to Willits, then home, after dinner with Erin at El Mexicano, I pondered the enormity of what we'd done, of what we were doing. This land, with its huge old oaks and rugged serpentine outcroppings and endless hillsides and forests had drawn us here. We had returned the favor by carving roads and a pond, bulldozing our favorite meadow and pouring tons of cement on its bosom. We were moving to the country. Erin had *already* moved.

"Hey, slab," I whispered softly. "Never surrender. Not to earthquakes nor floods nor fires nor terrorist assaults nor fear nor sickness nor vindictive CEOs nor searing self-doubts. Stay calm and carry on."

I drove slowly up the driveway, pausing to look back at our foundation so I could give Erin a full report at dinner, before we both headed back to our separate homes.

CHAPTER 24

HOUSE CALL

"Jesus!" I threw down the weed whacker and jumped back 10 feet.

"You okay?" Mike, Tom's tall, redheaded foreman, called from a ladder on the slab down below me, where he was framing walls.

Heart firing like an AK-47, I stared at the grass by the bay laurel stump a few feet away, where a tangle of moving rattlesnakes was writhing like Medusa's head. Were there such things as snake pits? Had I stumbled into one?

"I've never seen anything like this." Mike was next to me, drill in hand. "I can't believe the noise of the weed whacker didn't scare them away."

As we watched, riveted, I began to see that there were only two snakes, with unmistakable brown rattles, twisting before us.

Their movements were hypnotic--a graceful, slithering dance, their heads just above the grass, bodies spiraling around each other like the moving stripes on a barber shop pole. It was something out of *Indiana Jones* or The Animal Channel. We'd had a lot of freaky animal interactions since we'd bought our land. Coyotes had nabbed Woody. A boar had nearly charged Erin while she sat in the outhouse, door open. The wild horses had stomped on Woody's paws, requiring four surgeries for the little guy. But this had to be the weirdest.

"I think they're mating," I cried. "It must feel so good they can't stop."

The snakes kept at it, but I was done with weed whacking for the day. Who knew what other mating pairs were having sex in the grass? Stumbling on one rattlesnake tryst was enough for me.

Erin wouldn't be home from work for another few hours, and I felt guilty sitting around while the crew was still working. I'd driven up early on Friday to clear poison oak and cut the grass and see with my own eyes the stick frame of the house going up. Not that Erin hadn't kept me up to date. Every night when she got home from work, she'd take the cell phone and a flashlight over to the site, describing the changes as she made her way around lumber, toolboxes, table saws and compressors. Things were happening so fast that the house looked different each time I drove up.

The exterior and interior walls were fully framed by mid-September, when my father made his annual birthday trek to California. The roof trusses, which had been stacked for weeks next to the foundation, would go up soon.

Sobered by my tale of mating rattlesnakes, and a little wobbly on his feet, Dad stepped gingerly onto to the slab, walking stick in hand. At the site, his organized Virgo mind seemed overwhelmed by the apparent chaos of the job site. He knew a lot about many things, but home construction was not one, and he was out of his comfort zone.

I took his arm and led him through a doorway. "This is your room, Dad. And here's your bathroom."

He smiled. "No more outhouse?"

I shook my head. "You can still use it if you'd rather when the house is finished."

He gazed around wistfully. "Do you really think this will be done by Christmas?"

"That's what Tom says," I shrugged. "You'll be our first guest."

"How 'bout a drink?" he smiled.

It was a good visit, but Dad seemed frail and subdued. Atrial fibrillation, which sometimes made him woozy and short of breath, ruled out the hikes and bird-watching expeditions we'd often enjoyed together. With a long sigh, he told me he'd resigned from his trout fishing club in the Poconos because driving there by himself wasn't much fun anymore. Mrs. B. was far too unsteady on her feet now to accompany him, and most of the men friends who'd been his guests over the years had died or were too impaired, either mentally or physically, to go with him. For what seemed like the first time, Dad was feeling his 93 years.

I called him one Sunday in October to tell him the roof trusses were up and the walls were going in.

I heard a thud as the receiver crashed the floor. "P.H. Futcher, here," he said finally, in a low, hoarse voice.

"Dad, it's me. Janie."

"Hello, Janie," he said weakly.

"What's wrong?" My heart pounded. He was slurring his words.

"Drove to York, PA, today, to see a man with a...disease. Bad one. I'm. . ."

"Are you okay?" He was talking like a Western Union telegram.

"Feel fine. Tired. The. . .male. . .nurse paid house call this afternoon. Says vitals normal."

I glanced at the clock. It was 4 p.m. here, 7 p.m. in Baltimore. Too late for me to get on a flight today. "Who sent the male nurse?"

"Fought in Vietnam War, which I opposed. Pulse said to be normal."

"Dad." I spoke slowly and loudly. "I wonder if you've had a stroke or a TIA."

"No indication, Janie. Think. . . not."

"Okay, well, I'm going to call the nursing station now. You stay where you are. Be careful getting up and down, and I'll call right back. I'll come see you tomorrow."

"Ja. . .nie?"

"Yes, Dad?"

"Take. . .your time."

I called Mrs. B., who answered on the first ring.

"Have you talked to Dad today?"

"He's a little under the weather," she said. "We drove up to Pennsylvania to see my brother, who's very ill."

"Dad drove today? How could he? He's not himself at all."

"He's fine, Janie. The male nurse from Hallowell says his vital signs are normal."

"He doesn't sound normal, Mrs. B. He can barely talk. Something's terribly wrong."

"You're frightening me." She started to cry. "He's going to see his doctor tomorrow morning."

"Can you give me the nurse's number? I'd like to talk to him."

She gave me the number, and I told her I'd be taking the first flight I could get to Baltimore.

"This scares me, Janie," she sobbed. "The nurse said he's fine."

I called the male nurse. "My father needs to go to the ER," I said. "He's not able to talk."

"Your dad's vitals are fine. I'll check on him before I leave tonight if it makes you feel better."

"What would make me feel better is you calling an ambulance and taking him to the ER."

"That's not our protocol when vital signs are in the normal range."

"Screw your protocol," is what I wished I'd said. But I didn't. If they were certain he was okay, and he was seeing his doctor tomorrow, maybe I was overreacting.

I called Erin.

"I'm so sorry," she said gently. "Is he. . ." she paused. "Should I go with you to Baltimore? Do you think this is. . ."

"I don't know," I said, holding back tears. I didn't have much family. My sister wouldn't speak to me and my aunt was dead. "I'll call tomorrow from Baltimore."

By tomorrow, Dad was in the ICU, and I was camped out in his apartment, where mice scampered gaily across the living room, having made cozy homes in his closets, bureaus and sideboard. I called the management for pest control assistance, amazed that Dad had been coexisting so nonchalantly with a colony of *musculus*. It mattered little to him now.

He had a cranial bleed, caused, his cardiologist explained, by the blood thinner he'd been taking to reduce the risk of stroke and heart failure from atrial fibrillation. A craniotomy to remove his subdural hematoma could not be performed until his clotting factor improved. Otherwise, he could bleed to death. Each day that I sat by his bed, shivering in the hospital's sub-zero ICU, he became more and more confused and anxious, insisting there were bugs on the walls and that the clock needed relocating. I was cold and anxious as I sat alone by his bed watching him become a different person, haunted by a nightmare world of hallucination. I had no way to reach my sister, who wouldn't have come even if I could have gotten in touch.

Comforting calls from friends in California and the kindness of my childhood friends in Baltimore kept me grounded and sane as I waited for his clotting factor to improve. When that day came, Dad was wheeled away, returning a few hours later with a bandage around his head and his arms in a straight jacket. When he woke up, his awful fugue state returned. He begged me to help him to fight off the "pirates" he believed had kidnapped him and tied him up "below decks." He was so agitated that the only way I could calm him at all was by filing his nails. The touch and attention seemed to soothe him, so I did it for hours, starting over when I'd finished every finger. After a week, he came back to his right mind. In three weeks, he returned to the nursing floor of his life care community, where my Aunt Gwen and Mrs. R.'s husband had lived. He was wobbly but sane. In a week, he was able to return to his apartment. I flew home and went back to work.

Miraculously, over Mrs. B.'s strenuous objections, Dad made it to California for Christmas. But no guest room or bathroom or anything else was ready at the house. The place looked like a tornado had roared through. White plastic Tyvek paper covered the exterior walls. The door and window openings were draped in plastic. Thick brown paper covered the cement floor. Pieces of sheet rock, rebar, plaster and cardboard spilled out of a giant metal dumpster next to the muddy site. Rain dripped through parts of the roof and onto the cement slab. The appliances we'd bought months ago were still in boxes in the garage.

At Cherry Creek, Dad walked somberly through the chaotic construction site, then drank hot chocolate with me, huddling next to the heater in the cabin. Even with five blankets and the heat on, I couldn't get him warm that night. Back at our house in Marin, he slept late and went to bed early each night. On Christmas Day, he crawled back into bed in his jacket and tie before he'd opened all his presents. On his last day, I begged the goddess to give us a little more time so that he could spend at least one night, cozy and loved, in our new guest room.

A small squadron of my oldest friends in Baltimore met Dad at the airport after Christmas, helping him out of the airline wheelchair and driving him home to his life care community. A few days later, he began to cough. Soon after that, he was diagnosed with pneumonia and was back in the nursing wing where his sister had lived. I was back on a plane to Baltimore.

"Janie!" he whispered from his bed. "What are you doing here? Where are you staying?"

"I'm staying in your apartment," I said, kissing his cheek.

"My apartment?" He smiled. "You have an apartment in the hospital?"

"This is nursing wing of your life care community. Your apartment is two minutes from here."

"I see," he said uncertainly. "I hope you have everything you need."

"I do, Dad," I said, fighting my tears. "The most important thing is I have you."

He smiled and squeezed my hand, closing his eyes.

There was a flu outbreak in the community and everyone was at risk. The nursing floor was quarantined. No residents were allowed to visit the patients. Mrs. B., never a rule breaker, obeyed the edict. Mrs. R., always more daring, defied the caveat and sat with me and Dad and my friend Scotty, watching Dad go in and out of consciousness, at times convinced that he was on a boat on the Mississippi River, near where my mother had grown up, unable to reach the other side. Mrs. R. held his hand and kissed his cheek and left the room in tears.

I sat with Dad every day. My friend Scotty came often and we sat together with him, laughing and talking. He said the sound of our voices, so happy and alive, was comforting. Snow fell. Just beyond his window, dozens of black vultures perched eerily in the bare, bleak trees. I watched his chest rise and fall, rise and fall, bringing him water and ice cream and ice chips. I told him that all his bills were paid and that I had written my sister in West Virginia to tell her he was ill. He longed for her to come, but we both knew she wouldn't. Nanette called. My cousins called. Marny called. Erin and I spoke several times a day. Dinners and visits with Scotty and my other childhood friends made the sad, cold limbo bearable.

Alone by Dad's side, I thought about Erin and Cherry Creek and our new adventure. To my surprise, I did not miss my job or the newsroom or hospital politics or the grim new cancer data I regularly reported on. I was content at Dad's side, sleeping in his apartment--now happily mouse-free after visits from the pest controller--getting together with old friends in the evening. As Becky had said, there was life beyond the newspaper. What I realized I did miss and that I could not live without were deep and loving relationships with friends like Marny and Nanette, with my cousins, with Erin, with the Swallowtails of Cherry Creek, with my childhood friends from Baltimore.

Dad died at 6 a.m. on my sister's birthday-- January 29. Scotty came quickly, and we stood over his bed, his torso covered by a sheet and a blanket, his face calm and pale, his hands neatly folded on the covers. We prayed and sang and cried until the undertakers rolled him quietly down the hall under a sheet and slid him into their black SUV. At the funeral home we chose an oak coffin, a spray of yellow lilies and a limousine for Erin, Scotty, two cousins and I to ride in from the church to the graveyard.

For the first time, I understood why undertakers, like David and Nate on my beloved TV show, *Six Feet Under,* used unnaturally calm, modulated voices with their bereaved clients. It's what you needed when the ground was quicksand beneath you and your world was falling apart and you had to decide if you wanted a coffin lined with satin or silk or nothing at all. We planned the funeral with a woman minister from Dad's church, who amiably agreed to changes I requested in the service, including the removal of all references to God as "He."

We buried Dad in an ice storm so dangerous that few of his friends made it to the church and even fewer came to the graveyard. The undertakers lowered Dad into a hole next to my mother, buried 19 years before, and a few feet from my grandparents and my aunt and uncle. Mrs. B., who had not seen Dad in weeks because of the quarantine, nearly collapsed into her daughter's arms at the funeral and skipped the party after at my dear friend Kitty's. Mrs. R., whom Dad had written every night for so many years, didn't come at all. The weather was too awful.

"When in doubt, throw it out," Erin said as we undertook the job of packing Dad's apartment.

Under her determined supervision and with the

help of good friends, we finished the job in three days, having sorted through the layers of Dad's life and packed what I wanted to keep.

Dad had kept, recorded and filed every letter, detail and event in the lives of his family and friends. If I became too absorbed or tearful reading a letter or studying a file or photograph, Erin would repeat gently, "When in doubt, throw it out."

How could I throw anything away when everything seemed precious? I found jewelry of my mother's; there were letters to Dad from my dearest friend, Catherine, cut down by ovarian cancer in 1994. Photograph albums contained visual histories of my grandparents and aunts and uncles and my vanished sister.

"Janie-Baby, just pack it up and send it to California," Scotty would say softly. "Sort through it when you get home. It'll be easier. It's too sad right now."

The more I cried, the more I cried. I couldn't wait to get back to California. I had been raised in this cold, leafless, wintry Maryland landscape and would be forever grateful to my good friends here who'd seen me through this crisis. But California was my home, and I wanted to be back with my little dogs as soon as I could.

Two days after the funeral, Erin and I were on a plane home.

The dogs were ecstatic to see us. Woody's whole body wagged, although he backed away bashfully when I tried to scoop him up. Luna raced through the house, circling every room deliriously and finally stopping at my feet.

"My papa died," I said to Luna as she settled in my arms. "That's why I left you so long." She licked my face and tried to chew my nose. "My dear papa is dead," I repeated, as if saying it aloud would make it more real. "He was very sick, and then he died. And he never got to see the house." Suddenly, I was sobbing.

Erin held me on the couch. "He lived a good life, Jane. He loved the land and got a kick out of staying in the cabin, and you made him very happy and proud. He died well. You were there with him, and you took good care of him, and he knew you loved him, and that's what counts."

I was sad beyond words, relieved beyond words to be with Erin and the dogs, away from the cold, snowy East. My father's empty, dusty apartment and the long halls of the nursing facility where his defeated, often demented contemporaries sat in wheelchairs or lay in lonely rooms begging to go home, were history. Gone but not forgotten.

We drove home to Cherry Creek.

There was our house! It was a real house at last. Buckskin brown stucco had replaced the white Tyvek plastic paper that had wrapped the plywood walls like surgical dressings for so many months. We had a green metal roof now; double-paned, low UV-windows replaced the sheets of clear plastic. The sliding glass doors, covered in protective brown paper, had been installed along with the Craftsman-styled front door we had chosen a year ago. The front deck and side porches had been poured, and the three timber posts Erin had cut from a neighbor's land now held up the front porch roof. Left to be done were the interior painting, the trim, the counters, the cabinets and the appliances.

Dad's silver Ford Taurus, with a dent he'd put in the front fender, and his furniture and belongings, now ours, arrived at Cherry Creek a week after our return, on a clear, sunny February morning. I was happy they came so quickly, as if my father were as eager as we were to move into the new house.

Back at work, Rick bombarded me with questions: How was the house? When did we plan to move? Was there any chance the editors would let me telecommute?

"Nope," I told him. "The city editor said today that I can't cover my beat from two counties away. I'm quitting as soon as I know for sure when the house will be ready.

"I knew it," Rick said, walking the dog on his yoyo. "You're abandoning me."

"You're barely here anyway," I laughed. "And you'll be quitting as soon as your TV column goes global."

"I wish," Rick grumbled.

I couldn't wait to hand in my resignation, pack up our old house, move to the new house and wake up each day with Erin in my arms. The long ordeal was nearly over, and I was ready to embrace my new life.

Chapter 25

MOVING DAY

I called Erin from the Willits Safeway--40 minutes away from my new life. "Do you need me to pick up anything?"

"I need *you*. Hurry!"

"Did the movers make it?"

"They've come and gone. Dinner's ready and so am I."

"Wahoo," I grinned, flying up the last 16 miles of Highway 101 in our new truck with Luna and

Woody next to me on the seat. The four-by-four pick-up was piled so high with boxes of odds and ends I'd packed after the movers left that morning that I couldn't see out of the rear view mirror.

It had been a crazy 24 hours. A crazy couple of months. I'd buried my father; said farewell to Rick and the newsroom at the obligatory "quitter cake" party; celebrated my 54th birthday, and been legally married to Erin at San Francisco City Hall with 20 friends and family witnessing the union, then gathering afterwards for lunch at Cousin Anne's.

The day before, the movers I'd booked--the same guys who'd brought Dad's stuff from Baltimore--cancelled on me. After some frenzied calls, I found a company willing to come right to the house to give me an estimate. When I approved it, the guy started loading his rig on the spot. The truck had been so big and tall I'd been afraid to tell Erin that I didn't think it would clear the oak branches arching over our driveway. But obviously that hadn't been a problem. The entire contents of our house had been unloaded while I was still packing up golf clubs, beach chairs, and assorted junk in our garage.

"This is it," I said to the dogs as I turned down our driveway at Cherry Creek. "You've spent your last night in the suburbs. You don't ever have to be afraid to bark because you'll bother the neighbors."

Woody wagged his tail. Luna eyed me nervously. She didn't like changes and this was a big one. I looked at my watch. It was March 22, my mother's birthday. The sky was clear, the sun beginning to set as we passed the six wild horses grazing in our upper meadow. Slowly, I wound around the hairpin turns, down past the red reflectors that kept cars from driving off the cliff, then on to the last leg of road over to the home site.

And there it stood--our buckskin brown stucco ranch house with green metal roof and hand-hewn timber columns holding up the front porch. It was dusk now, and tiny pinpoints of light cascaded down the exterior walls from the copper stenciled sconces Erin had commissioned from an old Indian tin-worker in New Mexico two years ago. I caught my breath. It was magical. Magical.

"Here we are," I said, lifting Woody carefully from the front seat as Luna leaped over him and dashed ahead to the front door.

Standing on the threshold, my eyes widened. For the first time, the thick brown paper had been lifted from the acid-washed concrete floors as well as the doors and windows, revealing what had been hidden for months. The floors were dazzling, their swirling splashes of rusty red and deep orange and brown as rich and sparkling as marble. The high Douglas fir ceiling soared, opening and expanding the room. The yellowy tan leather couch, easy chair and ottoman I'd tested on scores of visits to Macy's furniture store looked perfect; so did the cherry wood kitchen cabinets, handmade by a carpenter in Willits.

The brushed nickel drawer pulls and knobs we'd sifted through in hardware stores for months perfectly matched the cabinets. The dramatic Nepalese granite counter tops we'd ordered last year from the toothless contractor in Laytonville were works of art, circling nebulae of yellow and gold, rust and onyx, giving the room and the kitchen island an earthy, regal glow. Above them, the hanging glass-and-steel café lights we'd selected after many debates were sleek and understated. The ceiling fans were in place at last, as were the skylights over the kitchen island and the two bathrooms. Even the stainless steel appliances I'd hauled up to Cherry Creek in a rental truck that I'd managed to drive off the road, looked great, perfectly matching and blending with the two kitchen sinks and faucets and cupboard hardware. Through the tall sliding glass doors along the south side of the room, I saw the last of drop of sunlight turning the far ridges golden.

"Welcome home," Erin said, taking my hand. "Do you like it?"

I looked at the familiar mahogany dining room table and matching chairs that I'd grown up with, at which I had sat across from my sister--my father on my right, my mother on my left--for so many years. Upon it were the two tall brass candlesticks that had been my grandmother's and then my father's. I smiled through tears. "It's a feast for the eyes. I can't believe you've unpacked and made this all happen since this morning. I'm in shock."

"I talked the movers into bring the dining room table in from the garage," she said. "They even assembled the wrought-iron bed you gave me as a wedding present."

"It's all fantastic," I said, entering every room: Erin's office, the guest room, bathroom, the pantry, and then our wing, with my office, our bedroom and bathroom and the walk-in closet. The walls, painted in marbled layers of gold and yellow, were perfect.

"Do you really like it?" Erin inched closer.

I held her hand, beaming as I tried to absorb it all. "I didn't know that buried under all that brown paper and Tyvek and plastic there was something so beautiful. It's. . .a religious experience." I wrapped my arms around her. "Thank you."

She pointed to a red casserole dish on the table. "I'm starved. Let's eat!"

We sat down at Dad's table and held hands. "Thank you, Goddess of 10,000 names," I began, "for this night, for this house, for our love, and for the love and support of so many friends and family members. Thank you for our many, many blessings, and for watching over us as we changed our lives and got married and made this move and saw Dad through. May we return to you as much as you have given to us. Blessed be."

"Blessed be," Erin whispered.

The roasted chicken and vegetables tasted better than anything I'd eaten in my life.

"To Erin," I said, lifting my glass of ginger ale. "For making our dreams come true."

That night, in the new bed, we held each other close, with Woody and Luna sleeping next to us under the comforter.

We turned out the lights, and through the sliding glass doors watched the moon rise in the East. "It's our first night in our new bed in our new house," Erin whispered.

"We're actually lying in the meadow," I said. "I can't get my head around it." It was overwhelming. We had really turned this wild land into a house and a home. "You know what I wish?"

"I bet I do," Erin said softly.

"Just one thing."

"Only one?" she laughed.

I gazed out at the moon, wiping my eyes. "I wish Dad could have spent one night in this house, in his very own room. I wish he could have been here and had dinner with us tonight. I wish in the morning he could have watched the birds with his binoculars and taken a hot shower in his own bathroom."

"Your father *is* here," Erin said, squeezing my hand. "He's here, and so are all the ones we've loved and lost." She pulled me closer and began to sing, ever so softly:

"Our house, is a very, very fine house,

"With two dogs and a cat. . .

"Life used to seem so hard," I sang with her.

"Now everything seems easier with you, babe."

Woody crawled up from the bottom of the bed, laying his head on Erin's pillow, and Luna curled against my leg. Hand in hand, we drifted into the first sleep of our new life in our new house at Cherry Creek. It was, indeed, a very, very fine house.

CHAPTER 26

INCH BY INCH

Erin donned her photo I.D. for work and loaded up the car as I followed after her in my pajamas.

"Go out and make it a great day!" I grinned, mimicking the annoyingly upbeat morning TV weatherman we watched on the news each day. There was a lump in my throat as I leaned into the window to give her a kiss goodbye, watching the Subaru disappear up our driveway on the first leg of her 70-minute drive to the community clinic in

Ukiah.

Back in the house, I considered which of the tasks on my to-do list to assault. We'd been in the house three weeks, and there were still stacks of boxes in the garage that needed sorting and unpacking. Or should I rumble through the Yellow Pages in search of a landscaper to help us transform the wasteland of rocky soil around the house into a garden? Or there was that contractor someone had told us about who might be able to build a kennel outside the doggie door so that Woody and Luna would have a place to pee without getting nabbed by mountain lions, bears or coyotes. Was it more important to call the new tenants in our house in Novato to find out if the cranky dishwasher had been fixed yet? Suddenly, it dawned on me as I dropped a load of laundry in the washing machine: I had become a housewife.

I swallowed hard, longing to go back to bed and sleep until noon. But I hadn't slept till noon in 30 years. Besides, Tom's crew would be back some time today to finish the redwood pergolas over the back deck. A nap was out of the question.

I dumped some kibble into the dogs' bowls and some cold cereal into mine. Okay, so, I had to get a handle on my feelings. But what were my feelings? I was angry, yes, that was it. But why? I was angry because here I was here in the middle of nowhere with Erin gone from 6:30 a.m. until 6:30 every night. But what's underneath the anger? I asked myself, trying to remember the self-help strategies that my snoozing, bike-riding shrink had taught me. *Uh-oh*, I thought. *I'm lonely, and being lonely makes me sad, and I have way too many daylight hours alone by myself to be safe from my brain.*

Erin and I had decided that I needed to make some friends now that I was a permanent resident of Mendocino County. But where did I start? Amazingly, Gina and Lin had moved up here, too, but not to Swallowtail Ranch, the 320-acre place at Cherry Creek that they owned with six other women. Instead, they'd bought a little farm close to the town of Laytonville, seven miles north of us. Gina was living there full time, with Lin coming up on weekends. The three of us had talked about reconvening our old Bay Area writers' group, but I wasn't sure what I would write. My novel was beyond fixing, and my journal notes and vignettes about moving to the country kind of depressed me now that I was finally here.

I felt a prickle of envy that Lin had managed to keep her Berkeley house *and* her magazine job and still live in the country on weekends. Not that I was pining for stomach-churning deadlines and forced marches to the publisher's office. But I missed the sense of purpose and connection the job had given me. Was it too late to take that reporting job I'd been offered at my former paper's sister paper in Ukiah? No, I told myself, I would have been miserable. They wanted me to cover night meetings, work every weekend and commute to Ukiah for an hourly wage that would barely have paid for my gas. I wanted to write something real and serious, I reminded myself, and one of these days, when I'd plowed through the myriad tasks on my list each day, I was going to do just that. When the words came cascading from my pen, I'd be grateful I didn't have a job to distract me from my brilliant endeavor.

I reeled in my mind and decided to focus first on making a friend. I didn't need a lot of friends, just a couple people to hike with every so often or drink a cup of tea with now and again when Erin was at work. My pal and I would talk about books and politics or maybe go to the independent film series in Willits on Thursday nights. Once I had a friend, I'd do my chores effortlessly and learn to love cooking dinner every night.

Should I call a neighbor? Which neighbor? Now that all the Cherry Creek Irregulars had real houses, hot showers, telephones and electricity, we no longer gathered at Jay's for Saturday night potlucks. The pioneer glue that bound us together in the days of tents, campfires and primitive infrastructure had evaporated. Meals with Mike and Robin were out because they were self-admitted vegetable-phobics, surviving on Diet Cokes and Hot Pockets. Cindy and Rod, who'd built a small but exquisite house by the creek, were chasing new dreams in the Bay Area and coming up less and less often. Cindy had acquired two horses and was learning to ride; Rod was constructing a lightweight airplane. And Jay, who'd retired from his telecommuting job in the travel business, was always busy at meetings, having joined the Mendocino Arts Council and been elected president of the board of the Willits Community Theater. Stephanie, whom we'd seen so much of in the early days, had become the theater's producer, and, if she wasn't directing, casting, building sets or preparing gourmet delicacies for theater fundraisers, she was nesting with Ken and the birds in their remote cabin near the Emerald Chasm.

My first call to recruit a friend would be easier, I decided, if I dressed, took the dogs for a walk and completed a maudlin march through some of my father's boxes in the garage. Those tasks under my belt, I called Gina, who agreed that reviving the writing group was a great idea, although she herself was so swamped with gardening chores, their new yaks and a growing flock of chickens that she wasn't writing anything. Lin, she said, was in the same boat, dashing madly up the freeway from the Bay Area each weekend to assist Gina with the farm tasks.

The call to Gina comforted me. It was good to know I wasn't the only country woman feeling so overwhelmed by the list of things to do that simply switching on the computer--we actually had Internet service via a satellite server--was like climbing Everest. Next up, I e-mailed the features editor at my old paper to say I'd like to write some freelance stories for him. He replied instantly, sending me a long list of Sunday profile ideas the paper was knocking around and asking me to pick a few I'd like to work on. I opted to start with a profile of a Mill Valley psychiatrist who'd written a book on cults, one of my favorite topics.

Feeling pretty good, I decided a friend-seeking call was in order and phoned Carolyn, a real estate agent and one of the Swallowtail Ranch partners who worked in Willits. I invited her to play golf with me on the nine-hole course in town. I hadn't been on a golf course in a decade, but she'd mentioned at a party that she played. When Carolyn said she could play that very day, I dusted off my clubs and raced down to the course, waving merrily to Tom and his crew as they bumped down our driveway.

We played horribly, laughed hysterically and ate afterwards at a burrito joint on Main Street. At a picnic table in the garden behind the restaurant, Carolyn showed me photos of her new motorcycle, and I asked her if she knew anything about plugging holes in leaky ponds.

"I know something about ponds," came a voice from the next table. We looked over at a tanned young woman in jeans and a work shirt, with pink cheeks, broad shoulders and an elderly black and gray Labrador retriever sitting by her feet.

"Really?" I said. "Does your pond leak?"

"Have you thought of getting a plastic pond liner?"

"Yeah, but they're expensive," I sighed. "The estimate from the irrigation store in town was $16,000, not including installation."

"Wow," she said. "Your pond must be a lot bigger than mine."

We asked her to join us, and she did, shaking our hands with a strong, warm grip. "I'm Antonia, by the way," she said. "Where's your pond?"

When I told her, she grinned. "I can practically see Cherry Creek from my road. I live across from you, on Shimmins Ridge."

It turned out Antonia, a horticulture graduate of the University of California at Davis, had recently launched a gardening and landscaping business that specialized in native, drought- and deer-resistant plants.

"Jane needs a landscaper," Carolyn offered helpfully. "Can you show her one of the places you've worked on?"

"Um. . . " Antonia looked down at her dog. "I don't know."

"I'd like to see something you've done," I said, watching a hummingbird flit among the orange trumpet flowers on the vines along the garden fence.

Antonia handed her dog a piece of her burrito. "My clients are very private."

Carolyn nodded, her clear brown eyes giving me a knowing look. "People up here are sort of protective of their gardens," she said carefully.

Mystified, I looked at Antonia. "We could come to your place."

Antonia scooped a last bit of guacamole onto a chip. "My place is. . ." she trailed off.

What was wrong with this woman? Did she want landscaping work or not? "Can you at least send me some photos of a garden you've designed?"

She folded her paper plate, dropping it into the recycling bin by the fence. "I always forget to take photos."

This wasn't turning out quite the way I'd hoped. Erin would never want a landscaper who couldn't show us any of her work. "You're not a very good sales person," I said, taking my last sip of lemonade. "How am I supposed to see how wonderful you are?"

She smiled, writing her phone number on a napkin. "Call me anyway."

That night, when I told Erin about my day, she was impressed with all that I'd accomplished, particularly finding a landscaper at the burrito place.

"Maybe she grows pot," Erin said. "That's why she wouldn't show you her place. Maybe all her clients are pot growers, too."

How could that be? I chewed my lip. Antonia was a Davis grad, really into native plants. She didn't seem like a pot grower.

"What's a pot grower seem like?" Erin asked. "Everyone up here is a pot grower. Let's invite her over to see our place and get her ideas."

Antonia came over and loved our place, bringing picture books of plants and trees and beautiful gardens she could create for us once we decided what we wanted.

That summer, the three of us studied dozens of garden books, eventually coming up with a landscaping plan for the south side of the house overlooking the ridge. We'd create a drought- and deer-resistant, California-style English country garden. We'd have a large, central flowerbed that included some ornamentals that "put on a show," as Antonia was fond of calling colorful bloomers, such as dahlias, and two side beds with a path winding through them. At the edge of the cement deck, we'd plant a postage-stamp sized swatch of green grass--Erin's idea--to contrast with the dry brown summertime hills beyond.

On the west side of the flower garden, separated by a decorative fence and archway constructed from little Douglas fir trunks that Antonia would harvest from her own land on Shimmins Ridge, we'd make four, 20-foot long raised vegetable beds. All the gardens and beds would be irrigated with an automated drip system that used our spring water, sparingly, we hoped, because we had no idea if our little spring had enough water to support an entire garden. It pumped several gallons a minute in the winter, when it was raining, but in the summer, when we were using it to irrigate a large garden, who knew?

"You and I can't put this garden in alone," I said to Antonia one late summer morning as we stood out in the dirt taking a soil sample to test for mineral deficiencies. "This ground is hard as a rock."

"That's because it is rock," Antonia laughed.

"We need a crew," I said.

She studied me with her gentle brown eyes. "Who did you have in mind?"

"Me?" I looked at her, puzzled. "You're the landscaper. Don't landscapers bring their own crews?"

She reached over to pick up Luna, holding her in her arms like an infant, something most of our visitors were afraid to do. "It's not that easy to find people who'll work in this county. I usually do the digging myself, but your soil is really hard."

I took off my Wild Women in the Garden baseball cap to scratch my head. "I see lots of strong guys buying dirt in at that nursery in Willits. Can't you hire some of them?"

"I'm not sure you understand," she laughed. I stared at her.

"Most young guys in this county don't do heavy labor."

"What do they do?"

"Um. . ." she inhaled.

"Hello?"

"They're growing and trimming pot."

I looked at her with amazement. "You're telling me every able-bodied male in this county is growing or trimming pot?"

"Pretty much." She kissed Luna's forehead and placed her gently back on the ground. "There's a high school kid in Laytonville who's worked for me, but he doesn't have a car, so you have to get his parents' permission and pick him up and drive him home, and he's only available on weekends."

I was astounded. "Let me get this straight. There aren't any workers in   Mendocino County we can hire to dig trenches and fence post holes and do the heavy lifting because they're making so much money growing pot?"

"Sometimes I can use my Woofers, but I don't have any Woofers right now."

"Woofers?" This was getting weird.

"It's an acronym for volunteers for World Wide Opportunities on Organic Farms. People give them food and a place to live in return for 20 hours a week of gardening. I use them at my place quite a bit. They always need money, so they'll probably work for you, under my supervision. But I won't have any Woofers for another month."

That night I told Erin that Antonia didn't have any Woofers, and we'd have to find our own crew to dig the irrigation trenches for the underground PVC pipes because all able-bodied men in Mendocino County were growing or trimming pot.

"That's not surprising," she said. "What are woofers?"

After I explained, she thought for a minute. "Why don't you hire someone with a backhoe or a tractor? Backhoes can dig faster than people, and there must be a million backhoes in this county."

I liked that idea and so did Antonia.

"I know a guy with a Kubota tractor in Laytonville," she said. "I'll call him."

"How come *he's* available?" I said.

Antonia smirked. "You didn't hear it from me,

but he grows indoor pot and doesn't harvest in the fall like everyone else."

"Sounds good," I said.

Antonia was relieved.

"I have a question for you."

She waited.

"Is the reason you wouldn't show us your garden because you grow pot?"

"Um. . ." she blushed.

"It's fine with me if you do. I'm just curious."

"Pot's easy to grow but not that easy to sell because everybody else is growing it, too. The reason I didn't invite you over to my place is because my place is. . ." she paused. "It's. . . in process. Not really a showcase. I mostly raise vegetables. I don't have a big ornamental garden."

I searched her eyes. "It's not because of the pot."

"Nope," she laughed. "I'm not a pot grower."

By late fall, our garden project was in full swing as Antonia and assorted Woofers and tractor operators pounded through our soil, one tractor breaking a bore on the rocks as Mike had when he'd dug the hole for our outhouse four years before. Once the trenches were made, Antonia laid down the PVC irrigation pipes, and we brought in several gigantic truckloads of fancy organic compost that the crew did their best to mix into the barely penetrable ground.

Day after day, Antonia arrived in the morning in her silver Toyota pick-up with Raider, her Lab, who hid in the truck most of the day, terrified of Woody and Luna, who barked at Raider from the moment she poked her timid head out the truck until the time she left at 5 p.m. with Antonia.

Two topics besides plants headlined my many, many conversations with Antonia: her boyfriends and the quirks of her complicated mother, who lived in Marin with Antonia's stepfather.

I called Marny. "When are you coming to visit? I've spent every day for months with a boy-crazy 30-year-old. I'm desperate for adult conversation."

She sighed. "I'd love to, Janie, but not until I figure out this bleeding."

"What bleeding?" I stared at the dirt that would soon be a swooning mix of decorative and edible plants, including artichokes, rhubarb and dwarf fruit trees.

"I think it's just an obstinate bladder infection," she said. "But I have an appointment with an oncologist next week."

"Oncologist?" My stomach tightened.

"We'll come soon, I promise."

I called Nanette, who was an M.D. and knew about medical things. "What do you think about this bleeding of Marny's?"

"Bleeding is never good. But we'll know more when she gets her lab and imaging results. What are we going to do about *you*?"

"What about me?"

"Are you writing?"

My writer's block seemed frivolous compared to Marny's bleeding. I explained that Gina, Lin and I had met several times, but we'd spent more time commiserating about how much we weren't writing because of our rural properties than we did sharing new work with each other. There wasn't any new work.

"I'm mostly a gardener now," I told Nanette.

"You need to write," she said. "And I want you

to edit my book."

"Your book?"

"*How to Say No in Ten Thousand Words Or Less.*"

"*Yes,*" I laughed.

"I haven't written it yet, but an agent has taken me on, and I want to hire you as my editor."

"Thank you," I said, resolving to be more like Nanette, who was organized, focused and disciplined in everything she undertook. If she had a vegetable garden, which she didn't, she'd have found time to take care of it as well as write, sell and promote her book, too. That's how she'd been able to run a private practice, conduct an ongoing longitudinal research study on the children of lesbian parents, and managed to travel the world with Dee, her partner. Her book would be a dream to edit because it would probably be perfect on the first draft. "I'm here when you're ready," I said.

"I don't want you to feel lonely and adrift, okay."

"Erin says I need to make more friends."

"You have friends. Come to San Francisco. We'll laugh and go to Eliza's for Chinese food and walk down by the Golden Gate Bridge at Crissy Field."

I scheduled a trip to San Francisco and felt better.

Out of the blue, Erin and I got some great news on the friendship front. Three of Gina and Lin's Swallowtail Ranch partners, all of whom we liked, had decided to build a one-room straw bale cabin on their land. *Deus ex machina,* we would have three funny, smart, independent, talented, and sympathetic weekend neighbors. Jane was an animated, warm-hearted film producer, who always brought great gourmet treats to our house when she visited. Kate was a Willits acupuncturist, physician assistant and musician extraordinaire. The third partner on the straw-bale project was Meaveen, a former schoolteacher and passionate Berkeley political activist who'd marched, protested, demonstrated and lobbied against war and corporate greed her entire adult life.

At last, we'd have like-minded, women-loving friends close by, sometimes staying with us, often making meals and breaking bread with us, entertaining us with fresh tales of the agony and ecstasies of constructing a home in the middle of nowhere. They were Goddess-sends.

The very bad news was that Marny's bleeding was cervical cancer. She needed a hysterectomy and probably chemotherapy.

I looked up at the ceiling and tried to stop the room from spinning when she told me the news. "I'm coming to see you," was all I could manage.

"Don't worry, Janie," she said glumly. "I'm not going to die right away. It'll take a little while."

"Stop it."

"I've had a good life. I have no regrets."

"I'm glad you have no regrets, but you have to stay alive. I need you. Susan needs you. Your clients need you. You're going to beat this. That's all there is to it."

I drove to San Francisco the day after Marny's surgery, nearly turning back in Ukiah because my back hurt so much from gardening. Even Antonia, who'd played rugby at U.C. Davis, was getting stiff from dealing with our rocks.

Marny was pale and weak and besieged by ports and drains and catheters and hissing pressure socks as she lay in her hospital bed.

"I'm okay, Janie," she said, seeing the panic on my face. "My lymph nodes are clear, and they didn't find anything in the surrounding tissue. I'm not going to die. Not right away."

I drove home ecstatic over Marny's good results. I knew what was important now. Gratitude, gratitude, gratitude. Gratitude that Marny would not be dying. Gratitude for our land. Gratitude for Erin and the doggies. Gratitude for three Swallowtails building a cabin on their land. Gratitude for the writing group. Gratitude for Antonia. Gratitude for the hard-packed soil around our house that by next summer would explode into an inviting cornucopia of color and edibles.

Pete Seeger's garden song became my mantra each morning after Erin left for work.

"Inch by inch, row by row," I chanted.

"Gonna make this garden grow.
Gonna mulch it deep and low,
Gonna make it fertile ground."

CHAPTER 27

RADIOACTIVE

Erin navigated the narrow, two-lane blacktop toward KZYX&Z radio station, hugging the road as we whizzed around heart-stopping hairpin turns and green gorges.

"I'm scared," I said, staring at two billy goats butting heads in a small fenced pasture. "I should never have volunteered for the station's board."

"It's going to be great," Erin soothed. She always drove on curvy roads because that way she didn't get so seasick. "The staff invited you out to see the place, and they'll love you."

I gripped the car door and took a deep breath. I'd been flat on my back and half out of my mind in November when I'd called the station to request an application for its board of directors. I blamed Antonia for my condition, but it wasn't her fault. She'd convinced me I could plant daffodil bulbs using the gorgeous overhead pickaxe swing that she had perfected, encouraging me to emulate her style. The result was a herniated disk in my low back. I could barely walk, let alone fly to Cincinnati where I'd planned to go door-to-door with Nanette and Dee to campaign for John Kerry and send George W. Bush packing. The day after the election, I lay on the couch in misery and isolation. Stoned and groggy from Percocet, I decided it was time I fought back against the corporate-owned news media that had meekly allowed George Bush, Dick Cheyne and Karl Rove to drag the country to war in Iraq, barely questioning the administration's specious claims that Saddam Hussein possessed "weapons of mass destruction."

Erin and I had been listening to KZYX&Z radio since we'd first stumbled across the station on our solar-powered portable radio. We'd procured medical marijuana for Erin's mother through the station's call-in show called *Trading Time* and enjoyed the weekend mix of Celtic music, bluegrass, jazz, National Public Radio news and talk shows. The station was wacky and innovative, a community treasure linking Mendocino County's far-flung, physically isolated residents to each other.

The station's headquarters were nearly two

hours away from our house in a tiny town called Philo, in the Anderson Valley, halfway between Ukiah, the county seat, and the Pacific coast. Since the Gold Rush, Anderson Valley had been an isolated ranching, farming and logging community that drew scores of hippies in the 1960s and '70s. The new arrivals soon learned what many locals who'd lost their lumber and mill jobs already knew—the climate and terrain of the valley were great for growing pot. Ditto grapes. In recent years, the valley's award-winning vineyards kept its B&Bs busy and its tasting rooms bustling.

The road ahead of us descended into a sunny green valley and the area's largest town, Boonville, population 1,500. Boonville was famous for its unique dialect of English, Boontling, which local historians speculated had been created in the nineteenth century as a diverting game by children, women and young men working in local hop fields and sheep shearing sheds. When the children grew into adults, they continued speaking their secret language, which was peppered with Scottish Gaelic, Irish, Pomo and Spanish words. "Bahl gorms" meant good food; a "buckey walter" was a pay phone; "harp" meant to talk or speak, and a "horn of zeese" was a cup of coffee.

Few residents spoke Boontling any more, but the community retained its reputation as an enclave of fiercely independent, proudly countercultural folks, who were very cool to tourists and other strangers.

Boonville looked like a set from *Gunsmoke*, with one- and two-story brick buildings and a handful of clapboard storefronts. I wouldn't have been surprised to see a bearded mountain man stationed at the end of town with a shotgun. But that day the only people we saw were some innocuous young guys in jeans and hoodies eating burritos at a roach coach, and two women in dreadlocks strumming guitars on the front porch steps of a lopsided clapboard grocery store. Three quick blocks later, we were cruising through a spectacular valley wedged between hillside vineyards and tree-covered ridges.

We overshot the driveway of KZYX&Z, hidden behind some trees, and, over my protests, Erin turned back. Moments later we were reading a spicy array of bumper stickers in the parking lot. "Grow your own dope--plant a man," read one. "Impeach Bush" screamed another. "Quiet! The President is trying to think" made both of us chuckle.

Prepared to meet my fate, we walked slowly up a rickety wheelchair ramp that opened into a run-down modular home smelling of wet dogs and moldy carpets. The place was *funky*. CDs, LPs, cassettes, coffee mugs, dogs, cats, and a muscular Beatnik with a goatee wearing a knit cap were crammed into a few tiny rooms. The sophisticated classical music show we'd heard driving to the station was emanating from a cramped broadcast booth behind a smudged glass window, where a gray-haired man in a white shirt, tie, and Air Force bomber jacket sat under headsets next to an enormous microphone and a jumble of wires and mixing boards.

"Is that Jane?" A woman with long black hair turning gray wandered by waving a CD.

"Hi," I croaked. "I've volunteered for the board and this is. . ."

"It *is* Jane!" The woman threw her arms around me. "Wonderful to meet you. I'm Athena. I do an education show and help out in the office once a week."

"Right," I stammered. "And this is Erin, my wife."

Athena hugged Erin, too. "We're thrilled you're here and that Jane is running for the board."

Running? I thought I'd simply volunteered. Wouldn't the board just accept me if my application passed muster? And why was she so thrilled about me? She didn't even know me. I could have been a mass murderer or a corporate media warmonger.

"Let me introduce you to Mary," said Athena, leading me by the hand through a dark hallway to a cluttered office. She left to look for some chairs.

"Mary's the program manager," I whispered to Erin as we waited in the cluttered office. "She's the one who invited me to come." The room was jammed with stuff--pledge-drive premiums, books by Amy Goodman of my favorite national news show, *Democracy Now!,* KZYX&Z T-shirts, CDs, a bobbing *Prairie Home Companion* dashboard ornament and NPR tote bags.

Mary arrived in a frenzy, pushing a cat from a chair so Erin could sit down and dragging a stool in from the back patio for me. Even seated, she was in constant motion, scrolling through e-mails, jotting notes to herself, stacking and re-stacking CDs and always listening with one ear to the speaker that broadcast the station live into her office.

"Things are a little interesting here at the moment," she said, twisting a strand of her long brown hair around one finger. "We haven't had a general manager in over a year, and there have been some. . ." She cleared her throat. "Some tensions on the board. That's why we're so excited you're running against the incumbent."

"Tell me about running," I said, trying to sound like I'd known all along I'd be attempting to unseat someone.

"No worries," she said, swatting a fly with an Excel spreadsheet. "Candidates for the three seats do one live, group call-in show and that's it. We take care of the rest, send out ballots, get the results from the auditor, that sort of thing."

"You mentioned a live broadcast?" I swallowed. Ever since a broadcast guy I'd known in Philadelphia years ago told me that I had a terrible radio voice, I was self-conscious about how weak and tinny I sounded. A live, on-air question-and-answer session with other board candidates could be terrifying. I didn't know anything about the station except that I liked its programs.

"You'll do great," she smiled. "We'll prep you."

"I don't want to take anybody's seat away from them," I squeaked. "Not if they want to stay."

"Don't you worry about that," Mary said, jiggling her knee. "The incumbent has created a little. . . turmoil here, publishing a document he calls 'The Secret Life of KZYX.' It attacks many staff by name and calls *me* imperious and abusive, among other things. So, I, for one, will be overjoyed if you win his seat. And you will."

"Who's electing me?"

Mary's big fluffy dog licked my hand. "Any station member who's current with their dues."

"Are Erin and I paid up?"

She turned to her computer, clicked on a file and scanned down a membership list. "Yep, you're current. So," she paused. "Would you like a tour?"

Without waiting for an answer, Mary jumped up, leading us out the back door and across a cement patio littered with ashtrays and old pizza crusts. We entered an ancient red railroad caboose, home of the membership and bookkeeping departments, then visited a dilapidated trailer that Mary said had recently been donated to the station. We waved to the station's one-person news department, a smiling, white-haired woman who was interviewing someone on the telephone and wearing a headset.

"That's Annie," Mary said.

"Cool," I said. "We listen to her every night."

"So, that's it." Mary led us to the front door. "We'll see you in two weeks. Come a little early so I can introduce you to some staff and programmers, and we can get a level on you. We'll ask you why you're running and what you want to accomplish and a little about yourself. Piece of cake." Suddenly, she looked up at a speaker in the hallway, heard dead air, and shot into the broadcast booth to rescue the programmer.

As we headed off to the coast for a celebration lunch, my back, neck and stomach began to relax.

"Boy, do they need you," Erin said, squeezing my hand, "If you win, which apparently you will if Mary has anything to do with it, you can knock some sense into them. I can't believe they took that old trailer. It's falling apart."

"Desperate times, desperate measures," I offered.

"You'll just have to raise some money then," Erin laughed.

JANE FUTCHER

I won my seat in a landslide, mostly because my opponent's former girlfriend, who had never met me, told everyone she knew in the county--and she seemed to know a great many people--to vote for me. Thus began my three-year term as a director of Mendocino Public Broadcasting.

At one of my first board meetings, the board was informed that a growing band of rodents was gnawing away at the station's infrastructure, ancient the day KZYX went on the air 16 years earlier, and now near death. What could go wrong did go wrong, it seemed, particularly in the rainy season, when the septic system flooded, transmitter problems took the station off the air for hours and sometimes days at a time, the electricity went out, the back-up generator failed, and the roof of the donated mobile home nearly collapsed on the news director. Those problems were nothing compared to some of the conflicts that raged among assorted staff, board and programmers, all of whom viewed the station as their baby, to be protected at all costs from malignant forces and meddling outsiders.

The board's greatest accomplishment that first year was hiring a station manager, a smart and capable media consultant named Belinda, who for more than a decade had hosted her own late-night music show, "Bubbles in the Think Tank," at a Cincinnati community radio station.

To our astonished relief, Belinda willingly took on the task of modernizing the station's infrastructure while attempting to guide staff and programmers away from boundary-free chaos to a more traditional organizational style that she and the board believed the station needed.

One morning Belinda called me at home to say that she had just given a warning to a nighttime disk jockey for leaving a shopping bag full of marijuana in the studio after his show.

The jock, whom she suspected of trimming buds while he spun records, explained to Belinda that he thought someone on the next shift might want the leaf he'd left behind.

"What if the FCC walked in?" Belinda asked, dumbfounded.

"Why would the FCC walk in?" The puzzled jock scratched his head.

"Because the Federal Communications Commission licenses and monitors this station. Those folks can drop in here any time they please."

The jock was incensed. "I've got a 215." He was referring to Proposition 215, a California state law, passed by voter ballot initiative in 1996, allowing California residents to grow or use marijuana for medicinal purposes if they had a letter or prescription--known as a 215--from a doctor saying their medical condition required it.

Our call was interrupted by shrill barking from Woody and Luna out near our new hot tub. I slammed down the phone, ran outside and stopped dead. Woody and Luna were inches away from a big, fat, coiled rattlesnake.

I screamed. Luna glanced at me and kept right on barking. Little Woody, too blind to know what he'd cornered but delighted to hear I'd arrived on the scene, stepped closer to the snake. Taking a deep breath, I swooped both of them up in my arms, locking them in the house as I grabbed Dad's 12-gauge shotgun from the front closet. I'd never shot anything with that gun except for few clay pigeons decades ago, but I loaded the two barrels with buckshot, covered one eye with my sleeping mask and headed grimly outside, heart pounding. The snake hadn't moved.

Praying for forgiveness for myself and for a peaceful journey to the other side for the snake, I peered down the barrel, pointed at its midsection, prepared my stance for the horrendous noise and kickback that would follow, and pulled the trigger. Boom! As the gun recoiled against my shoulder, the snake bounced a foot in the air. I looked down. I'd blown his body nearly in two, but the snake was still moving and rattling. I lined its front section in my sites and pulled the trigger again. Crack! The snake was still writhing. What was I supposed to do? Was he immortal? I looked around. A few yards away, on the far side of the gate, stood Antonia, her dog Raider and two Woofers, who'd just pulled up in her truck.

She opened the gate to inspect the rattler, whose two halves were still writhing in the grass.

"It's dead," she said. "You can put the gun away."

While the Woofers started their day's assignments, Antonia and I sat at the kitchen counter and shared some tea. I was a wreck, my hands and legs still trembling. Like everyone in Mendocino County, I would later find out, Antonia had her own rattlesnake story to tell, about the time a neighbor had tried to teach her to skin a rattlesnake she'd shot. Technically dead, the snake had coiled around her arm like a living bracelet when she'd tried to slit open its belly. Three times it coiled around her arm, and after the third time, she'd had enough, putting the snake down and resolving never to try to skin or eat a rattler again.

I was still shaky when Erin pulled into the garage that night. Out back, we looked at the two halves of the snake, now pitiful and sad, life force gone, its once powerful body covered with flies. We cut off its venomous head with loppers, sealed it in a mixed-nuts can that Erin would drop in the dumpster at work the next day, and tossed the snake's body away on a far hillside for the ravens and vultures.

That night I slept fitfully, seeing rattlesnakes everywhere and imagining what might have happened if the dogs had gotten a step closer.

I called Belinda to explain why I'd hung up so abruptly. She listened sympathetically, obliquely suggesting there were as many human snakes in public radio as there were rattlers in the hills, then, ever so gently, guided me on to her favorite topic—how to raise money for the station.

Mysteriously, I'd been appointed chair of the board's bylaws committee, undertaking a rewrite of the obsolete portions of the station's legal documents—a painstaking task for which I was singularly unsuited--and chair of the major-donor fundraising committee. Suddenly, I was a busy woman, meeting and talking to committee members, organizing house parties, asking people in the community to write large checks to the station. Dozens of station-related e-mails now popped up daily on my computer screen. My office phone actually rang several times a day with calls about solicitation mailers or on-line seminars or board workshops I'd organized on making "the big ask."

A few months into the board job, I regained a

portion of that sense of mission and contribution that I'd lost and missed after leaving the paper. At Safeway or the post office or in the library, people stopped to talk to me about radio shows they liked or hated. The station's board had no control over those decisions, but I was happy to listen to their comments, passing them along to Belinda and Mary. Sometimes, people thanked me for working to keep our great little station on the air. It felt good to know that in some small way I was helping make a unique community resource a little better. If I had to fire at a snake every so often, that was okay. Farmers and radio soldiers needed every tool in the arsenal.

CHAPTER 28

HOMEGROWN

When we first bought our land, we often asked people we met what they did for a living. But what would have been an innocuous icebreaker in the Bay Area drew suspicion in Mendocino County. Some people simply walked away. One guy mumbled something about being a caretaker. A woman from Laytonville whispered that she was a caterer. Another rolled her eyes and said she taught herbal medicine classes. Many of these jobs didn't seem to add up to a living, as far as we could tell. But in this county so committed to sustainable agriculture, we'd met many hardy folks who had apparently learned to live on a shoestring.

Now that we actually lived in Mendocino, we were beginning to get the picture. Lots and lots of people here grew pot. No one was ever going say, if we asked their line of work, "Well, as a matter of fact I grow a potent strain of Train Wreck. Would you like a pound?" Eventually, we stopped asking people what they did.

Antonia, our gardener, had warned us about the situation when she admitted that she couldn't get a landscaping crew together because all the able-bodied males she knew were making so much money in the pot industry. Since that time, I'd studied the police blotters in the local newspapers, noting that there were constant arrests each month for possession or transport of controlled substances, usually marijuana. I'd always assumed that these folks were probably kids who'd never been to college or dealers passing through Willits from wild and wooly Humboldt County to the north, where the grass was very green.

Once our eyes were open, evidence of the pot culture in our own backyard stared us in the face. Nearly all the roadside billboards posted on the north side of Willits as you drove into town promoted pot-related businesses--a head shop, a nursery, two hydroponic gardening supply stores, an irrigation outfitter.

Still, we didn't actually *know* any growers. We were sure there weren't any in the Willits chapter of our new anti-war group, Code Pink, with whom we'd marched in the town's Fourth of July parade.

And we doubted many growers attended the Willits Community Theater, where Jay was now board president and Stephanie was a fellow board member and the theater's producer. And surely they weren't working at Erin's clinic or volunteering in Willits' new economic localization group, WELL, which was earning a global reputation for inspiring communities to become more self-sustaining and less dependent on foreign oil.

"Maybe *you* should try growing pot," said Marny, who was healthy and very much alive. Her scrape with death and a tiny boost from Lexapro had transformed her. She wasn't gloomy anymore. At that moment she was sitting on our patch of green grass beyond the deck, tears of joy in her eyes, grateful to be alive and overflowing with praise and appreciation for the slice of heaven we'd created at Cherry Creek. She loved our clusters of lavender, red and purple penstamon, plumes of white and yellow Mullen, delicate pink Mexican primrose, and blue buddleia plants, irresistible to butterflies. A bubbling terra cotta fountain gurgled next to a dwarf nectarine tree.

"Grow pot?" I stared at her.

"I'd consider it," Erin said, glancing at me. She was longing to quit her clinic job. Trying to convince lifelong diabetics to take their meds and forgo Cokes, Snickers bars and smoking was getting to her. It wasn't like being a home birth midwife, where most of her clients were healthy, motivated and excited about their lives.

"We don't even smoke pot," I protested. "We could lose this place if we were busted."

"You don't know what you're talking about." Erin yanked a dandelion from the grass. "They'd have to prove we paid for the land and the house with drug profits, and, of course, we didn't and they can't."

Marny drifted off to admire the string beans climbing a pole in the raised beds.

"So exactly how many of your friends grow?" I asked Antonia one morning after we'd picked a real live artichoke from one of the bare root plants we'd put in the ground last fall.

She kept on weeding. "I'll plead the fifth on that."

"I'll take that to mean a lot."

She headed to the garden shed for a shovel.

Even if the whole county grew pot, no one at Cherry Creek did, I was sure of that. Until one Saturday, when Rod and Cindy invited us down to their place by the creek for a barbecue.

A big, silver Toyota truck roared by their house, heading up the road past Liz's old cabin and parcel, which she'd now sold, toward the steep, wooded parcel formerly owned by someone called Doctor Lee, a chemist whom no one had met.

"That guy's growing," Rod sighed.

I perked up. "Really? What's he like? Have you ever talked to him?"

"He avoids talking to me. He and his friends drive too fast and bring in truckloads of dirt."

Eyebrows raised, I glanced at Erin. A grower at Cherry Creek. A bona fide outlaw who drove too fast and didn't speak to his neighbors. That was a sure way to piss folks off.

One day at our place a pleasant but wasted-looking kid in his twenties whom Antonia had persuaded to help in the garden, handed me a small, clear plastic box with a dozen round specks inside. "Since you're so interested in gardening," he grinned, "I brought you these."

I stared into the plastic box. "What kind of seeds are they?"

He laughed. "You know."

I looked into his sweet blue eyes. "Pot? For me? What do I do with it?"

He laughed. "Plant it. Put the seeds in dirt and give them some water like any other seed. It's a weed. Grows like gangbusters. Just be sure to pull out the males so they don't pollinate the females."

"Pull out the males?" I scratched my head. "How do you tell a male plant from a female?"

"No worries," he shrugged. "The boys have little sacks for sex glands and the girls have tiny white hairs. The girls are what you want because they have buds and resin and all the THC."

That night I showed Erin the little plastic box of seeds.

"Cool." She opened the box. "They're big."

"Should we plant a few? "

She stared at me. "I thought you were dead set against it."

"Maybe we ought to grow a few as a kind of self-initiation into the Emerald Triangle. We can give it away to people who need it."

"Great," Erin laughed. "Raise enough pot so I can stop working."

"No way. If we plant the seeds it's just for fun. Just to see if we can. We're not trying to sell it or manicure it or anything. Right?"

"Sure," she said. "It's an experiment."

"To see what the plants are like."

"Absolutely."

I had three empty wine barrel planters out by

the raised beds, next to the zucchinis and cucumbers and squash. Kissing each seed, I placed five in each pot, watering them every couple of days. I waited for them to become the tall, bushy, monster plants I'd seen in *High Times* magazine. When the little things popped through the soil, I was awestruck.

"Should we sex them?" I asked Antonia.

She shook her head. "They're just babies. They won't differentiate for a month or two."

Six weeks later, when the babies were pretty green adolescents, I asked Antonia to sex them.

"It's not all that easy," she said, pointing out some invisible hairs that apparently affirmed the womanhood of several plants. "I think these three are girls. That one's a boy." She pointed to what she thought was one of the sacks. "We'd better wait a little longer before cutting them down."

By July, seven female marijuana plants had sprouted up in our wine barrels.

One night some of the Irregulars came for a party. I showed my new crop to Rod.

He frowned. "Are you going to smoke it?"

"I don't smoke," I said.

"Neither do I." He rubbed his beard. "What are you going to do with it?"

"Give it away, I guess. "Would you like some?"

He reddened. "What would I do with it?"

"Make a remedy? Use it as medicine? They say it's good for pain and inflammation."

He and Cindy hurried into the house.

When the Irregulars were gone, Erin shook her head. "You shouldn't show everyone your pot plants."

"It's a joke," I said. "We're not going to sell it."

"Not everyone thinks it's a joke. I don't think Rod did."

"Oops," I said. "I'm sorry."

Our pot grew taller and taller, but the next time Antonia's guy came, he took one look at my plants and declared that they were far too yellow.

"What did I do wrong?"

"You might have overwatered them. And they need more nitrogen."

I felt bad. "Where do I get nitrogen?"

"Add some bat guano."

"I don't have any bat guano."

He smiled. "Pee on the soil."

I laughed. "Hard for a woman to pee in a four-foot barrel," I said. "Why don't you?" There were three guys working with Antonia that day building our new wood shed. I lined them up for a photo as they added their nitrogen to the plants, but they'd only let me shoot them from the backside. A few days later, the plants still looked yellow and scraggly.

Still, by the fall, the plants had buds. That was about the same time we began to notice a lot of strangers driving too fast on the Cherry Creek roads. They never stopped to say "hi" or catch up on news like most neighbors did when we passed each other.

"Where you headed?" Erin would ask in a friendly way if she saw one of these folks opening the main gate to Cherry Creek.

"Just up the road," they might say if they replied at all.

"Which parcel?" she'd persist.

"Don't know the number."

"What's the owner's name? Is it . . ." By the

time she'd finished her sentence, they'd have sped off.

Antonia told us that some of these people could be trimmers, the seasonal workers who prepare pot for market by removing the big leaves and clipping the colas into neat nuggets.

One night, Erin came home from work brandishing a copy of *The Willits News*. "Guess what?" she said. "The guy at the end of Rod's road was busted."

"At Cherry Creek?"

She opened the paper. "Listen to this." She read aloud: "'The County of Mendocino Marijuana Eradication Team seized nearly 2,000 cannabis plants. . .'"

"Two thousand plants?!"

"Listen! "'Seized nearly 2,000 cannabis plants with an estimated weight of 4,000 pounds Thursday from the Cherry Creek subdivision in Laytonville, resulting in arrests for conspiracy to manufacture marijuana. Law enforcement officials served a federal search warrant Thursday at the remote property for gardens that were located during the Drug Enforcement Administration over-flight school held in June.'"

"Let me see." I tried to grab the paper away. "Helicopters were spying on Cherry Creek. Do you think they saw my barrels?"

"No way." She pulled the newspaper back and read aloud. "'Agents found $20,000 in cash on the parcel, two rifles and some methamphetamine. Two Mexican nationals were arrested on the site, and the owner was arrested by agents at his home in Sonoma County.'"

We called Terrie, a new neighbor who lived near

the bust parcel. She said she had seen close to a dozen black DEA vehicles roll up Cherry Creek Road on Thursday. Later, she saw a 10-wheeler hauling away hundreds of pot plants.

We called Woody, a neighbor who'd lived at Cherry Creek for years. He gave us the lowdown on every bust that had ever happened at Cherry Creek, starting with a meth addict on Parcel 45, off Black Bear Road, a decade earlier. Woody and other neighbors had often seen him prowling the roads near his place carrying an Uzi and stopping anyone he saw to ask what they were doing there. The partners originally selling the parcels didn't tell the police for fear the subdivision would get a bad name. But to keep the guy from intimidating prospective buyers, they tried, unsuccessfully, to evict him. The grower was finally arrested because of a sort of fluke, when the California Highway Patrol stopped him on the street for driving under the influence. The CHP discovered two loaded Uzi magazines on his front seat, later searching his parcel. They never found the Uzi, but they discovered dozens of pot plants and arrested him. When he defaulted on two payments, the partners foreclosed.

Woody also told us more about that female caretaker who preceded Stephanie on Liz's parcel. She'd been a grower whom neighbors disliked because she had all sorts of nasty people around who stole stuff from neighbors and cut the main gate lock more than once. That woman was found dead in the road near Liz's house from an overdose of meth.

"Found dead?" I was shocked.

"Stephanie told us that," Erin said. "When she

first showed us the land."

"Yep," said Woody. "And there's one more. The former owner of Parcel 58, off Black Bear. He had thousands of plants."

Woody said he and some other neighbors had gone over to the parcel after the owner got busted to look at what they called "the house that Mary Jane built." They were spooked by five huge water tanks with pipes going every direction and six trails leading through dense overgrowth to flattened spaces large enough for sleeping bags and a propane burner.

"Why a propane burner?" Erin asked.

"So the workers could stay warm, I guess. Maybe cook? They also found booby traps made of mousetraps and shotgun shells. The DEA destroyed thousands of plants."

"Who were they trying to catch with the booby traps?" I asked.

"Rats or mice," Woody said. "Who knows? Maybe people."

We put down the phone, dazed

A few days later, an idea began percolating in my head. "I'd like to see what a pot grow looks like," I said to Erin. "Want to drive over to the parcel that was busted and look around?"

"Really?" She was surprised because I was usually too scared to do anything risky.

The entrance to the bust parcel was just past Rod and Cindy's, not far from our new friends Nadine and Janelle, who had also bought land from Liz and were camping with some friends by the creek that weekend.

"We're going up to see the drug bust place," we told their friends. "Want to come?"

A couple of them hopped in the back of our truck.

The gate to the pot bust parcel was wide open. I guess I thought there'd be a lock and police tape and maybe a guard on duty. But the place was deserted. We drove slowly in, wondering if the feds or maybe some lingering criminals would take shots at us with machine guns. It was eerily quiet. After parking in a cleared area in the Douglas fir trees, we hiked up a rugged hillside road. Halfway to the top, we saw plumbing pipes spray-painted with green camouflage poking out of a manzanita grove on our right.

We all stopped dead. There, in the manzanitas, in the filtered light, were hundreds of 200-gallon plastic pots, each with quarter-inch irrigation lines connected to them, and each with nothing left inside but a stump. It was beautiful and haunting in a strange way, even with the rat traps every few feet and boxes of rat poison everywhere. Sections of black, half-inch plastic tubing were stacked in circular piles all over the place. We explored the area in nervous, breathless fascination, sure that somebody was about to take a shot at us. We talked softly at first; when nobody came after us, we used our normal voices.

"Hey, look at this! Over here," one of us would call, and we'd gather around to examine a generator or a case of bat guano or a fat, forgotten bud left on a stem.

"The paper said there was a house," I said. "Let's find it."

Halfway down the road we'd just walked up, we spotted a steep driveway veering up into the woods. Back in the truck, we crept up the hill, still expecting to be killed. And there it was. In front of us in a fir grove was a long, two-story plywood house with no windows. The front door was wide open.

Erin jumped from the cab.

"We'd be trespassing if we went in," I said, courage fading.

"We're already trespassing."

We all went in.

The door looked like it had been jimmied and kicked in by the DEA. The place was trashed. Garbage was strewn across the long, open downstairs room. There was an open kitchen with running water, a stove, a microwave and several long plywood tables that Erin said were for trimming, although how she knew I wasn't sure. A television and a VCR and dozens of Spanish-language videos were strewn across a table by some unzipped sleeping bags and two cots. Clearly, the residents had left in a hurry.

"Mexican nationals," someone mumbled.

"Hey, look." Erin pointed to the refrigerator by the front door. "A bear's been in here." The fridge was on its side, the door dangling from its hinges. The bear had tossed jars of tomato sauce and salsa onto the floor, biting and flinging everthing from beer to whipped cream cans around the place.

We tiptoed upstairs, which was one big room like the downstairs with long wire clotheslines stretching from one end to the other.

"Drying lines," Erin whispered.

On a shelf were a dozen little white-handled scissors, Reynolds turkey roasting bags, scales for weighing pot and rolls of seal-a-meal plastic wrap.

"They must eat a lot of turkey," I said.

One of Janelle's guests laughed. "They're for transporting the pot. Turkey roasting bags cut the smell."

It was both terrible and intriguing at the same time. This was no hobby garden. This was the real thing. A criminal operation. Lives had been interrupted, like Pompeii after the volcano, with the tableau frozen in time. The police had come and taken the perps and trashed the place, with help from the bear. It was weird and unreal. What were the lives like of the Mexican guys who'd been arrested? Were they really bad guys or were they just immigrants trying to make money to support their families in Mexico? Was the owner in jail? Was he going to sell this place? Would it be confiscated? My imagination was on fire.

A week later, a friend of Erin's, who was toying with the idea of buying land at Cherry Creek, found the owner's phone number through information and called him to ask if he were interested in selling his parcel. He said he was, told her the price, and said no charges had been filed against him.

For the longest time I could not get the scene out of my mind--that eerily beautiful manzanita forest with its slaughtered pot plants, and the chaotic plywood house where panicked workers had been surprised by the police.

Our pot studies continued that winter, when a young man named Matthew bought the pot-bust parcel. He seemed very nice, with a neatly cropped beard and a white Subaru station wagon, like Erin's.

"Do you think he's a grower?" we asked Rod.

"I hope not."

"He seems really nice," Erin said.

We invited him to Erin's birthday party, but he didn't come. By late summer, at harvest time, guys who didn't live at Cherry Creek were once again roaring along the roads, many heading toward Matthew's parcel and leaving the subdivision gate open. They never made eye contact with neighbors they passed on the road.

One weekend morning Janelle called in a breathless state. A friend of theirs was camping with them and had taken a jog that morning. Somehow he'd wound up running on Matthew's part of the road. A guy on an all-terrain vehicle had come roaring down the road demanding to know what he was doing there.

"There are three guns pointed at you right now," the guy in the ATV told their friend. "Get off this land now or they'll open fire."

"They said what?" We were stunned.

"He threatened to shoot our houseguest and followed him all the way down the hill in the ATV. He was terrified."

A week later, Erin and I were leaving Cherry Creek as Matthew was unlocking the gate. Erin jumped out and hurried over to him.

"Do you have a screw loose, Matthew?" she said. "Why did you threaten Janelle's friend with guns?"

He reddened. "Word travels fast here."

"You bet it does," Erin glared.

"The guy was trespassing."

"But you told him you had three guns pointed at him. What were you thinking? You can't threaten people with guns."

"There weren't any guns," he reddened. "We wanted to scare him. He was on our property and shouldn't have been."

Erin looked like she was about to shake him by the collar and bite his head off. "I don't care what you do with your land. If you grow pot that's your business. But threatening to shoot someone is unacceptable. Everyone at Cherry Creek has heard the story, and people are angry. If you get busted, don't be surprised, because you screwed the pooch, Matthew."

She turned back for the car, as he stood speechless by the gate.

Three weeks later, Matthew was busted by the federal Drug Enforcement Agency. So were two other Cherry Creek owners we didn't know who lived close to the main gate.

In no time, professionally painted signs popped up all over the roads at Cherry Creek. "Warning: Marijuana Growers Will Be Reported," they said.

The community was in a furor--over the pot busts as well as the new signs. Quite a few Cherry Creek residents, it turned out, were growing pot legally, with doctors' prescriptions. They didn't like the signs, said they were threatening and hostile. They wanted the signs taken down, predicting they would lower property values and invite retaliation against us by outsiders. The buzz in Laytonville, they said, was that Cherry Creek was unfriendly to pot growers.

Other neighbors loved the signs and hoped they'd deter new buyers from planting marijuana gardens.

A couple of years back, Cherry Creek residents had elected Mike to the three-member board of the road association. I stopped by his house to voice my opinion about the signs. "They're mean-spirited," I said. "They make it look like Cherry Creek is at war with all growers, including legal ones, like the 'Mom and Pop' gardeners with 215s."

Mike was calm but firm. He had canvassed a number of owners, including Erin, and all thought the signs were a good idea.

"Erin has changed her mind," I said. "You caught her by surprise. Why didn't you call a community meeting to discuss the signs? Wouldn't this be a good time to convene as a group?"

He shrugged. "The road association manages the roads, not the community. Our bylaws don't require us to hold community meetings. Besides, the signs weren't a road association action. A group of us paid for the signs out of our own pockets."

Could anyone post signs along the road? I asked. If I wanted to post a sign in support of legalizing marijuana, could I do that?

He said he wouldn't recommend it.

Since the road association board wouldn't call a meeting, Erin and I and several other neighbors organized a community gathering at our house to discuss Cherry Creek issues, including fire preparedness and the new anti-pot signs.

Nearly 50 people squeezed into our living room. Many of the neighbors had never met before. Almost everyone was friendly and civil. There was no consensus on the anti-pot signs, so it looked like the signs were staying up. Mike and his unnamed allies were adamant.

"We're never growing pot again," I told Erin that

night. "My life of crime is over."

She rolled her eyes. "So the self-appointed Cherry Creek posse has intimidated you?"

I nodded. "Those helicopters and those busts and those signs scare me."

She rolled her eyes. "You think the DEA would have come after those six puny plants of yours?"

I shook my head. "I'm not going to tempt fate."

"Whatever," Erin sighed. Her long commute, the diabetics who wouldn't take their medication, and tensions at the office were getting to her. I didn't want her to suffer, but if she quit, she sure as heck wasn't going to raise homegrown at Blind Dog Ranch. Case closed.

CHAPTER 29

NIGHT CROSSINGS

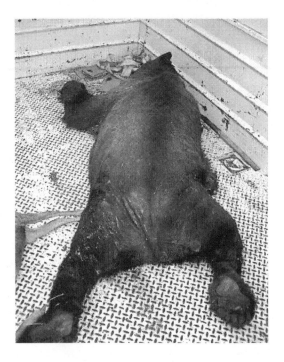

Erin and I had seen a few California black bears

at Cherry Creek, but they were always running the other way, which was how we liked them. Still, it was always exciting to see a bear if it wasn't too close.

We were both ready for a break from life on the ranch. The furor over the busts and the marijuana signs had taken its toll. So had our recent disappointments in the quest to find more water. Our supply was running out. We'd paid many thousands of dollars to a well digger who'd dug two wells for us, both of which went dry weeks after we'd installed a solar pump and solar panels and trenched nearly half a mile of PVC pipe from the wells to our storage tanks. We'd finally resorted to buying water by the end of the summer. To our relief, Bob, our neighbor who scared bears away with Christian music, offered to let us tap the spring on our property that was actually deeded to his parcel. Finally, an extra trickle was flowing into our tanks.

At the urging of dear friends in Florida, who sensed Erin's need for a vacation and my eagerness to escape life off the grid, we left Stephanie and Ken in charge of Luna and Woody and the house and garden to embark on a cruise from Sitka, Alaska, to Vancouver, Canada, along the Inside Passage. The guidebooks all said Alaska was full of bears and that we'd probably see members of the *ursus* family at several of our stops along the route. But the most exotic land mammals we encountered were two newlyweds we visited in Canada after the cruise. They lived on a small island six hours and three ferry rides from Vancouver.

Angel, a dear friend of Erin's from her Sikh days,

was a statuesque, six-foot, white-haired, blue-eyed beauty whose ex-husband owned a wildly successful potato chip company and whose new man, Ernie, was a rugged, half-Iroquois songwriter who played six instruments, maintained Angel's fleet of motorboats and had an incredible green thumb, growing unnamed crops on unnamed islands nearby.

"Hurry, before we lose the light," Angel yelled as we yanked our duffels from the rental car. We had missed the last ferry to her island, and, at twilight, she'd insisted on crossing the channel in her motorboat to pick us up. "Keep your eyes out for big logs. I can't see a thing because my glasses are fogging up. We're headed for that blinking green light."

The faint green light and dark silhouette of land across the straights seemed frighteningly far away as the bow of the little skiff slammed into icy, four-foot swells, and rain pelted our faces. Erin and I glanced longingly at the orange life vests piled in a wet, unreachable heap behind us.

Erin sang sea tunes to bolster our spirits, which soared when at last we neared the blinking green light, then sagged when our nearsighted captain told us that unless we found two unlit buoys fast, we'd crash on some nearby rocks.

"Over there," I cried, pointing a dark object off the bow. "The other's just beyond it."

"Right on," Angel shouted. "Now pray we don't hit the islands as we pass through the gorge near the oyster beds."

"Should we ask Ernie to turn on your dock light?" I squinted through the rain at a dark mass that looked like the shore.

"Can't," Angel said. "My cell doesn't work here."

In an instant, Erin found her cell phone. The thing worked, and Ernie answered, promising to wave us into the dock with flashlights.

Later that night, we sat around Angel's cozy kitchen table, our hostess shaking her long white mane and pouring a little more Amarula into Erin's chai. "I've never crossed by myself in the dark before," Angel giggled. "But we made it, didn't we girls?"

"Right on," Ernie said, rolling a spliff. "A toast to the travelers."

Canada had been sunny and hot all summer, but it rained so much during our five-day visit that Ernie disappeared for 24 hours, taking Angel's launch out to an unnamed island to harvest his unnamed crops.

We flew home to San Francisco without ever having seen any bears, or for that matter, any of Ernie's tomatoes. But we learned quite a bit about life off Vancouver Island.

Our car crammed with luggage and provisions from Costco, Trader Joe's, Whole Foods and Target, we drove north from San Francisco airport in Dad's Ford Taurus, happy to be back on solid ground. On that moonless night, we were cresting the long grade between Ukiah and Willits on Highway 101 when a huge, unearthly creature appeared in front of us. There was no time to scream or to swerve. Bam! We collided. The airbags deployed, the windshield shattered, the horn blared maniacally into the night.

"What happened?" Erin whispered from the driver's seat.

"I'm not sure," I said. "But I think we're on fire." Smoke was filling the car. I reached for my seatbelt with trembling hands. "Get out fast."

We climbed out, huddling by the highway, praying my Dad's faithful car would not explode. A bearded man with gleaming eyes jumped from his pickup. "You all right?" he asked kindly.

"They hit a bear," said a woman who had stopped to check on us. "A big one."

"A bear?" Erin gulped. "Is he okay? Is he. . .?"

"Died instantly," the woman said, pointing into the darkness. "Some guys are pulling him off the road right now."

A highway patrol officer approached carrying a megaphone to shout gawkers away. "What happened here?"

"We hit a bear." Erin wiped her eyes. "He came out of nowhere."

"I need your license, proof of insurance and registration," he said.

Erin looked uncertainly at the car that we'd shipped from Baltimore to California. The left fender was smashed and the hood was curled up toward the windshield, a spider web of fractures. "It's in the car. We saw smoke and thought we might blow up."

"That's the powder they put in the airbags to keep them from sticking," the officer said brusquely. "Looks like smoke but it's not. You're safe to go in."

The guy from Triple A, a boy really, craned our car up behind his tow truck, dropping us at a 24-hour café in Willits. "You were lucky," he said. "The highway patrol officer said he's hunt bears all his life and that's the biggest he ever saw. I've towed four bear accidents myself, three of them this year, but I never seen one that big."

Our friend Melinda left her houseguest alone at home watching a video and drove to Cherry Creek. When she swerved to avoid a jackrabbit, we panicked, a queasy feeling of déjà vu making us weak with fear. But we arrived in one piece, surprised to be alive.

Woody and Luna barked and yipped, circling us joyfully when we walked in the front door.

"We hit a bear," I told Woody, capturing the prancing boy and holding him in my arms. "He's gone to heaven. So has my papa's car."

Woody wagged his tale and licked my nose.

"It was sad and scary, but we're home and we're safe and we love you." I squeezed his little body close to my chest.

On Monday morning, I called the highway department. "The California Highway Patrol said you removed the bear that we hit on Highway 101 near Ukiah Saturday night. Do you still have him? We'd like to come visit, maybe do a little ritual for him. It happened so fast we never actually saw him. We'd kind of like to say goodbye."

"I'm sorry," he said. "'Fraid it's too late for that. We've buried the bear already. He was a big old guy. Measured five feet from paw to shoulder and weighed about 500 pounds. You were very lucky. I wouldn't have wanted to run into that bear, not on the road *or* in the woods."

But run into him we did, which may be why they say be careful what you wish for. We cruised Alaska looking for bears and killed one 20 miles from home.

Chapter 30

MURDER SHE WROTE

With time to kill in Ukiah before a KZYX&Z fundraising lunch with the general manager, I climbed the steps of the Mendocino County Courthouse to have a look around. I'd been wanting to do that for some time. Courtrooms were a strange other world, a kind of living theater with unique sets and scripts, rules and players. They were also great places to get to know a community; I was still trying to feel like I belonged in mine.

"Any interesting cases today?" I asked a security guard checking briefcases at the metal detector.

"Murder upstairs," he yawned. "Courtroom E."

As I found a seat in the crowded courtroom, it took me a moment to get my bearings. In the witness box, a sheriff's detective was describing the night that he'd brought in the two prisoners now sitting in front of the courtroom in orange and red jumpsuits. The detective said that both men had initially denied involvement in the murder of the victim, 42-year-old Kevin Henry of Albion, but that later one of the suspects claimed that, high on methamphetamine, they'd encountered the victim at a nearby lake, where he'd offered them cocaine.

"He felt that the victim was making advances toward him," the detective told the court. "He stated that he felt uncomfortable because he was heterosexual and had a girlfriend."

I sat up. The victim was gay? Had he really made a pass at the two young men--one scared, one defiant--sitting in the jury box?

The courtroom was dead quiet save for the whispers of several women in the first three rows. They were part of a group of more than a dozen people, many wearing purple lapel buttons bearing a photograph of the victim stamped with the words "Forever in Our Hearts." In the seat next to me, a tall, gray-haired woman wearing a loose woolen sweater and blue jeans took detailed notes on a yellow legal pad.

"That's Kev's family," she whispered to me at the break. She told me these same people had disapproved of his sexual orientation when he was alive and were hoping to appear more accepting than they really were.

I looked at her, surprised. "You're not a reporter?"

She shook her head. "Those rotten punks killed my best friend."

"Wow," I said. "I'm sorry."

That day in court haunted me. A gay man had been brutally murdered. The family and friends of the victim were devastated. The lives of the perpetrators--charged with murder, robbery, carjacking, kidnapping and initially a hate crime-- were ruined. For what--a few hundred dollars they managed to steal with the victim's ATM card?

The image of the two young tweekers stabbing and kicking a man to death was at odds with the Mendocino County I knew. My friends were environmentalists, psychotherapists, health care providers, human rights activists, gardeners and contractors who co-existed peaceably with flag-waving Republicans and hard-core libertarians.

Was the murder, as I feared, a hate crime fueled by drugs and paranoia? Was it a cocaine deal gone wrong, as the public defender argued? And what did the crime say about Mendocino County? Was my new home the tranquil, safe place Erin and I had assumed it was?

"E-mail the editor at the Chronicle magazine," Nanette urged me. "I know her. Use my name. I bet she'd be interested in a story about that murder. The timing's perfect."

Nanette had a point. The garden was thriving. My back was much better. My novel was mothballed. And my work for the KZYX&Z board was less radioactive than usual.

The Chronicle editor was interested.

For the next year and a half, I followed the case, interviewing anyone who'd talk to me about the victim and the perpetrators and the confluence of social and economic circumstances that played a role in what had happened that November night in 2005.

Talking to lawyers and mental health professionals, going to court, meeting people who'd lived in the county far longer than I was a giant step toward understanding and connecting with my new community.

I was in court the day the medical examiner declared that methamphetamine had been found in the victim's bloodstream and that he had been stabbed 17 times, the death blows being two deep knife wounds to his back and chest, as well as blunt-force trauma to his head. I listened as the first prosecutor on the case dropped the hate crime charge, arguing that the defendants' claim that the victim had tried to grab his genitals was "probably self-serving and false." I was there when both suspects pled guilty to second-degree murder, waiving their rights to a trial.

I talked often with one of the two defendants, mostly by phone, but once at the jail, where he spoke to me through a Plexiglas window. Although I'd toured San Quentin with my old newspaper, I'd never interviewed an alleged murderer before. Both defendants blamed the other for the murder. Legally it didn't matter; each man was linked to the crime, and under California law, to aid and abet a homicide makes you as culpable as committing the act itself. On August 31, 2007, a judge sentenced both men to 15 years to life in prison.

The Mendocino County scene in which the two murderers hung out was, in part, I learned, the result of the decline of well paying blue-collar jobs that occurred when the already waning timber and fishing industries collapsed in the 1980s and early 1990s. With only minimum wage jobs available, young people with motivation, resources and education left the county and didn't return. Increasingly, the residents who remained were drawn to the underground economy fueled by drugs.

Methamphetamine was the rising star in this underground economy, as it was in most other rural California communities. Mendocino's relaxed attitudes toward marijuana use and cultivation may have contributed to meth's success, according to a county substance abuse counselor I knew in Willits. In our county, she said, "casual multigenerational acceptance of drug use is the norm."

After the story came out, I received e-mails from lots of people, including the publisher of a colorful and hard-hitting local newspaper--the Anderson Valley Advertiser in Boonville.

"I think you got the parallel universes sense of Mendocino just perfectly," AVA publisher Bruce Anderson wrote me after reprinting my story in his own paper. "There's a serene world of nice, well educated people. Then there's this large, violent underclass that suddenly looms up in ways we don't expect. Looking at the Sheriff's on-line booking log every day, and having lived here since 1970, I've seen the deterioration. In 1970 the timber and fishing industries still employed several thousand unskilled men. These people and their descendants are now in the drug trade and whatever else they can find, lawful or not. You know all this, I'm sure, but your story is the first I've read that captures two textbook cases."

That letter made me feel good, like I'd gotten it right, written something of value that had nothing to do with my daily life involving composts and seedlings, soil amendments, squash and solar electric systems.

After the article came out, I kept writing every day. Gina and Lin and I were meeting regularly. Lin was researching and writing an historical novel set during the Civil War. Gina had created a Web site for their budding heirloom seed company, Laughing Frog Farm, and was struggling to wrest enough time from the chickens and garden chores to create her whimsical, poetic blog about farm life. The three of us pledged we'd find time to write no matter what needed watering, planting, fixing, feeding or cleaning.

Through Gina and Lin, Erin and I met Jude and Lucinda, who had moved here from Sonoma to find and develop their own raw land. They were smart and fun, cosmic, surprising and warm. Our budding friendship added playfulness and intimate connection to our lives—something we'd missed since moving away from friends in the Bay Area.

From the comfort of our cozy, finished home, we cheered on Jude and Lucinda as they entered a complicated land purchase agreement, grappled with digging a pond, installed their off-grid electrical system, built two shed cabins similar to ours, constructed a two-story straw-bale barn that would become their home and dealt with the relationship tensions the whole process inevitably generated. I could see, from my new distance how all-encompassing and stressful creating life off the grid can be.

Hungry for some time away from the demands of Blind Dog Ranch--from weed whacking and plant management to troubleshooting our water and solar electric systems. With Erin's blessings, I flew off to an artist's retreat in New Mexico. Ironically, the casita I was assigned in the high-desert town of Taos was far busier and noisier than Blind Dog Ranch. But with no responsibilities, I could write every day without interruption for as long as my neck, shoulders and brain could stand it. At the end of a month, I had finished a draft of *Women Gone Wild.* I flew home renewed and happy and eager for the clear air and mountain silence of Cherry Creek.

The terrible news that the daughter of one of my dearest childhood friends had jumped off a building in Baltimore and that an old love from San Francisco had leapt from an overpass there shook me. I counted my blessings. I could not help thinking that the opportunity to live peacefully among the hills and trees and awesome quiet of the country might have helped both women heal the sorrow, depression and desperation that led to their final acts. Might living on this land, I wondered, have also kept two young men strung out on meth from taking the life of a lonely gay man looking for fun and companionship?

I kept writing. As long as I kept writing I was able, line by line, "bird by bird," as my friend Annie Lamott would say, to feel more alive and connected--with myself, with Erin, with the land and with my new community. When I wrote every day, I could make sense of the sad, shocking losses of life, cope with the suffering all beings experience, and enjoy Earth's unexpected delights, from the smallest yellow calendula to the spectacular array of stars I could see in the night sky. More than ever, writing made me grateful for my two- and four-legged soul mates--Erin, Luna and Woody.

CHAPTER 31

R.I.P.

Erin's mother fell in the shower at her assisted living facility and was taken on a gurney to an ER in Santa Rosa. She had broken her hip and needed emergency surgery.

With every ounce of energy she had, Erin had tried to make her mother's last years happy. She had taken days off from work to drive her to doctors' appointments, buy her clothes when she complained she had nothing to wear, then return the same clothes when Maggi changed her mind about her own choices. No matter what Erin did or said, she couldn't put her mother back together again.

Confused and disoriented after her surgery, Maggi was moved to a nursing home, where she developed pneumonia. Back in the hospital, her confusion grew. Sometimes she told the staff that Erin was her mother; sometimes she asked the staff to pack her bags so she could go home. Erin's daughter Nam Kirn tried to comfort her grandmother. We, too, sat by her bedside, singing and chanting and praying for her release. After a week of morphine-assisted sleep, Maggi died.

We packed up her apartment, as we had my father's, holding a memorial for Maggi under the crooked oak at Blind Dog Ranch. Jiwan came from New Mexico. Nam Kirn and her son, Forrest, came from Santa Rosa. Erin's ex-husband and his wife arrived from the Bay Area. So did many of our friends. It was healing for all of us to sing and cry and break bread together, remembering Maggi, letting go of old hurts and misunderstandings, releasing together purple and white helium balloons that ascended into the sky.

Luna barked through much of the ritual. Rio, the handsome new black Great Pyrenees mix, who'd adopted Erin by jumping in her car at the gate, sat quietly next to Erin in the circle. Woody stayed inside. Something was wrong with him. He had new little lumps on his head and neck, which the vet diagnosed as mast cell cancer. In early December he was so weak we'd asked the two guys who'd begun doing yard work for us every two weeks to dig him a grave near the crooked oak. We wanted a place ready for Woody in case the ground was too hard to dig when he died. By Christmas he was so much better that we filled in his grave, planting narcissus bulbs in the soil where he would have lain.

He still pranced gaily when Erin came home from work at night and danced his little jig when we set down his food bowl down at mealtime. But in a few weeks, life seemed to drain out of him again.

"Should we take him to the vet?" Erin said after several days of his lying from morning to night in his bed by the wood stove. "Do you think it's time to, you know. . ."

"If you can assist people with dying at home," I pleaded, "surely we can help a little doggie stay in his own bed. You're a hospice nurse."

"But I don't know about dogs," Erin said. "I don't want him to suffer."

"Of course, you don't, but please, let's keep him here. You and I can see him through."

Erin agreed. She'd found some liquid morphine in her mother's medicine cabinet. If his pain got too bad, she'd put it in his mouth to keep him comfortable.

We were crying as we gazed down at our thin little boy, curled in his bed. We didn't want to let Woody go. We'd been through so much with him-- the shock of learning he was blind at two years old, the kidnapping by coyotes, his paws smashed by wild horses and umpteen heart-stopping disappearances into the hills. Through it all, he'd been our brave little love child, our North Star-- happy, courageous and uncomplaining. He'd moved to the middle of nowhere with us, to the wilds of Mendocino County, and survived.

Swallowtail Kate spent the night with us that last weekend of January 2010. She was exhausted from two months in Texas caring for her sister, who was critically ill.

All day Saturday Erin and I sat in the living room with Woody. Luna was in her usual spot on the couch, Woody in his little bed by the wood stove, barely able to open his eyes, breathing slowly and heavily, sometimes moaning slightly, not drinking or eating. Erin gave him the liquid morphine, which seemed to calm him. We took turns lying in the big leather easy chair holding him in our arms, watching his breath, telling him how much we loved him, thanking him for his life and for being such a strong and loving companion who was always by our side (except when he ran away). He would sigh heavily, sometimes fully opening his white, cloudy eyes, moaning almost inaudibly, then drifting back to sleep, eyes half open, half closed.

On Sunday morning, Erin and Kate talked in the living room as I lay on the floor next Woody watching his lungs rise and fall. He didn't want to be picked up that day. He was too weak and sore, his breath barely a whisper.

I touched his head. Erin and Kate were still talking.

"He's gone," I said.

"Woody?" Erin kneeled by his motionless little body, stroking his head. "Woody? Are you there? I love you. Are you okay?"

He was okay, I guess, because he was dead. All three of us were crying. We cried and chanted and asked that Woody's friendly, dear, warrior spirit travel peacefully toward the skunks and squirrels and gophers and coyotes and the wild horses he so dearly loved to chase.

"Goodbye, sweet boy," we said again and again. "Goodbye, dear friend."

Luna hurried out the doggie door.

That afternoon we carried Woody up to the new grave the guys had dug for him beside the first one. Luna sniffed the site and wandered off as we placed his body in the hole near the oak tree where Maggi's ashes rested in a brass box.

"Goodbye, little Woody. Goodbye, Goodbye," we sobbed. "Thank you for your life. Thank you for your courage. Thank you for being our beloved friend and companion for 12 years."

There was a hole in our hearts.

The house was way too quiet without Woody barking and wandering through the house knocking into the dining room table legs and the big leather chair by his little bed. At mealtime it seemed completely weird that there was only one little dog to feed. Only one little dog to put outside at night for a last pee. Only one little dog to cuddle with in the morning.

Woody had been with us at Cherry Creek from the very beginning, exuberantly sniffing every square inch as he danced through the fields and around the pond and up the driveway. His crazy, stubborn spirit, his will to keep on hunting and chasing horses and eating and barking and smiling despite his blindness and later his hearing loss, had made us fall in love with him again and again. Now his suffering was over, and that was good. We reminded ourselves how he'd shown us that the size of one's body does not reflect the depth and grandeur of the heart. How we would miss that crazy black ball of love.

Maggi's death, so closely followed by Woody's, was a turning point for both of us. Erin made the decision to quit her home health and hospice-nursing job in Willits. She wanted to be at Blind Dog Ranch full time, growing all of our vegetables, swimming in the pond, watching her grandchildren swing exuberantly off the rope swing at Outlet Creek, hunting for black trumpet and chanterelle mushrooms in the woods with the Swallowtails. She'd had it with death and dying. She wanted to embrace life and the home we'd worked so hard to create.

CHAPTER 32

FULL CIRCLE

Thirteen years have passed since Erin and I "died" in our Year to Live group. Eight years ago we moved to our house at Blind Dog Ranch.

A lot has happened in those 13 years, and much more, Goddess willing, is yet to come.

Erin is now a full-time biodynamic gardener, working at home, saving seeds, planting, harvesting and cooking all sorts of amazing dishes with vegetables from our own beds.

After digging two dry wells, we now irrigate the garden, from squash and tomatillos to fruit trees and fennel, with water from our still leaky pond. A pump run by solar electricity sends water up from the pond to a new storage tank above the field where Woody was kidnapped by coyotes. The water flows from the tank down to the garden by gravity feed.

The last time I went swimming in the pond, on a hot August day two years ago, the water was full of reeds and weeds and was very low. I lowered myself down the pond's steep sides with the rope we'd tied to the oak tree by the far bank. At the water's edge, I gasped. A fat rattlesnake was stretched on the packed mud where I was about to step.

"What's wrong?" Erin called. She had entered the pond from the other side and was paddling into the deep water. "It feels great."

"Um . . ." I mumbled, backing up the bank. "There's a rattlesnake right here."

"Come in over here. It's wonderful."

"Nope," I said. "I'm done." The rattlesnake was too much for me.

"Time to get a pool," Erin said that night. She'd been threatening for years to buy a plastic aboveground pool. But we could never figure out where to put the ugly thing, which we'd have to look at all year round.

"What about a new pond?" I said. "One that doesn't leak?"

She shrugged. "Can we afford it?"

I called Bud, the heavy equipment operator who had graded our driveway and flattened the ground for the new water tank and trenched a water line down from our spring by the road.

Bud dug some soil samples with his backhoe, looking for a spot with enough clay to cover whatever rock was in the area. If he could find enough clay, he said, he could build us a pond that held water.

He took a few samples from the field above the new water tank overlooking the ridges and he liked what he found. It was a beautiful spot with plenty of clay. For a price we could afford he was almost positive he could build a pond that wouldn't leak.

As I write this today, my sister's birthday and the day my father died eight years ago, the new pond is filled to the brim. It's too cold and rainy to swim. And too early to know if it leaks or holds water. But we're crossing our fingers that it will, offering us the same breathless thrill that the first pond did 12 years ago.

That lush new oasis of water reminds us once again how lucky we are to have come here to the middle of nowhere.

Nowhere is home now.

The land has stretched us, and we have stretched the land. It has driven us crazy and kept us alive. It has asked more of us than we ever thought we'd be able to give. It has tested our relationship and deepened our love. It has sustained us through losses and challenged our assumptions. We plan to live here until we die. Will we be able to? Hard to say. A ranch in the middle of nowhere is a lot to take care of. But just for today, which is all we have, we're not going anywhere.

In New Mexico, Mabel Dodge Luhan, a writer and friend to many artists from the 1920s until her death in 1962, describes the process of creating a home on the frontier in her memoir, *Edge of the Taos Desert*.

"*Of course, acquiring a piece of this land here was a symbolic move, a picture of what was happening inside me,*" she writes. "*I had to have a place of my own to live on where I could take root and make a life.*

"*The day the place became mine, it was as though I had been accepted by the universe. In that day I became centered and ceased the lonesome pilgrimage forever.*"

I'm not sure my lonesome pilgrimage will ever be over, but I'm very glad I'm here and very grateful that Erin and I went wild together.

We let go of our old lives, and new doors opened. That's the way it should be. And that's the way it was.

ACKNOWLEDGEMENTS

"You've got to have friends," Bette Midler sings. How right she is.

I want to thank not only the many friends and family members who helped us through the adventure of creating a life off the grid, but also the carpenters, contractors, heavy equipment operators, house painters, plasterers and assorted craftspeople who made this new life possible.

My biggest, fattest thank you, of course, is to Erin, my wife and best friend. Erin was the wind beneath my sails, to steal another cliché from Bette. Without her courage, sense of humor, energy, vision, kindness, compassion and determination, I'd still be in the suburbs scrolling through real estate ads for a country spot so close to home that we would still be living exactly as we had—near Costco, noise and traffic jams.

I also credit three people with keeping me vertical and laughing as I wrung my hands over our venture into the wild. Marny Hall and Nanette Gartrell offered love, humor, literary advice and their psychotherapeutic insights every step of the way. My cousin, Anne Rightor Thornton, has been and continues to be a loyal cheerleader; she has kept the porch light burning since we were classmates at school in Baltimore 50 years ago.

We first met Stephanie Chatten when she was the warm and welcoming guide who showed us Cherry Creek and Parcel 39. She remains our dear friend, neighbor, intrepid house sitter and guide to the mysteries of iPads, iPhones, iMacs, iWeb, e-publishing and assorted baffling technologies. More than a year ago, as we talked on the road, Stephanie suggested that I e-publish this book and offered to help me. Her support, understanding, dedication, aesthetic vision, love and technical skill have allowed me to publish electronic and print versions of this book.

I am grateful to the Swallowtail Ranch women for the community and companionship their presence brings to our lives. Gina Covina and Lin Due, the original Swallowtails, led us to Cherry Creek and have remained close friends and literary inspirations, providing invaluable editorial help with this book. The inimitable Jane Hernandez ("La Cubana," as her partner calls her) cooked, talked and kibitzed her way into our hearts during her many stays at our house when she and her partners were building their straw-bale cabin down the road. Kate Black's voice, music and heart have lifted our spirits time and again just as her acupuncture skills and medical expertise have alleviated our aches and pains. The willowy Meaveen O'Connor, with her red hair, precious heart, passion for justice and flash-mob "Occupy Oakland" dances, inspires us to do a little more than we might for social and economic justice and the environment. Renita Herrmann, aviatrix and homeopath, began her Swallowtail house as the straw-bale women were finishing theirs, and keeps Erin, me, Luna and Rio happy with her hospitality, mushroom walkabouts and determination to find remedies for anything that ails us.

When you live off the grid on a six-mile dirt road, 16 miles from town, the word *neighbor* takes on new importance. Who do you turn to when you run out of gas, need a tire jack, get stuck in the snow? Our first neighbors, the Cherry Creek Irregulars, have been saving our lives since the beginning. They are, of course: Jay Gordon, who hosted many happy weekend potlucks in the early camping years; Rod and Cindy Panzer, whose gourmet contributions to our Irregulars' gatherings kept our bellies and hearts full; Mike and Robin Carter, who made our little cabin livable and still keep the roads of Cherry Creek safe; and Stephanie Chatten and Ken Dixon, artists to their cores, who dream the impossible dreams.

I send a special shout-out to our nearest neighbors, Sue and Peter Poncia, guardian angels who have given us a shelf in their freezer, changed flat tires for us and shot a rabid skunk wandering in our yard.

Other neighbors who have added immeasurably to our lives are: Peggy Weber and Shana Byrne, Sandy and Larry Onderdonk, Janelle Elliot and Nadine Silva, Tracy and Ray Losee, Glen and Lorrie Cowell, Terrie and Richard Dukes, John and Shari Fisher, Sue and Steve Enjayan, Linda and Woody Hendrick, Art and Sheila Butterfield, Laurel March, Lin Talkovsky, Judith Lerner, Bill Clarke, Bob Davis, Sue and Phil Cruz, Mary Porter and Vic Magnotti and Martha Collins.

We're also grateful to the following fantastic contractors: Tom Allen, homebuilder; Nancy Simpson, architectural designer; Ralph Pisciotta, electrician; Mike Trevey and Richard Pauli, plumbers; Gary Owen, landscaper; Dave and Gloria Thomas, general contractors; Kerry Bell, contractor, and Timbermill Sheds.

My greenest gratitude goes to Antonia Partridge, who taught us how to garden and turned our pile of dirt into an oasis.

Reference librarian Theresa McGovern in Marin County provided fantastic research assistance. The Willits Library lends us all kinds of stimulation for our deprived minds.

Two portions of *Women Gone Wild* were published in the *San Francisco Chronicle* magazine in articles entitled "The Way It Would End" and "Rough Crossing."

I would like to thank the publishers of the following songs and poems for permission to reprint several lines in this book: "Casey Jones," by Jerry Garcia and Robert Hunter, Copyright © 1969 by Ice Nine Publishing; "Althea," by Jerry Garcia and Robert Hunter, Copyright ©1979 by Ice

Nine Publishing; "The Stolen Child," by William Butler Yeats, Copyright © 1889, by A.P. Watt and Company; "Our House," by Graham Nash, Copyright ©1970 by Sony/ATV Music Publishing LLC, EMI Music Publishing, and "Garden Song," by Dave Mallett, Copyright © 1975 by Cherry Lane Music Publishing.

For your friendship, love and support over the years and across the miles, thank you to: Jean Scott Prema, Anne Santos Paxson, Ellen Reeder, Kitty Santos Harrison, Esther Rothblum, Brian Kellman, Steve Martin, Douglas Schmidt, David Lebe, Annie Thornton, Jane Thornton, Charles Thornton, Kristy Thornton, Henry Thornton, Mary Jane Olney, Chris Olney, Anne Bevan, Gareth Bevan, Nick Olney, Sasha Olney, Becky Larsen, Rick Polito, Paul Liberatore, Pam Moreland, Mike Townsend, Jackie Kerwin, Jeff Prugh, Brent Ainsworth, Sandy Miller, Janet Kornblum, Holly Woolard, Brad Breithaupt, Alison Bigger, Robin Bentel, Amrit Khalsa, Jiwan Khalsa, Nam Kirn Khalsa Davenport, Forrest Davenport, Sarib Jot Khalsa, Siri Atma Khalsa, Siri Nirong Kar Singh Khalsa, Sat San Tokh Singh Khalsa, Johnna Carney Foster, Gene Foster, April Carney, Jack Carney, Diane Carney, Jennifer Beard Badger, Rosie Powell, Bill Barksdale, Martha Rightor Crutchfield, Mary Jane Rightor Olney, Chris Olney, Laura Lee Kent, Sherman T. Kent, Jane Lee Wolfe, Frederick B. Lee, George N. de Man, Drew de Man, George de Man, Mary Aswell Doll, Bettie Anne Doebler, Helen Vendler, Lisa Zimmerman, Julie Beach, Sylvia Israel, Sheryl Goldberg, Jane Spahr, Sandy Lee Nelson, Ardas Grene, Jane Gurko, Abigail Hemstreet, Pat Holt, Fee Hughes,

Sarah Harrison, Clancy Rash, Helen Falandes, Judy Nagel, Lucinda Dekker, Beverly Rich Kahn, Bob Kahn, Susan Kennedy, Belinda Rawlins, Mary Aigner, Anne Lamott, Teresa Lozoya, Jane Lawton, Ruby Holladay, Lynnsy Logue, Sharon Lieser, Lynne McNabb Walton, Barry Morris, Dee Mosbacher, Caroline Merrill, Paul Newman, Catherine Hopkins, Joan Alden, Debigail Mazor, Nora Sage Murray, Cindy Morninglight, Angela Graystar, Judy Luria, Melinda Clarke, Ann Norsworthy, Gwen Norsworthy, Kiloran Russell, Elisa Odabashian, Kitty Norris, Creek Norris, Paula Murray, Robert Oster, Katharine Baetjer Pilgrim, Cally Cochran, Caroline Cochran Boynton, Alice Cochran, Tolly Brown Lewin, Pratt Remmel, Elizabeth Scoville, Mary Ann Shaefer, Ina Silverwood, Mie Toyokawa, Haruyo Toyokawa, Margaret Winter, Bill Winter, Louise Whitney, Jen Pennington, Holly Barnard, Wolfgang Rennefeldt and Laura Wilensky.

Lastly, I honor my sister, Marjorie Chaparral Futcher, and my parents, Palmer Howard Futcher and Mary "Sissy" Viola Rightor Futcher. My going wild was born of our time together.

Jane Futcher
P.O. Box 939
Willits, CA 95490
janefutcher@me.com
womengonewildpress.com & janefutcher.com

PHOTO CREDITS & CAPTIONS

Cover

A playful Jane with antlers -- *Photo by Stephanie Chatten*

Dedication

Jane and Erin in the lush of spring -- *Photo by Nam Kirn Khalsa Davenport*

Chapter 1 -- Looking for Land

Erin, left, holding a very young Woody Von Woodruff Woodpecker the Third, and Jane, holding Woody's sister, Princess Luna del Mar, around 1997, when they began looking for a country place. The dogs are miniature longhaired dachshunds. *Photo by Marion Little Utley*

Chapter 2 -- Eat, Drink and Be Merry...

Erin and the dogs and Jane with the Year to Live Group in an Olema, CA, graveyard, November 1998. Finding land in the country topped both of our bucket lists. *Photo by Joyce Creswell*

Chapter 3 -- North to Mendocino

Jane at the top ridge on Parcel 40 at Cherry Creek, 1999. You could see forever, but was it too remote? *Photo by Erin Carney*

Chapter 4 -- Welcome to Cherry Creek

Stephanie with the Kawasaki Mule, Puppy Schnoodles and Ruff at the top of Parcel 39, 1999. We felt like Spin and Marty playing in our very own ranch or national park. *Photo by Jane Futcher*

Chapter 5 -- On the Beat

Rick and Jane in the newsroom in 1999 viewing additions to Rick's "Planet Becky: Where Nice People Say Nice Things About Nice People." A favorite entry was: "Dogs just love you. They don't care how much money you make." *Photo by Becky Larsen*

Chapter 6 -- Horses Make a Landscape More Beautiful

Raven, Splash and Rowdy, three of the dozen-plus wild geldings Liz released on the land in the early 1990s, grazing at Cherry Creek. *Photo by Ken Dixon*

Chapter 7 -- Consider Yourself at Home

Enjoying breakfast at our first campsite on Parcel 39 at Cherry Creek. Months before we held title to the land, we'd camped there, dug a pond and built two road extensions. *Photo by Erin Carney*

Chapter 8 -- Breaking the News

Marny, left, and Jane, dressed for a costume party in Novato, CA. It wasn't easy telling close friends and family that we'd bought rural land three hours away from San Francisco in the middle of nowhere. *Photo by Erin Carney*

Chapter 9 -- Shock Treatment

Mrs. R., Palmer--Jane's father--and Jane at the 1987 Lesbian/Gay/Bisexual/Transgender March on Washington, D.C. Mrs. R. became depressed when Palmer moved to a life care community in Baltimore and was pursued by many widows. *Photo by Catherine Hopkins*

Chapter 10 -- Jane Acres

A dream come true--our first tent site on Parcel 39 in the summer of 1999. *"Oh, Jane, Willits is no place to be,"* sang Rick, my newsroom buddy. *"Outhouses, no 'lectricity." Photo by Erin Carney*

Chapter 11 -- Eureka!

The Cherry Creek Irregulars, our eccentric band of new friends, at a Scorpio birthday party at Jay's house in November 1999. In the foreground, left to right, are Rod, Cindy and Erin (holding a pumpkin on her head). Behind are Stephanie, Jay and Ken. *Photo by Jane Futcher*

Chapter 12 -- Beat Change

Erin and Jane with party-goers at a Y2K New Year's Eve party in Novato, CA. Despite predictions of global catastrophe, the transition from 1999 to 2000 was nearly seamless. *Photographer unknown.*

Chapter 13 -- Labor Pains

Doug, the backhoe guy, creating a new leg of the driveway over to the home site on Parcel 39. A few months later, in New Mexico, Erin's daughter went into early labor on Valentine's Day. *Photo by*

Jane Futcher
Chapter 14 -- This Little Piggy
That's Jane next to the new pond in Spring 2000. When I wasn't panicked about what we'd done, I was thrilled that we had our own place in the wilderness. *Photo by Erin Carney*

Chapter 15 -- Woody, Come Back!
Woody, our longhaired doxie mini, age five at the time, resting on his pillow on his faux grass lawn at Cherry Creek a few minutes before he was snagged and nearly eaten by two hungry coyotes. *Photo by Jane Futcher*

Chapter 16 -- SSSnakes
A shrink was convinced I was obsessive-compulsive when I told him I was afraid of the rattlesnakes at Cherry Creek. I took this photo of a gopher snake on our woodpile in July 2000. *Photo by Jane Futcher*

Chapter 17 -- Stephanie's Visitor
This may have been the California Black Bear that traumatized Ken, Stephanie and her mother at Jay's place. One neighbor kept bears away by playing loud Christian music on the radio. *Photo by Jay Gordon*

Chapter 18 -- Pondificating
We hired a guy called Tony to mix Bentonite clay powder into the bottom and sides of the pond, which we drained, to try to stop the leaking. There was too much rock in the spot we picked, and that rock kept the pond walls from sealing. *Photo by Erin Carney*

Chapter 19 --Karmaceudicals
Erin, her mother Maggi, and a friend, at our house in Novato in 1999. We were hoping the medical marijuana that Prof. Ping-Pong gave us

would ease Maggi's excruciating hip and leg pain, but the cannabis didn't help. *Photo by Jane Futcher*

Chapter 20 -- No Time to Waste

The attack on the World Trade Center, along with reduced oil supplies and the fear that California might be attacked, created a sense of urgency about building a house on our land, growing a garden and learning to live off the grid, sustainably. *Wire photo.*

Chapter 21 -- Ch, Ch, Changes

Erin, the dogs and Jane in front of their new cabin at Cherry Creek in 2001. Erin pressed resolutely ahead with plans to move to the cabin, get a nursing job and watch Tom, the contractor, build our house. I stayed behind in Novato. *Photo by Mike Carter*

Chapter 22 -- Detox

Erin and Jane swimming in Outlet Creek at the Swallowtails' swimming hole. We both spent some time in another body of water, the hot tub at a health institute near San Diego in 2002, prepping ourselves for the changes ahead. *Photo by Gina Covina*

Chapter 23 -- Pouring it On

Despite my jitters, we poured the foundation of our house in July 2003 with the help of an enormous boom that moved easily across the footprint. *Photo by Jane Futcher*

Chapter 24 - House Call

Excited but frail, Jane's father, inspects the framing of the house on his 93rd birthday in September 2003. I shot this from the future guest room, where we hoped he'd soon be staying. *Photo by Jane Futcher*

Chapter 25 -- Moving Day

The roof of the front porch of the new house was supported by Douglas fir trees cut from a neighbor's land and cured for a year under tarps. Landscaping still to come. *Photo by Jane Futcher*

Chapter 26 -- Inch by Inch

The months we spent planning and planting the garden with Antonia paid off. By spring of 2005, we had a flower garden and four raised beds for vegetables. *Photo by Jane Futcher*

Chapter 27 --Radioactive

Joining the board of directors of KZYX&Z in 2005 got me out of the house and meeting new people. I'm in the back, in a plaid jacket, behind Belinda, the general manager, in the red and white striped shirt. Photographer unknown.

Chapter 28 -- Homegrown

For fun we tried our hand at growing medical marijuana, with seeds from one of our gardener's helpers. We discovered that some of our neighbors were growing a lot more than a couple of barrels. *Photo by Jane Futcher*

Chapter 29 -- Night Crossings

We never managed to see a single bear on our Alaskan cruise, but driving home from the airport we hit this black bear on Highway 101. The impact killed the bear and totaled my father's Ford Taurus. Erin and I were fine. *Photo by CalTrans*

Chapter 30 -- Murder, She Wrote

In 2007, I stumbled into a Mendocino County courtroom to entertain myself for an hour and ended up writing a story about the brutal murder of a gay man for the San Francisco Chronicle. *Photo by Jane Futcher*

Chapter 31 -- R.I.P.

Little Woody, who'd been kidnapped by coyotes and trampled by wild horses, died of natural causes on Jan. 31, 2010. *Photo by Jane Futcher*

Chapter 32 -- Full Circle

We were never able to fix our leaky pond, so we now use it to irrigate the garden. We built this new swimming pond in Fall 2011. *Photo by Jane Futcher*

Acknowledgements -- Jane with kale -- *Photo by Erin Carney*

Photo Credits -- View from our garden -- *Photo by Jane Futcher*

About the Author – Jane & Rio -- *Photo by Ken Dixon*

ABOUT THE AUTHOR

Jane Futcher

Jane Futcher was raised in Baltimore, MD. She began her professional writing life as a scriptwriter and producer of live, high school multimedia auditorium shows for Rick Trow Productions in Philadelphia. Later, as a project editor for Harper & Row Media in New York, she wrote and produced educational programs for the science and society curriculum. In 1977, after moving to San Francisco, she wrote her first novel, **Crush**, published in 1981 by Little, Brown. That same year, Holt, Rhinehart and Winston released **Marin: The Place, The People**.

In 1991, Avon Books published her young adult novel, **Promise Not to Tell**. After teaching English for several years, she joined the staff of the Marin

Independent Journal, where she was an editorial writer and reporter for nearly a decade. In 1999, she and her partner, Erin Carney, bought 160 acres in the mountains of inland Mendocino County, moving there with their dogs in 2004. **Women Gone Wild** is about that experience.

Made in the USA
Charleston, SC
30 September 2012